RESEARCH METHODS FOR THE SELF-STUDY OF PRACTICE

Self-Study of Teaching and Teacher Education Practices

Volume 9

Series Editor
John Loughran, *Monash University, Clayton, Australia*

For further volumes:
http://www.springer.com/series/7072

RESEARCH METHODS FOR THE SELF-STUDY OF PRACTICE

Edited by

Deborah L. Tidwell
University of Northern Iowa, Cedar Falls, IA, USA

Melissa L. Heston
University of Northern Iowa, Cedar Falls, IA, USA

and

Linda M. Fitzgerald
University of Northern Iowa, Cedar Falls, IA, USA

 Springer

Editors

Dr. Deborah L. Tidwell
University of Northern Iowa
Dept. Curriculum & Instruction
618 Schindler Education Ctr.
Cedar Falls IA 50614-0606
USA
deborah.tidwell@uni.edu

Dr. Linda M. Fitzgerald
University of Northern Iowa
Dept. Curriculum & Instruction
618 Schindler Education Ctr.
Cedar Falls IA 50614-0606
USA
linda.fitzgerald@uni.edu

Dr. Melissa L. Heston
University of Northern Iowa
Dept. Educational Psychology & Foundations
617 Schindler Education Ctr.
Cedar Falls IA 50614-0607
USA
melissa.heston@uni.edu

ISBN 978-1-4020-9513-9   e-ISBN 978-1-4020-9514-6

DOI 10.1007/978-1-4020-9514-6

Library of Congress Control Number: 2008940336

Printed on acid-free paper

9 8 7 6 5 4 3 2 1

springer.com

Series Editor's Foreword

This series was initiated as an extension of, and support for, the International Handbook of Self-study of Teaching and Teacher Education Practices (Loughran, Hamilton, LaBoskey, & Russell, 2004). As such, the books that comprise the series are designed to offer new and engaging ways of examining issues (both theoretical and practical), associated with self-study research.

Through this text, the editors have taken a bold stand in holding up to scrutiny the work of a number of scholars in ways that shed new light on the methods, practices and outcomes of their self-study endeavours. They have assembled an outstanding array of authors that demonstrates well the way in which the self-study community functions as a collaborative and supportive enterprise in the work of teacher education.

Deborah Tidwell, Melissa Heston and Linda Fitzgerald are an experienced and talented team of editors who have accepted responsibility for a number of the recent Castle proceedings (Fitzgerald, Heston, & Tidwell, 2006; Heston, Tidwell, East, & Fitzgerald, 2008; Tidwell, Fitzgerald, & Heston, 2004, the bi-ennial conference of AERA's S-STEP SIG). Through that work they have been fortunate to be fully immersed in the most up to date and influential research conducted by members of the self-study community. As a consequence of that involvement and leadership they have been exceptionally well placed to be familiar with, and therefore attract, authors that have a great deal to offer by sharing their work through this exceptional text.

As the editors and authors make clear, self-study as 'inquiry-guided' research demands a great deal from participants. However, an issue at the heart of this book is the need to demonstrate that self-study can, and must, move beyond the individual and impact other teacher educators, and teacher education programs more generally, if it is to be truly effective. In their introduction to the book the editors draw attention to the notion of trustworthiness. This is an interesting and important issue because the nature of self-study means that it is far from 'recipe driven,' rather, it tends to evolve and develop over time, all of which require confidence skill and expertise by the researcher. Therefore, when done well, it is a demanding task.

Deborah Tidwell, Melissa Heston and Linda Fitzgerald have done a remarkable job in supporting the authors and developing this text into a coherent and well-conceptualized body of work that has much to offer both the novice and the experienced self-study researcher. This is an important book developed by a strong group of scholars who have worked together to offer a range of insights and new possibilities for those interested in supporting and further pursuing the work of self-study.

It has been a pleasure to work with the editors in bringing this book to fruition. As you work your way through the myriad of new, challenging and exciting ideas encapsulated in each of the chapters, you will no doubt see that the editors' efforts have been well rewarded by the quality of this text.

This is a fine piece of work by a fine group of teacher education scholars.

References

Fitzgerald, L. M., Heston, M. L., & Tidwell, D. L. (Eds.). (2006). *Collaboration and community: Pushing the boundaries through self-study. The Sixth International Conference on Self-Study of Teacher Education Practices. Herstmonceux Castle, East Sussex, England.* Cedar Falls, Iowa: University of Northern Iowa.

Heston, M. L., Tidwell, D. L., East, K. K., & Fitzgerald, L. M. (Eds.). (2008). *Pathways to change in teacher education: Dialogue, diversity and self-study. The Seventh International Conference on Self-Study of Teacher Education Practices. Herstmonceux Castle, East Sussex, England.* Cedar Falls, Iowa: University of Northern Iowa.

Loughran, J. J., Hamilton, M. L., LaBoskey, V. K., & Russell, T. (Eds.). (2004). *International handbook of self-study of teaching and teacher education practices.* Dordrecht: Kluwer.

Tidwell, D. L., Fitzgerald, L. M., & Heston, M. L. (Eds.). (2004). *Journeys of hope: Risking self-study in a diverse world. The Fifth International Conference on Self-Study of Teacher Education Practices. Herstmonceux Castle, East Sussex, England.* Cedar Falls, Iowa: University of Northern Iowa.

J. John Loughran

Contents

Contributors

Clive Beck   Ontario Institute for Studies in Education, University of Toronto, Toronto, ON M5S 1V6, Canada, cbeck@oise.utoronto.ca

Amanda Berry   Faculty of Education, Monash University, Wellington Road, Clayton, Victoria 3800, Australia, amanda.berry@education.monash.edu.au

Robyn Brandenburg   University of Ballarat, Ballarat, Victoria 3353, Australia, r.brandenburg@ballarat.edu.au

Rosa T. Chiu-Ching   Department of Educational Psychology, The Hong Kong Institute of Education, Counselling and Learning Needs, 10 Lo Ping Road, Tai Po, NT, Hong Kong, tlchiu@ied.edu.hk

Lesley Coia   Agnes Scott College, 985 Wesley Drive, Macon, GA 31210, USA, lcoia@agnesscott.edu

Alicia R. Crowe   Kent State University, Teaching Leadership and Curriculum Studies, 404 White Hall, Kent State University, Kent, OH 44242, USA, acrowe@kent.edu

Katheryn East   University of Northern Iowa, 617 Schindler Education Center, Cedar Falls, IA 50614-0607, USA, katheryn.east@uni.edu

Linda M. Fitzgerald   University of Northern Iowa, 618 Schindler Education Center, Cedar Falls, IA 50614-0606, USA, linda.fitzgerald@uni.edu

Morwenna Griffiths   The Moray House School of Education, University of Edinburgh, Hollyrood Road, Edinburgh, Scotland EH8 8AQ, UK, morwenna.griffiths@ed.ac.uk

Mary Lynn Hamilton   University of Kansas, Room 344, 1122 W. Campus Road, Joseph R. Pearson Hall, Lawrence, KS 66045, USA, hamilton@ku.edu

Melissa L. Heston   University of Northern Iowa, 617 Schindler Education Center, Cedar Falls, IA 50614-0607, USA, melissa.heston@uni.edu

Julian Kitchen   Brock University, Faculty of Education, Hamilton, Ontario, L8K 1V7, Canada, jkitchen@brocku.ca

Clare Kosnik   Ontario Institute for Studies in Education, University of Toronto, Toronto, ON M5S 1V6, Canada, ckosnik@oise.utoronto.ca

Vicki Kubler LaBoskey   Mills College, Education 219, Oakland, CA, 94613, USA, vickikl@mills.edu

Heather Malcolm   The Moray House School of Education, University of Edinburgh, Hollyrood Road, Edinburgh, Scotland EH8 8AQ, UK, heather.malcolm@ed.ac.uk

Mary P. Manke   University of Wisconsin, River Falls, College of Education and Professional Studies, River Falls, WI 54022, USA, mary.p.manke@uwrf.edu

Claudia Mitchell   McGill University, Faculty of Education, Montreal, Quebec H3G 1Y2, Canada, claudia.mitchelll@mcgill.ca

Stefinee Pinnegar   Brigham Young University, 201W MCKB, McKay School of Education, Brigham Young University, Provo, UT 84602, USA, stefinee@byu.edu

Kathleen Pithouse   McGill University, c/o Claudia Mitchell, Faculty of Education, Montreal, Quebec H3G 1Y2, Canada, Kpithouse@gmail.com

Monica Taylor   Montclair State University, 7 Morningside Road, Verona, NJ 07044, USA, taylorm@mail.montclair.edu

Deborah L. Tidwell   University of Northern Iowa, 618 Schindler Education Center, Cedar Falls, IA 50614-0606, USA, deborah.tidwell@uni.edu

Sandra Weber   Concordia University, Department of Education, 1455 de Maisonneuve West, Montreal, Quebec H3G 1M8, Canada, sandra.weber@education.concordia.ca

Jack Whitehead   University of Bath, Department of Education, Bath BA2 7AY, UK, edsajw@bath.ac.uk

Zoè Williamson The Moray House School of Education, University of Edinburgh, Hollyrood Road, Edinburgh, Scotland EH8 8AQ, UK, zoe.williamson@ed.ac.uk

Esther Yim-mei Chan The Hong Kong Institute of Education, Department of Early Childhood Education, 10 Lo Ping Road, Tai Po, NT, Hong Kong, echan@ied.edu.hk

Introduction

Deborah L. Tidwell, Melissa L. Heston and Linda M. Fitzgerald

Self-study as an established genre of educational research has grown dramatically over the last 15 years, and in 1999 was acknowledged by Zeichner as research that could potentially have the greatest impact on teacher education and the transformation of practice. Self-study is a methodology that embraces multiple methods of research. While drawing heavily on traditional qualitative methods of data collection, self-study generally transforms those methods by taking them into a new context and using them in ways that often depart from the traditional. These transformations highlight the fact that the role of the researcher in self-study and the role of teacher educator are closely intertwined and generally inseparable. Thus, self-study is centrally concerned with seeking to "understand the relationship between the knower and the known" as well as seeking "to understand what is the form and nature of reality" (Kuzmik & Bloom, 2008, p. 207).

Self-study as inquiry-guided research must be sufficiently trustworthy (Mishler, 1990) for others to be able to find that research both meaningful and potentially generative in relationship to the readers' own teacher education practices. This trustworthiness can best be achieved by making the data visible and by clearly presenting and illustrating the "methods for transforming the data into findings, and the linkages between data, findings, and interpretations" (LaBoskey, 2004, p. 1176). This can be a challenging task for a variety of reasons. While self-studies are embedded with an overarching research question – How can I improve my practice? – some self-studies do not begin by formulating a formal and clearly defined research question in the traditional sense. Indeed, only about half of the studies in this book have clearly defined questions from the outset of their particular work. Among those that do have an initiating question, the process of self-study can provoke a significant change in the nature of the question being asked. Thus, the methods selected for use in a study are not solely or inevitably driven by the nature of the research question as is the case in more traditional forms of research. Rather, the particular methods used in self-study emerge as a function of the particular context within which the study is being pursued, which is evident in each of the studies in this book.

D.L. Tidwell (✉)
University of Northern Iowa, Cedar Falls, IA, USA
e-mail: deborah.tidwell@uni.edu

Other factors can make establishing the trustworthiness of a self-study somewhat more difficult than is the case with studies using more traditional kinds of qualitative methods. In self-study, the data-generating and data-analysis processes are often mutually interdependent and can even occur simultaneously. In addition, even the practice which is being examined in a self-study can itself evolve during the study. That is, in the course of a given study, important and yet subtle aspects of the researcher's practice as a teacher educator may actually be transformed without conscious awareness, and such transformations may only come to be recognized through post hoc reflections.

Finally, self-study is often conducted collaboratively. In fact, the findings of any given collaborative study depend critically upon who the collaborators are and what they individually and collectively bring to the research process. This is quite different from more traditional research in teacher education where there is an a priori agreement among members of the research team regarding how data will be gathered and analyzed; rigor in this type of research depends upon adhering carefully to that agreement in all its aspects. In self-study, however, rigor, in the sense of maintaining a critical stance towards one's practices, can demand that self-study researchers negotiate, adapt, and change research methods, processes, and even the research questions as the study unfolds.

Every self-study unfolds in a somewhat fluid and unpredictable manner. We believe it is important to illustrate more explicitly how self-study researchers have examined their education practices. In particular, how do their ways of gathering and analyzing data relate to their education practice and their understandings of that practice? The 13 self-studies in this book were selected to provide readers with concrete and authentic illustrations of self-study as it naturally unfolds. In addition, while the studies have been grouped into four broad areas, even within a given area, the specific methods used for collecting and analyzing data related to practice are somewhat different.

We begin with a set of studies that all emphasize or describe the use of text as the central prompt for the self-study process. Text has been used extensively in self-study work; sometimes the texts are self-generated by the teacher educators engaged in the study, while other times, the texts arise from published sources. In either case, the text offers a critical lens through which teacher educators can problematize their practice, seeking insight into the implicit assumptions that may be more influential on those practices than is the propositional understanding these teacher educators have about practice. In Part I, *Self-Study Through the Use of Text*, three self-studies present different ways in which researchers use texts chronicling accounts of their personal experiences to elucidate the meaning within their practice. In *Co/autoethnography: Exploring Our Teaching Selves Collaboratively*, Monica Taylor and Lesley Coia provide an in-depth examination of co/autoethnography, a distinctive method they have developed and used to conduct a number of self-studies (Coia & Taylor, 2006; Taylor et al., 2006). Striving to be accessible to all audiences, they discuss co/autoethnography in two sections: conceptual and application in real-life contexts. In the first section they explicate co/autoethnography, focusing on the distinctive nature of collaboration and collaborative research undertaken with the aim of understanding the present through the use of past experiences. They use what they describe as a thick description of the self, serial and simultaneous writing, and a research method that evolves from personal experiences. These methods have been drawn from various sources, including self-study of teacher education, anthropology, literacy theory, autobiography, narrative inquiry, and qualitative research. In their chapter, they explain the ways in which their co/autoethnography method emerged within the context of their teaching collaboration and was built upon their own teaching histories and disciplinary backgrounds in philosophy, English education, and literacy. In the second section of the chapter, they guide readers through the process of co/autoethnography, highlighting appropriate types of pedagogical contexts, demonstrating the ways they were able to recognize emerging research questions from their teaching or collaboration, sharing the various possible collaborative methods of data collection (in particular technological tools such as google.docs and email), and providing guidelines for data analysis strategies.

In the second chapter of this section, *Teaching and Learning Through Narrative Inquiry*, Rosa T. Chiu-Ching and Esther Yim-mei Chan explore the use of teacher stories to promote teaching and learning of child development. Instead of teaching the grand theories of child development, their description of their teaching begins in the sharing of their family stories of their fathers with their students. Students are then invited to reflect on these stories and resonate with their own father stories. Chiu-Ching and Chan adopt Clandinin's (1993) view of teacher education as narrative inquiry and ground their work in self-study (Loughran, 2004b) via their use of father stories as narrative inquiry (Clandinin, & Connelly, 2000; Connelly & Clandinin, 1988). Through sharing stories, they investigate their own practice to learn how their fathers have shaped their development and views toward students and teaching. In stimulating students' reflection (Schön, 1983) and resonance (Conle, 1996), they suggest that child development can be learned via an experiential and a narrative approach. Storytelling, then, becomes a tool for understanding the meaning of lived experiences and for the construction of knowledge that informs professional practice. In this self-study, the authors discuss how they made sense of their teaching, validated their narrative inquiry process as a way of knowing, and found new ways to story and restory the teaching and learning of child development in teacher education programs.

The work of Clandinin and Connelly (2004) also sets the focus for the third self-study in this section, *Passages: Improving Teacher Education through Narrative Self-Study*. In this chapter Julian Kitchen focuses on narrative knowing as a means of improving teacher education practices. Narrative knowing, which has been at the heart of his self-study practices for a decade, has enabled Kitchen to navigate a meaningful passage for preservice students. He juxtaposes how narrative knowing informed his practices as a neophyte teacher educator (Kitchen, 2005a, 2005b) with his present efforts as a reflective teacher educator in another university. Through his research question, How does narrative knowing inform my practices as a teacher educator? he illustrates the "living of teacher knowledge in action" (Clandinin & Connelly, 2004, p. 582) by drawing on artifacts of practice (e.g., lessons, reflections, observations, feedback by students) from his experience as a neophyte and at present. Through this process Kitchen formulates the resolution of tensions between belief and practice as an action research project aimed at improving classroom practices. In constructing meaning from these artifacts of experience, he draws on multiple frames including Schwab's (1970) four commonplaces and Loughran's (2006) *Developing a Pedagogy of Teacher Education*.

The studies in Part II, *Self-Study Through Discourse and Dialogue*, provide different ways in which teacher educators have used dialogue as a data generation tool, and even an analysis tool. In *Talking Teaching and Learning: The Use of Dialogue in Self-Study*, Katheryn East, Linda M. Fitzgerald and Melissa L. Heston describe their use of dialogue as a methodological tool which poses some unique challenges in terms of both its creation and its analysis. They found that as they engage in dialogue for collaborative self-study, they must be thoughtful, intentional, and earnestly adhere to a set of specific conversational practices and principles. Through the resulting dialogue they uncover tacit beliefs together, which they then subject to focused examination. At unpredictable intervals in this process they reach points where they recalibrate, as an individual and as a group, due to an insight in a moment of clarity or through a gradually dawning realization. In this chapter they describe how they go about structuring their self-study work using dialogue, what they believe to be essential for the creation of useful self-study dialogue, and how they in turn have used that dialogue as data. They conclude the chapter with a set of cautions and caveats.

According to Brown (2004), "Self-study is uniquely suited to contribute to an understanding of race and social class issues in education" (p. 520). Vicki Kubler LaBoskey agrees that self-study has the potential to enhance our knowledge and implementation of social justice education, but it is a potential yet to be fully realized (LaBoskey, 2004). In *"Name It and Claim It": The Methodology of Self-Study as Social Justice Teacher Education*, LaBoskey examines the language of inquiry in making explicit the issues of social justice in teaching and learning. LaBoskey's study was designed to help fill the gap by examining the learning outcomes of a student teacher inquiry project focused on race/racism in their teaching contexts. Additionally, the aim was to explore ways in which self-study methodology might be strengthened by incorporating methods more consistent with and thus contributory to social justice education. The findings in her study support the notion that the essence of social justice education is inherent in the conceptualization of self-study, particularly with regard to its personal responsibility for both self and student learning and for the enactment of that learning; for its insistent attention to affective, as well as cognitive growth; and, for its aim of learner empowerment. She explains how this potential can only be realized if the implicits are made explicit, if hard questions are asked about issues like race/racism; and if social justice criteria are incorporated into measurements of progress.

In *Many Miles and Many Emails: Using Electronic Technologies in Self-Study to Think about, Refine and Reframe Practice*, Amanda Berry and Alicia R. Crowe describe their collaboration through the use of Information Communication Technologies (ICT). Their chapter explores the development of a long distance critical friendship between two teacher educators, each seeking to better understand how she might improve the quality of her students' experiences of learning to teach. The research approach is based on collaborative inquiry conducted via email dialogue. Using this approach, "Each participant in the collaborative research is helping the other identify and interpret his (sic) professional knowledge as a teacher [educator] by reading and commenting on email accounts of teaching-learning experiences" (Beck, Freese, & Kosnik, C., 2004, p. 1269). They describe how email offers a form of ICT that supports the development of thinking about, refining, and reframing practice. They discuss the development of their collaboration through email, issues they encountered through the use of email as a tool for both collaboration and analysis in self-study, and implications for the use of this methodological tool in studying teacher education practices.

The studies in Part III, *Self-Study through Visual Representation*, explore the use of various kinds of visuals both as data and as prompts for reflection in the self-study process. These studies draw upon pictures, video, drawing, and collage as ways of documenting practice and professional experiences, which can then be analyzed for what these visual representations can tell us about practice. In *Faces and Spaces and Doing Research*, Morwenna Griffiths, Heather Malcolm and Zoè Williamson describe their collaborative work which highlights the significance of space and place for research processes and research culture. The authors worked together to develop an inquiry into the question, How do we make places and spaces for research, and how do they influence how and what we research? An iterative and collaborative research design was developed using photos, videos, and other visual representations to create an exhibition with the intention of developing a greater collective understanding of the available spaces and places and their significance for research. The process of analysis is itself done visually through small group presentation and discussion, and then, in more depth, in the process of creating the public exhibition. These visual and discursive dynamics are documented and presented through an in-depth description of the analysis process.

In *Facing the Public: Using Photography for Self-Study and Social Action*, Claudia Mitchell, Sandra Weber, and Kathleen Pithouse look at ways in which working with the visual through the participatory construction and performance of a 'curated' photo album can contribute to the public face of self-study in education. Visual approaches facilitate a meaningful engagement with the social and political as well as the professional and personal dimensions of education. In this chapter, their focus is on professional practice in what might be described as 'the face of change,' a context in which social issues and 'going public' are integrated as an inevitable part of self-study. They illustrate the processes and potential of working with photo albums in self-study with concrete examples from their work with teachers in South Africa, where the practices of teachers and teacher educators are critical in relation to addressing the impact of the HIV and AIDS epidemic. What emerges from their work is the realization that some forms of self-study not only involve changing individual practice and perspectives but can also illuminate critical social challenges and stimulate creative, context-specific responses to those challenges. Building on previous writings (Mitchell & Weber, 1999; Pithouse & Mitchell, 2007; Weber, & Mitchell, 1995, 2004), what they develop (and theorize) further in this chapter is the social and educative value of going public through participatory and performative visual approaches to self-study.

In *Making Meaning of Practice through Visual Metaphor*, Deborah L. Tidwell and Mary P. Manke describe their use of drawn metaphors as a means to examine their professional practice in administrative work in teacher education programs. Their chapter describes the process they used to develop visual representations of challenges they experienced in their administrative work. Having drawn visuals representing key moments in practice (Tidwell, 2002; Tidwell, & Tincu, 2004), they used these drawings to discuss, deconstruct, reconceptualize, and analyze that practice. Guided by their research question, How can we use metaphorical drawings of nodal moments to inform our practice?, they focused on specific archetypal nodal moments that captured experiential commonalities across typical events in each of their administrative lives. The use of the archetype resonated with similar moments across time and space, which then became the metaphoric representation upon which they focused their discussions and reflections. Tidwell and Manke chronicle the process that unfolded when using nodal moments for self-study research. They describe the impact that drawn metaphorical representations have on understanding their practice and on influencing their professional decision making.

In *Creating Representations: Using Collage in Self-Study*, Mary Lynn Hamilton and Stefinee Pinnegar argue the importance of stepping beyond the veil of tradition to use imaginistic tools to help them see what is absent, important, or unimportant in their texts. Within self-study research they identify three important conversations – dialogue, trust, and ontology. Their work with images combines their interest in all three, especially ontology, as a way to establish the value of the imaginistic in self-study. For this study they return to their early work in collage with a critical eye as they collaboratively explore possibilities and construct analyses. They looked at their previous work for themselves and others with whom they write and think. Imagistic representations like collage are symbolic narratives which force the creator and viewer to think beyond interpretation and tradition. In their chapter they discuss how collage (and other art forms, like poetry and painting) offer levels of nonlinearity facilitating simultaneous understanding of cultural models and praxis (Weber & Mitchell, 2004).

Finally, the book closes with studies that step back, to some extent, from self and examine more explicitly the impact of practice on students while maintaining a reflective stance toward that practice. While the studies in Part IV, *Self-Study on the Impact of Practice on Students*, may use methods similar to those used in the other sections, they differ in that they focus specifically on the impact of their practices on others. *How Do I Influence the Generation of Living Educational Theories for Personal and Social Accountability in Improving Practice?* chronicles Jack Whitehead's self-study of his working life in the Department of Education at the University of Bath. In this study, Whitehead analyzes the impact his work with educators has had on their professional growth through examining his distinctive academic approach to the education of professional practitioners. In particular, his approach focuses on the generation of a new epistemology for educational knowledge from living educational theories in inquiries of the kind, How do I improve what I am doing? The living theory research methodology used to address this question emerged in the course of his inquiry and includes action reflection cycles from the work of Whitehead and McNiff (2006) and McNiff (2007), methodological inventiveness from the work of Dadds and Hart (2001), and narrative inquiry from the work of Clandinin and Rosiek (2007).

In *Assumption Interrogation: An Insight into a Self-Study Researcher's Pedagogical Frame*, Robyn Brandenburg seeks to contextualize Dewey's (1909/1933) attitude of "responsibility" (p. 12) through identifying and interrogating taken-for-granted assumptions about learning and teaching mathematics in preservice teacher education. Beginning with a framed yet flexible research design, Brandenburg used a triad of written reflective tools, ALACT (Korthagen, Kessels, Koster, Lagerwerf, & Wubbels, 2001), Freewrites (LaBoskey, 1994), and Critical Incident Questionnaires (Brookfield, 1995) to foster reflection in and on learning among her students. She came to see that as a self-study researcher she needed to be responsive to the data, and in some cases be creative about data gathering so that more could be understood about how teacher educator/preservice teachers were making sense of learning through reflection. In this chapter, she presents new understandings that emerged as a result of interrogating assumptions about reflective practice in preservice education which, in turn, relate to understanding 'reflective traction,' and the impact of understanding sub-assumptions in learning about teaching through reflective practice.

The final chapter, *Teacher Education for Literacy Teaching: Research at the Personal, Institutional, and Collective Levels*, Clare Kosnik and Clive Beck describe how following 22 graduates helped them identify strengths of the program (e.g., focus on engaging the pupils, creating a class community, incorporating children's literature). Linking the new teachers' practices to their preservice program resulted in the identification of seven priorities for teacher education: program planning; assessment; classroom culture and classroom management; vision for teaching; inclusive pedagogy; professional identity; and subject specific knowledge. While they found the design of the study worked well, overall, they found two challenges: analyzing the interviews and developing a classroom observation form that was both focused and suitable for use by the entire research team. Their self-study examines the processes by which they made sense of the data, the process in identifying the seven priorities for teacher education, insights they gained from examining their research practice within a longitudinal research frame, and issues they uncovered when attempting to disseminate their results to the university community.

As Berry and Crowe point out, self-study is often quite messy. In the 13 chapters that follow, the authors present their work in ways that highlight what is problematic for them, not just as teacher educators but as self-study scholars. Moreover, looking across these chapters, we see a wide variety of methods being used within this broad methodology called self-study. Clearly there is no single best way to engage in self-study. Yet as diverse as these chapters are in the specific methods being used, all of these studies use a highly recursive process in which data are revisited, reinterpreted, reframed, and restoried. We agree with Parker Palmer (1998) and Tom Russell (1997). Palmer argues that we teach who we are, while Russell asserts that how we teach is the message. Self-study provides a means for examining the messages we give as compared to the messages we intend to give, paired with a critical examination of the self that is the medium of those messages. In pursuing self-study, even familiar and comfortable practices become suspect. We cease to be naïve about our practice and increasingly recognize our individual and collective roles in the success or failure of teacher education. External factors (e.g., the students, the curriculum, the administration, colleagues, government mandates, socio-cultural contexts) can no longer excuse us from being responsible for our impact, and thus we are called to change.

References

Beck, C., Freese, A., & Kosnik, C. (2004). The preservice practicum: Learning through self-study in a professional setting. In J. J. Loughran, M. L. Hamilton, V. K. LaBoskey, & T. Russell (Eds.), *International handbook of self-study of teaching and teacher education practices* (Vol. 2, pp. 1259–1294). Dordrecht: Kluwer.

Brookfield, S. D. (1995). *Becoming a critically reflective teacher.* San Francisco: Jossey-Bass.

Brown, E. (2004). The significance of race and social class for self-study and the professional knowledge base of teacher education. In J. J. Loughran, M. L. Hamilton, V. K. LaBoskey, & T. Russell (Eds.), *International handbook of self-study of teaching and teacher education practices* (Vol. 1, pp. 517–574). Dordrecht: Kluwer.

Clandinin, D. J. (1993). Teacher education as narrative inquiry. In D. J. Clandinin, A. Davis, P. Hogan, & B. Kennard (Eds.), *Learning to teach, teaching to learn: Stories of collaboration in teacher education* (pp. 1–15). New York: Teachers College Press.

Clandinin, D. J., & Connelly, F. M. (2000). *Narrative inquiry: Experience and story in qualitative research.* San Francisco: Jossey-Bass.

Clandinin, D. J., & Connelly, F. M. (2004). Knowledge, narrative and self-study. In J. J. Loughran, M. L. Hamilton, V. K. LaBoskey, & T. Russell (Eds.), *International handbook of self-study of teaching and teacher education practices* (pp. 575–600). Dordrecht: Kluwer.

Clandinin, J., & Rosiek, J. (2007). Mapping a landscape of narrative inquiry: Borderland spaces and tensions. In J. Clandinin (Ed.), *Handbook of narrative inquiry: Mapping methodology* (pp. 35–75). London: Sage.

Coia, L., & Taylor, M. (2006). Moving closer: Approaching educational research through a co/autoethnographic lens. In L. M. Fitzgerald, M. L. Heston, & D. L. Tidwell (Eds.), *Collaboration and community: Pushing boundaries through self-study. Proceedings of the Sixth International Conference on Self-Study of Teacher Education Practices, Herstmonceux Castle, East Sussex, England* (pp. 59–62). Cedar Falls, IA: University of Northern Iowa.

Conle, C. (1996). Resonance in preservice teacher inquiry. *American Educational Research Journal, 33*, 297–325.

Connelly, F. M., & Clandinin, D. J. (1988). *Teachers as curriculum planners: Narratives of experience.* New York: Teachers College Press.

Dadds, M., & Hart, S. (2001). *Doing practitioner research differently.* London: RoutledgeFalmer.

Dewey, J. (1933). *How we think: A restatement of the relation of reflective thinking to the educative process.* Chicago: Henry Regnery. (Original work published in 1909).

Kitchen, J. (2005a). Conveying respect and empathy: Becoming a relational teacher educator. *Studying Teacher Education, 1*(2), 194–207.

Kitchen, J. (2005b). Looking backwards, moving forward: Understanding my narrative as a teacher educator. *Studying Teacher Education, 1*(1), 17–30.

Korthagen, F. A. J., Kessels, J., Koster, B., Lagerwerf, B., & Wubbels, F. A. J., Kessels, J., Koster, B., Lagerwerf, B., & Wubbels, T. (2001). *Linking practice and theory: The pedagogy of realistic teacher education.* Mahwah, NJ: Erlbaum.

Kuzmik, J. J., & Bloom, L. R. (2008). "Split at the roots": Epistemological and ontological chal-
lenges/tensions/possibilities and the methodology of self-study research. In M. L. Heston,
D. L. Tidwell, K. K. East, & L. M. Fitzgerald (Eds.), *Pathways to change in teacher education: Dialogue, diversity and self-study. Proceedings of the Seventh International Conference
on Self-Study of Teacher Education Practices, Herstmonceux Castle, East Sussex, England*
(pp. 207–212). Cedar Falls, IA: University of Northern Iowa.

LaBoskey, V. K. (1994). *Development of reflective practice: A study of preservice teachers.* New
York: Teachers College Press.

LaBoskey, V. K. (2004). The methodology of self-study and its theoretical underpinnings. In
J. J. Loughran, M. L. Hamilton, V. K. LaBoskey, & T. Russell (Eds.), *International handbook
of self-study of teaching and teacher education practices* (Vol. 2, pp. 817–869). Dordrecht:
Kluwer.

Loughran, J. J. (2004a). History and context of self-study of teaching. In J. J. Loughran, M. L.
Hamilton, V. K. LaBoskey, & T. Russell (Eds.), *International handbook of self-study of teaching
and teacher education practices* (Vol. 1, pp. 7–40). Dordrect: Kluwer.

Loughran, J. J. (2004b). Learning through self-study: The influence of purpose, participants and
context. In J. J. Loughran, M. L. Hamilton, V. K. La Boskey, & T. Russell (Eds.), *International
handbook of self-study of teaching and teacher education practices* (Vol. 1, pp. 151–192). Dordrecht: Kluwer.

Loughran, J. J. (2006). *Developing a pedagogy of teacher education: Understanding teaching and
learning about teaching.* London: Routledge.

McNiff, J. (2007). My story is my living educational theory. In J. Clandinin (Ed.), *Handbook of
narrative inquiry: Mapping a methodology* (pp. 308–329). London: Sage.

Mishler, E. (1990). Validation in inquiry-guided research: The role of exemplars in narrative studies. *Harvard Educational Review, 60*(4), 415–442.

Mitchell, C., & Weber, S. (1999). *Reinventing ourselves as teachers: Beyond nostalgia.* London:
Falmer.

Palmer, P. J. (1998). *The courage to teach: Exploring the inner landscape of a teacher's life.* San
Francisco: Jossey-Bass.

Pithouse, K., & Mitchell, C. (2007). Looking into change: Studying participant engagement in
photovoice projects. In N. de Lange, C. Mitchell, & J. Stuart (Eds.), *Putting people in the
picture: Visual methodologies for social change* (pp. 141–151). Amsterdam: Sense.

Russell, T. (1997). Teaching teachers: How I teach IS the message. In J. Loughran & T. Russell
(Eds.), *Teaching about teaching: Purpose, passion and pedagogy in teacher education*
(pp. 132–151). London: Falmer.

Schön, D. A. (1983). *The reflective practitioner: How professionals think in action.* New York:
Basic Books.

Schwab, J. J. (1970). The practical: A language for curriculum. *School Review, 78,* 1–23.

Taylor, M., Coia, L., Hopper, T., Sanford, K., Smolin, L., & Crafton, L. (2006). Making collaboration explicit in self-study research in teacher education. In L. M. Fitzgerald, M. L. Heston, &
D. L. Tidwell (Eds.), *Collaboration and community: Pushing boundaries through self-study.
Proceedings of the Sixth International Conference on Self-Study of Teacher Education Practices, Herstmonceux Castle, East Sussex, England* (pp. 247–251). Cedar Falls, IA: University
of Northern Iowa.

Tidwell, D. L. (2002). On stage: The efficacy and theatrics of large group instruction. In C. Kosnik,
A. Freese, & A. P. Samaras (Eds.), *Making a difference in teacher education through self-
study. Proceedings of the Fourth International Conference on Self-Study of Teacher Education
Practices, Herstmonceux Castle, East Sussex, England* (Vol. 2, pp. 111–116). Toronto, Canada:
OISE, University of Toronto.

Tidwell, D. L., & Tincu, M. (2004). Doodle you know what I mean? Illustrative nodal moments as
a context for meaning. In D. L. Tidwell, L. M. Fitzgerald, & M. L. Heston (Eds.), *Journeys of
hope: Risking self-study in a diverse world. Proceedings of the Fifth International Conference
on Self-Study of Teacher Education Practices, Herstmonceux Castle, East Sussex, England*
(pp. 241–245). Cedar Falls, IA: University of Northern Iowa.

Weber, S., & Mitchell, C. (1995). *"That's funny, you don't look like a teacher": Interrogating images and identity in popular culture*. London: Falmer.

Weber, S., & Mitchell, C. (2004). Visual artistic modes of representation for self-study. In J. J. Loughran, M. L. Hamilton, V. K. LaBoskey, & T. L. Russell (Eds.), *International handbook of self-study of teaching and teacher education practices* (pp. 979–1037). Dordrecht: Kluwer.

Whitehead, J., & McNiff, J. (2006). *Action research living theory*. London: Sage.

Zeichner, K. M. (1999). The new scholarship in teacher education. *Educational Researcher, 28*(9), 4–15.

Part I
Self-Study Through the Use of Text

Co/autoethnography: Exploring Our Teaching Selves Collaboratively

Lesley Coia and Monica Taylor

Last night Monica recounted her interactions earlier that day with a teacher education candidate who behaved disrespectfully toward her and toward the students with whom he was working. We talked, telling stories from our past experience, sometimes connecting directly with the current situation and sometimes not. We discussed our reactions to this type of student behavior. We talked about what we thought we were doing as teacher educators, what our vision of a good teacher is, and we discussed our and the student's role in his development as a teacher. In essence, we responded to the scenario as teacher educators, teachers, and women, as people with multiple identities who bring their whole selves to the situation at hand.

This conversation about professional matters is not unusual. It is the kind of conversation that frequently occurs between colleagues and is most valuable when occurring with other teacher educators. It is the kind of conversation necessary to continue to develop as professionals. These conversations should occur more often as a natural part of our professional development, but we struggle to find time and space for them. In our self-study research we take seemingly normal everyday conversations such as this seriously. We take them as revelatory, with the appropriate work, of important themes and structures in our work.

In this chapter we discuss the collaborative analysis of our teaching experience using a method we have come to call co/autoethnography. We start, in the first section, with the assumptions we make in order for thinking, talking, and writing about our everyday experience of teaching to be significant. In the second section we show, through detailed explanation and the use of examples from on-going co/autoethnographies, how this type of research is conducted.

We are teacher educators, but no matter how it might feel at times this is not all that we are. None of us is solely defined by our identity as teachers, and our identity as teachers is not solely defined by us. This conceptualization of identity as complex and culturally informed motivates our development and use of co/autoethnography. A corollary, central to our methodology, is that identity is dialogical. We maintain our identity in relation to others (Taylor & Coia, in press).

L. Coia (✉)
Agnes Scott College, 985 Wesley Drive, Macon, GA 31210, USA
e-mail: lcoia@agnesscott.edu

D.L. Tidwell et al. (eds.), *Research Methods for the Self-study of Practice*,
Self-Study of Teaching and Teacher Education Practices 9,
DOI 10.1007/978-1-4020-9514-6_1, © Springer Science+Business Media B.V. 2009

Identity is a central concern in self-study of teaching practices (Loughran, Hamilton, LaBoskey, & Russell, 2004), and more specifically co/autoethnography. Because researching ourselves assumes a certain understanding of the relation of self to self and self to others, it is important to be explicit about the theory of self underlying our approach, but that is not sufficient. It is also important to discuss epistemological perspectives of self. The purpose of self-study, after all, is to improve or at least better understand our practice (LaBoskey, 2004). We do this, in co/autoethnography, through the narrative process (Lyons & LaBoskey, 2002) when we make sense or interpret our experience by telling stories. We tell stories about ourselves and others in order to understand what we are doing or what we have just done. Below we look briefly at each of these underlying rationales for the use of co/autoethnography. We start with the importance of 'auto,' connect it with 'ethno,' move on to the 'co' and complete the section with a short discussion of 'graphy.'

Auto

Recently, Griffin (Monica's youngest child) saw his teacher in the supermarket. He could not believe it. He laughed and laughed. He could not believe that she shops or eats. We are all aware of this construction of the teacher as one who lives and breathes school, a person who is barely a person, someone with few personal attributes or emotions. Although we find this understanding of the teacher frustrating and baffling, we also play into it with our own lack of acknowledgment that we do, in fact, bring our whole selves to the classroom.

We started this chapter with the story of a professional conversation, making the point that this type of interaction provides a vantage point to enter a discussion of co/autoethnography. We are accustomed to thinking of conversations about our practice as professional if they are essentially an impersonal account of teaching and meet certain ethical and confidentiality standards. We make the stronger claim that when two teachers are talking about their practice it is not and never can be a purely professional conversation in that sense. There is no such thing as a discussion of the disembodied or impersonal practice of teaching. All discussions of practice involve the personal whether or not this is explicitly acknowledged. All practice is undertaken by persons: our questions are about our teaching, our dilemmas, our joys, and our triumphs. We cannot divorce our lives from our teaching. We can learn, for example, about discussion methods and theories behind active learning, but the issues we face when we are teaching are those generated by the intersection of us as fully fledged people, the text (theoretical or actual), and the students.

In order to understand our practice, the role of ourselves as persons has to be in the forefront where persons are seen as temporal beings with complex identities (Palmer, 1998). The auto of co/autoethnography refers to the self, and most particularly to the self as agent. We can never understand our own practice until we have some measure of understanding of our place in the execution of that practice. All practice is personal in this sense. Our pedagogical choices, our perceptions of the challenges we face, all involve our values, beliefs, and prior experience. But clearly this is not all that is involved. It is not that we are all there is in the world, but that we are in the world (Donnelly, 1999). Our subjectivity can not be excised from our practice (Levering, 2006). As we study our own practice, we grapple with how to capture our experience of teaching in a way that acknowledges its personal nature. In so doing, it is important to acknowledge the impact of the world on constructing the personal.

Our identity as teacher educators and our identification with this role is important if we accept that understanding our practice as teachers, the decisions we make and the actions we perform, involves looking at the values and reasons underlying our actions. In other words, our actions cannot be understood in a purely impersonal way. A recognized way to uncover our values, beliefs, and motivations is through autobiographical inquiry (Zeichner & Liston, 1996).

In its most general and simplistic terms, the idea behind the usefulness of autobiographical reflection is in the process of reflecting on the past from the perspective of the present where one achieves understanding that will hopefully lead to a better future (Abbs, 1974). This is possible because of the central identification of the author and protagonist in autobiography: the person being written about and the person writing are one and the same. This identification is the root of the epistemic privilege of autobiography (Bruss, 1976). Rarely in education is this identity relation made problematic. Yet, the intractable and common problems associated with the use of autobiography come from this defining feature. We are all aware of the problems of responding to autobiographies, or even more problematic, grading an autobiography. If, on the other hand, we recognize that the conception of the self underlying autobiography is culturally constructed and informed, then we open a space between the I writing and the I being written about. In the space opened up, we can see a looser relation that privileges the interpretative self, the author, and the present over the past (Coia & Taylor, 2002).

The value of autobiography in researching our own practice lies in our ability to understand how our past impacts our present. This is really a manifestation of agency. Teaching is an act which involves choices. The questions which trouble us on the way home and the joys of making a connection with a student are a result of seeing ourselves as agents. The conversation with which we started this chapter could be characterized as addressing the question, What do I do in this situation? None the less, we have to be aware that our sense of ourselves as actors, as agents, is constrained. We almost have to act as if we are agents. The idea of teacher which forms the basis of our work is a cultural construction. Our dilemmas and questions come from the specific and inescapable cultural context within which we live and breathe. We start from our experience of acting in the world as individuals. This is the ideal and what we strive for, but it is very complicated. Co/autoethnography provides us with a vehicle to make explicit the complexity of self-construction, self-identity, and agency.

Just as 'professional' has certain connotations, so does 'personal.' It can imply private, it can imply ownership, and it can imply the epistemological isolation we associate with solipsism, ample reasons why work on one's self is sometimes considered suspect in the world of educational research. We enter a classroom not just clothed in our teacher identity, but inhabiting all the identities we have formed over time. In any attempt to understand our experience of teaching, of being teacher educators, we must capture the tension between being an agent, being the author of our actions, and being constructed by the cultural norms and expectations within which we act. In co/autoethnography this tension is always apparent and allows for a more complex understanding of practice. It is apparent because the cultural aspect of experience plays along side the personal interpretation of that experience. This takes us to the 'ethno' of co/autoethnography.

Ethno

Co/autoethnography starts from the view that our identity and identification as teacher educators is not only important, it is culturally informed. A teacher educator is a complex of socially constructed individual enactments that form part of a person's identity. Our understanding of ourselves as teacher educators draws on and adds to its social and cultural meaning. There are aspects of this role with which we identify and aspects with which we struggle. While the role itself operates under social and cultural norms and expectations (Britzman, 1986), and to that extent is more or less clearly defined and thus constraining, it is a role we have accepted and made our own. Each teacher educator is constructed by others in that the role has meaning in a society, a meaning that is enacted in every experience we have as teacher educators. Each teacher educator, in so far as she exercises her agency within that role, makes it her own.

Just as with other social meanings of roles taken by persons, the meaning of teacher educator is malleable. There is space for new meanings as we each make it our own. This is a vital part of co/autoethnography. While autobiography is always at least implicitly interpretative, co/autoethnography insists on pulling the interpretative aspect to the surface. Co/autoethnography forces us to look at our lives through a cultural lens. Teaching is a social practice with cultural norms. Teacher educators are part of this practice and are not outside these norms. Co/autoethnography provides a means of making sense of this complexity from the inside, for ourselves.

Co

We bring the personal into the teaching whether we want to or not because teaching is about interpersonal connections between teacher and student. There are some teachers who strive to be impersonal, who give or accept advice such as, "Do not smile until December." And while we do not judge this view of the teacher or the view of teaching and learning on which these impersonal admonitions are based, we want to stress that for us this flies in the face of the idea that teaching is a relationship. If teaching is a relationship, we have no choice but to bring some of ourselves to our students. In fact, we must.

We start with the idea that teaching is interpersonal, because self-study research builds on an important idea: all self-study research is collaborative (Loughran & Northfield, 1998). As teacher educators who conduct research together, it would seem obvious that we meet this criterion. However, we want to make a stronger claim: We can research ourselves only within the context of others. Our notion of self is formed along a dynamic continuum. When we look at self, we move from the self that is constructed individually to the self in relation to others. This framework for self construction easily fits our selves as teacher educators. Although we believe that this framework can be applied to all teacher educators, we realize that part of our self-conceptualization stems from our foundational beliefs about teaching and learning. We value relationships in our teaching. We strive to build caring relationships with our students that support, guide, and nurture their own development as caring teachers. We are explicit about relationship building and model the process for our students with the hopes that they will do the same with their own students. Because relationships take center-stage in our teaching, it is only logical that they would also take center-stage in the research that we do on our teaching. We have also found, however, that the very process of undertaking autoethnographic research has helped us develop a collaborative method that allows us to weave our narratives together in a way that opens new opportunities for understanding our practice. This takes us to the narrative, the writing of our stories, the 'graphy' of co/autoethnography.

Graphy

So far, we have established that teaching is a relationship between teacher and student, each of whom does not and cannot leave their lives at the classroom door. We have also claimed that the identity of the teacher, of the teacher educator, is complex and is to some extent socially constructed. The question now becomes, How do we analyze and understand the personal experience of teaching? If we are to improve our practice, it is necessary that we have a way of reflecting on and making sense of our own teaching acts. We make sense of our work as teacher educators, as we make sense elsewhere, by narrative. We tell stories of our teaching in order to understand and improve it. Co/autoethnography involves writing about one's self, exploring the past in the effort to understand the present and prepare for the future. In drawing attention to the cultural and narrative aspect of experience we draw on Bruner's (1990, 2002) argument that narrative is not only a primary mode of thought but one that must be situated within a cultural context. It is via culture, our shared symbolic systems, that meaning is "rendered public and shared" (Bruner, 2002, pp. 12–13). Thus, as Bruner argues, experience is only intelligible if it is in narrative mode.

Stories are interpretations but they also need continual interpreting. In co/autoethnography, our stories become texts of experiences that are interpreted.

These interpretations change as our identity changes. The experience may be past, but the meaning or interpretation of the experience is from the present, and this is what is significant. The sense we make of the past is through the stories we tell today.

Drawing on the power of Bruner's (1990) argument that mind and experience are cultural narratives, our perceptions of experience (and the processes of remembering them) are ordered by narratives and narrative schemas. No conversation we have is solely in the present. We draw on our memories of past experiences in order to make sense of the present, but the very act of remembering and making sense is according to cultural stories and conventions. We strive to make sense of our experience, but we can only do this through the cultural symbols and systems we live in through the narratives we construct and by which we are constructed. As Ellis (2004) states, "[t]here's nothing more theoretical than a good story" (p. 23).

Co/Autoethnography

There are three central ideas behind co/autoethnography. In this section we have argued for co/autoethnography as an important method for researching our own teaching practices on the following grounds.

1. We are more than teachers. Our self-characterization always involves more than one facet of our identity, though it privileges certain parts of our identity depending on context. Identity is complex.
2. We are defined by others. Our identities as teacher educators are socially constructed. To be a teacher educator at this time in this culture has a specific cultural meaning. People react to us, and we respond based on this cultural understanding of what it means to be a teacher educator. This is not totally determined of course. There are multiple meanings and we have room within these meanings to change them, but they are there and they are constraining. Identity is cultural.
3. We are defined by our relationships with others. A fundamental tenet of our approach to self-study is that it is collaborative in a deep sense. Dialogue and conversation are vital to us in understanding ourselves and our practice. This is based on several positions concerning the nature of the self, knowledge, and the role of language in constructing knowledge. Identity is dialogical.

With this background in place, we now turn to consider how we carry out our co/autoethnographic research.

Co/Autoethnography Is Rooted in Collaboration

As we mention above, co/autoethnography relies on collaboration between at least two people. In our experience, this relationship must develop over time. We had been working together for 2 years before we began to develop our research methodology. We realized early on in our work that we had much in common. We both were influenced by feminist pedagogy and had studied and taught issues of language and literacy. We shared commitments to urban education and social justice teaching and had both been urban teachers in London and New York, respectively. We were both interested in the use of autobiography and personal narrative as vehicles to explore beliefs about teaching and learning. While this commitment to autobiography could probably be attributed to our interests in feminist teaching, language and literacy, we would also contend that it was an instinctual pedagogical choice as much as it was deliberate. Working together, we also acknowledged that we were quite different: Lesley is a philosopher of education, and Monica formally studied language, reading and culture, and qualitative research. We grew up in different parts of the world, during different decades, immersed in different cultures and experiences. On the other hand, our collaboration also seems to work because we share a similar work ethic. We are doers. We tend to volunteer and are not afraid to get our hands dirty. We would guess that this is the case for many teacher educators. We knew some of this before we began our work together, but truthfully we learned a tremendous amount about each other once we began our research together.

Our writing styles, however, were quite different, stemming from our different disciplines, although that has changed some over the past 8 years. Through insisting on writing together, rather than allocating sections of each piece we write, we have developed a collaborative voice. This was not an easy, smooth, or quick process but our trust seemed to navigate us through the rough spots. We have combined a variety of stances, including personal narratives, philosophical argument, theoretical discussion, research review, and qualitative research to form our collaborative voice. This voice is not a fully blended voice nor is it made up of our two voices alongside one another. More specifically, we each write pieces for every section of a text. We write them alone at our own computers and then talk about what we have written and we write together either face to face or over the telephone with a shared text in front of us. In some ways, writing collaboratively has liberated us from some of the stress and anxiety that we feel when we are writing solo. This process of writing collaboratively is essential to our analysis and explanation. We will talk in more detail about the actual writing process below.

The Social Contexts for Co/Autoethnography

Over the past 8 years, we have been conducting co/autoethnographic research. Our methodology has morphed and changed to accommodate changes in our pedagogical contexts and has been facilitated by emerging technologies. This malleability is one of the more important characteristics of co/autoethnography. We began developing this methodology as we worked together in an education department at a small liberal arts college on Staten Island. Most of the narrative sharing and analysis took place face to face, in our offices, classrooms, public schools, and homes, at lunch, and in the parking lots. These conversations continued over the phone but we had the luxury of relying on time together to participate in the research. Our encounters were taken for granted, however. We knew we would see each other each day. There was no need for scheduling.

Unfortunately, the end of that year brought change. Monica moved to a larger state university, in a curriculum and teaching department. Because of the proximity of the schools, we were able to continue to meet face to face. This time, however, we scheduled bi-weekly meetings that spilled over beyond the allotted time. We also relied more heavily on the telephone between our meetings. After all, we were teaching every day and had much to share and analyze.

A new year brought another new situation. This time Lesley moved down to Georgia to begin teaching at a small women's college. We fretted over whether or not we would be able to find a way to continue our collaborative research. But we found ways to support ourselves and ways to continue working with other. We realized we relied on each other just as much in our efforts to understand and improve our practice. We began to depend more heavily on the telephone, as well as email narratives and drafts of collaborative writing. Although we are not in constant communication, our pedagogical work drove the frequency of our discussions. We laugh now at our primitive use of email, shared files with italicized responses, and extended phone calls. (We had some mishaps with email where only one of us could receive files from the other.) We were always on the look out for ways to make our communication more effective.

Of late we have discovered and experimented with two important tools. We used and rejected *track changes* (a word processing function that allows the writer to track any comments and changes made in the paper). At first we saw it as an excellent way for us to respond to narratives and add text to a shared piece. But we became frustrated with the tool since it was antithetical to our method. The imposing style and color felt judgmental as if we were editing one another's writing rather than building it together. We have been working with *google.docs,* a shared writing program on Google that allows access by invitation only. This Internet format for writing complements our research style in that it lends itself well to collaborative writing. As a shared work processor, we each open the same file and either write individually or write together while on the phone. If both people have the file open, you can watch each other add and edit text. As we become more fluent with this technology, we use it to both share our individual narratives and write collaboratively.

But even with this interactive and engaging technology, we continue to have long, extensive phone conversations. The beginnings of these conversations are maintenance of our personal and professional relationships. We share personal updates as well as reports or frustrations about our teaching. We rely on each other to process through our personal and professional lives. We do not know if we could do co/autoethnography without talk. It is really an essential piece of our process.

Recognizing Emerging Co/Autoethnographic Questions

Our co/autoethnographic questions can address a variety of different scenarios and content. Sometimes, our questions emerge "from a frustration, a practice puzzle or a contradiction in a setting" (Anderson, Herr, & Nihlen, 2007, p. 125). These questions tend to feel like typical action research, practitioner research, or self-study.

In this case, we are looking for ways to explicitly improve our practice or our understanding of our teaching. Other times, we find ourselves grappling with more abstract concepts or situations that are not necessarily solution directed. We may discover new perspectives, or view a narrative from a different light, be led to a whole slew of new questions, or feel more confused and uncertain. Co/autoethnographic questions do not necessarily lead to linear investigations. They are at times messy and complicated and take extensive time to articulate and contextualize. Often we write about a particular topic and then feel as if we have come to a dead end and need a new direction to follow. We abandon strands of narratives that are examining a particular question that does not seem to take us anywhere. Our questions are generated from our dynamic situations as teacher educators and as people. As messy people, we can at times have messy questions.

For example, we are currently conducting a co/autoethnography examining the roots of our methodology. We are examining our history of researching language and literacy to better understand where we currently stand on co/autoethnography. This particular co/autoethnography emerged not so much from a problem or challenge in the classroom but from an appreciation that for each of us our particular understanding of literacy and language has profoundly affected our approaches to teaching and self-study. This has been a background to our work since we began our collaboration 8 years ago, yet, until now we have not explicitly addressed it. A co/autoethnographic project is an investigation into the teaching relationship, and in line with other qualitative methods, need not start with a fully and carefully defined research question. It can start with a general interest in an issue and curiosity about its relevance to our practice. Thus, while we have sometimes started with a problem in our past or present, we do not think of teaching as solely concerned with problem solving. We start with the idea that teaching is a relationship that occurs in a social, historical, and cultural context.

Consistent Qualities of Co/Autoethnographic Method

Throughout our different co/autoethnographic research studies, several consistent characteristics have emerged. Co/autoethnographic research is generated from the lived experiences, past and present, of teacher educators. We explore these lived experiences collaboratively with at least two researchers through the cyclical sequence of a variety of literacy practices including (a) writing, re-writing, and sharing personal narratives; (b) talk and discussion before and after the narratives are shared; (c) reflective writing and response; (d) reading theory, research, and other narratives; (e) more discussion and talk; (f) collaborative analysis through talk and writing; and finally, (g) writing up research through individually writing, talk, collaborative writing, talk, and collaborative editing. Our process does not necessarily follow this sequential order. It ebbs and flows depending on upon our particular context and topic of exploration. These literacy practices generate our data for analysis. We now describe these seven practices in a holistic fashion which mirrors the actual process. To describe each of these seven practices discretely would falsely represent our method. To illustrate our method we shall use our on-going self-study on language and literacy.

We started this self-study as a result of thinking about how we came to co/autoethnography and realized that while we 'knew' each other's background in language and literacy, we had never explored the impact of this shared lens on our work together in self-study. In short, the topic initially came up in conversation about self-study. We talked about it several times before deciding to explore it more systematically. We began to write, keeping in mind that for us, as co/autoethnographers, there is no such thing as writing autobiographically in the sense of purely personal writing. Our autobiographies are autoethnographies because social and political interpretations are built into the autobiographical narrative. We ground ourselves in the belief that our thinking and writing are deeply informed by the idea that the self is socially and culturally constructed. In this self-study we started with the question/idea of exploring how our current practice in language and literacy is informed by the social and intellectual context of our early experiences of teaching. So, for example, as we started writing we not only reflected on our past readings but more importantly on our lived experiences in urban communities. As we unpacked our particular understanding of the role of language and literacy in our practice, these past experiences naturally emerged as significant.

We respond to each other's initial writing by writing into each other's work. This stage is exploratory and affirmative and looks like a conversation. We respond in a variety of ways. Sometimes we are direct when we ask questions for clarification. Sometimes we give a personal response when we react in a true aesthetic fashion by sharing emotional connections. Sometimes a response is triggered by links with our own experience. Sometimes we give a response that shows how the writing is opening new perspectives for us. Sometimes the response is associative and helps us explore alternative avenues. These written responses lead us into many phone conversations. It is not enough for us just to write, we need to talk in real time throughout the process.

Then we start to write together. We post our combined document on *google.docs* and then, as we are now, we write while cradling phones on our necks, talking to each other. We take turns writing while we are talking. We read aloud and conduct the rest of the self-study, including data analysis and reporting, collaboratively. This way of working has evolved to meet our particular needs. For others, different modes of collaboration may well work better.

Our process is messy. Sometimes the writing flows and other times it is labored. Our conversations often help us to get through tensions. Below is an excerpt of our most recent co/autoethnography on language and literacy. We provide this snapshot of the initial writing and response stage of a co/autoethnography.

Lesley: *I have been reading Harold Rosen again and it reminded me of my first and foremost stance to language – that is a personal/political form of expression. Kids in London, at least then in the early '80 s, had the right to tell their stories in their language and to be heard. It is integral to*

> the anti-racist and anti-sexist education which is at the core of what I do although I see my approach has changed over the years. We really worked with the students not only on helping them tell their stories but understanding the structures of society and working with them. A lot of that work had to do with showing students the political nature of language (who gets to speak; who gets to tell you who is right and who is wrong; who gets to tell you that your story is not worth telling). A lot of the work we did was on self-respect as an individual and as member of a class, and appreciating that you have to tell your story in order to understand other people's stories.

Monica: *My life has revolved around language. I know that sounds clichéd – well of course, language is all around us – but for me it is true. I have spent much of my life trying to figure out the language of others whether it was other children my age from different cultures, grown-ups, my own middle schoolers at the alternative school who came from a very different New York, or the gang girls in my dissertation, or even people I encounter socially. Deciphering language and communicating with others allows me in. I am always trying to break the code and be able to communicate as an outsider/insider and an insider/outsider. I am talking about the all encompassing Language: i.e. body, visual symbols and signs, words, music, art, dance, dialect, expressions, jargon, etc... I am talking about the language of the streets, of the market, of the club, of the world.*

These excerpts from our first narratives on language and literacy may look polished and smooth but in actuality we struggled to write them and they took several weeks of phone conversations to emerge. We each had difficulty thinking back to our beginning interests in language and literacy. It felt like so long ago. We had trouble separating our current beliefs from our past beliefs and yet we had faith that something about language and literacy began early on for us. We knew that our collaborative narrative method had roots from the past; we just could not find the proper way to express them. Our conversations over the course of those weeks helped us to plod through our discomfort. We realized that our language awareness was heightened when we starting teaching kids in urban communities. Ironically there was quite a bit of overlap in the themes of our pieces. As we wrote earlier, the more we write narratives about the past, the more we identify common experiences and perspectives. We have begun to trace our intellectual histories and find there are multiple intersections.

Tailoring the Data Collection Methods to Meet the Needs of the Co/Autoethnographic Study

As we illustrate above, our data collection methods are tailored to meet our contextual and pedagogical needs. We have adapted our data collection methods to our location as well as the scope of our studies. When we taught and lived in the same location, we relied more heavily on face-to-face meetings, sharing narratives, discussing ideas, examining and analyzing data together, and organizing and writing research reports. In those days, we were also able to audio-record our discussions as another source of data. We used many of these data collection methods informally, as part of our day-to-day teaching and living. We view this as an extension of our daily lives as teachers where sharing narratives and discussing ideas were the primary means of support and community. These methods developed organically from our needs as teacher educators to find ways to learn about our teaching.

Over the past 6 years, during which we have lived and taught in different contexts within the United States, we have devised ways to continue these narrative sharings and conversations. Our data collection methods are more formalized, deliberate, and scheduled. No longer do we find ourselves in the restroom sharing stories. Rather we schedule deadlines for personal narrative sharings via email and *google.docs,* we organize times to have phone conversations to discuss narratives, share ideas, readings, theories, analysis, and writing format, and we schedule time to work on our studies. The vehicle of google.docs has been an enormous benefit as we now can work on the same piece together or individually. Also for scheduling, we use email, cell phones, text messaging, and land phone lines to communicate our plans. Barring a power outage, which we both experienced recently, our method is relatively smooth. Although we would prefer a more informal stance to our method, the value of our collaboration greatly exceeds the inconvenience of constantly scheduling. We are committed to this work and therefore make the time and effort to be productive together.

Although our written communication plays a vital role in our process, our talk and discussions are the most important methods of co/autoethnography. Without our discussions, there would be little deep analysis. It is often during our conversations that we discover or rethink our understandings of our teaching. This can take one conversation or often multiple conversations and some writing time around the same topic. We both take field notes either during the phone conversations or directly afterward so that we can record the essential points and the process of getting to those ideas. Our talk serves two purposes: it is a way that we generate data but it is also a method of data analysis.

Co/Autoethnographic Data Analysis

The goal of our analysis is to peel back the layers of our teaching and teaching identities to reveal new insights into how our past informs our present and future. We strive to deconstruct, as Anderson et al. (2007) write, "the dualisms of theory and practice, subject and object, and research and teaching" (p. 25). Our analysis is collaborative, reflective, and participatory where we both are involved in the analysis of the data. Our data collection method is recursive; as we collect the data we also attempt to analyze them. We analyze the data inductively by means of constant comparison (Glaser & Strauss, 1967; Strauss & Corbin, 1998). As we search for common patterns and themes (Bogdan & Biklen, 1998), we also check to make sure that they are identified as emerging by both of us. We triangulate the data, looking for patterns in multiple data sources and across both of our narratives and discussions, to ensure validity (Gordon, 1980). Once we have identified the patterns, we return to the literature to see if there is consistency with other research. Our goal is to develop a theory from which to continue teaching.

We look at the data from multiple lenses: researcher/researched, subject/object, and insider/outsider. We believe these varying perspectives lead to trustworthiness. Much of this analysis occurs through examining the data, theorizing by writing collaboratively, and talking, whether it is face to face or on the telephone. The value of our analytical talk again reminds us of why we do this type of research together. Without one another, we might not be able to find the same types of insights. Specifically, we move backwards, forwards, and sideways from reading individual narratives and the responses that have been written into them, talking, and theorizing and analyzing the narratives through writing collaboratively. The direction of this spiral movement is determined by where we are in our findings. For example, after analyzing some of the narratives we may decide that we need to revisit the literature and/or the first narratives written on a particular topic. Narratives by their nature are open to multiple interpretations and fixing on one interpretation is superficial. We do this because we need to report on our research for the moment, but we are aware that an interpretation can change with time. Knowing this encourages us to reflect on the data over long periods of time so that multiple interpretations can emerge. The interpretation serves the purpose for which it was constructed. There is an important sense in which no co/autoethnography is ever complete, although the findings of each co/autoethnography can be valid.

Conclusion

The use of co/autoethnography acknowledges the personal while recognizing the social construction of our identity and practices. This leads to a stronger learning experience for us and our students by making explicit the relational and cultural aspects of teaching. This has led to concrete changes in our practice such as an increased focus on trust-building and a willingness to honestly grapple with the complexity of teaching identity with our students.

There are challenges with this approach to our own practice. By working with the personal, by bringing it into our teaching, we risk opening ourselves to our students by admitting into the classroom a more expansive understanding of professional identity. While this can be uncomfortable for us and our students, it is necessary in order to embrace the complex human dynamic that is teaching and learning.

As all self-study researchers know, researching one's own practice is never straight forward or easy. Investigating one's self in relation to one's teaching where one focuses on one's past, one's relation to others, and one's relation to cultural norms, as one does in co/autoethnography, can seem daunting. One thing it is not, however, is self-indulgent. The focus while apparently on the teacher self, is always on the student and how to create a meaningful learning environment. When this hard work is undertaken with others it can help us make sense of our experience, and lace our conversations with even more significance.

References

Abbs, P. (1974). *Autobiography in education*. London: Heinemann.

Anderson, G. L., Herr, K., & Nihlen, A. S. (2007). *Studying your own school: An educator's guide to practitioner action research* (2nd ed.). Thousand Oaks, CA: Corwin.

Bogdan, R., & Biklen, S. K. (1998). *Qualitative research for education: An introduction to theory and methods*. Boston: Allyn & Bacon.

Britzman, D. (1986). Cultural myths in the making of a teacher: Biography and social structure in teacher education. *Harvard Educational Review, 56*(4), 442–456.

Bruner, J. (1990). *Acts of meaning*. Cambridge, MA: Harvard University Press.

Bruner, J. (2002). *Making stories: Law, literature and life*. Cambridge, MA: Harvard University Press.

Bruss, E. W. (1976). *Autobiographical acts: The changing situation of a literary genre*. Baltimore: Johns Hopkins Press.

Coia, L., & Taylor, M. (2002). Writing in the self: Teachers writing autobiographies as a social endeavor. In D. L. Schallert, C. M. Fairbanks, J. Worthy, B. Maloch, & J. V. Hoffman (Eds.), *The 51st yearbook of the National Reading Conference* (pp. 142–153). Oak Creek, WI: National Reading Conference.

Donnelly, J. F. (1999). Schooling Heidegger: On being in teaching. *Teaching and Teacher Education, 15*, 933–949.

Ellis, C. (2004). *The autoethnographic I*. Walnut Creek, CA: AltaMira.

Glaser, B. G., & Strauss, A. L. (1967). *The discovery of grounded theory: Strategies for qualitative research*. Chicago: Aldine.

Gordon, R. L. (1980). *Interviewing: Strategies, techniques, and tactics*. Homewood, IL: Dorsey.

LaBoskey, V. K. (2004). The methodology of self-study and its theoretical underpinnings. In J. J. Loughran, M. L. Hamilton, V. K. LaBoskey, & T. Russell (Eds.), *International handbook of self-study of teaching and teacher education practices*, (Vol. 2, pp. 817–869). Dordrecht: Springer.

Levering, B. (2006). Epistemological issues in phenomenological research: How authoritative are people's accounts of their own perceptions? *Journal of Philosophy of Education, 30*, 451–462.

Loughran, J. J., Hamilton, M. L., LaBoskey, V. K., & Russell, T. (Eds.). (2004). *International handbook of self-study of teaching and teacher education practices*. Dordrecht: Kluwer.

Loughran, J., & Northfield, J. (1998). A framework for the development of self-study practice. In M. L. Hamilton, S. Pinnegar, T. Russell, J. Loughran, & V. K. LaBoskey (Eds.), *Reconceptualizing teaching practice: Self-Study in teacher education* (pp. 7–18). London: Falmer.

Lyons, N., & LaBoskey, V. K. (Eds.). (2002). *Narrative inquiry in practice: Advancing the knowledge of teaching*. New York: Teachers College Press.

Palmer, P. J. (1998). *The courage to teach: Exploring the inner landscape of a teacher's life*. San Francisco: Jossey-Bass.

Strauss, A., & Corbin, J. (1998). *Basics of qualitative research: Techniques and procedures for developing grounded theory* (2nd ed.). Thousand Oaks, CA: Corwin.

Taylor, M., & Coia, L. (in press). Co/autoethnography: Investigating teachers in relation. In C. Lassonde, S. Galman, & C. Kosnik (Eds.), *Self-study research methodologies for teacher educators*. Rotterdam: Sense.

Zeichner, K. M., & Liston, D. P. (1996). *Reflective teaching: An introduction*. Mahwah, NJ: Erlbaum.

Teaching and Learning Through Narrative Inquiry

Rosa T. Chiu-Ching and Esther Yim-mei Chan

Our Context

As teacher educators, we work at The Hong Kong Institute of Education (HKIEd), a major provider of teacher education in Hong Kong. The HKIEd provides teacher education for about 80% of early childhood education teachers (HKIEd, 2007a) and about 80% and 25%, respectively, of new primary and secondary school teachers with degree and postgraduate qualifications (HKIEd, 2007b). The institute was founded in 1994 through an amalgamation of four former Colleges of Education and the Institute of Language in Education. As a single-purpose teacher education institute, learning and teaching are central to its mission, and HKIEd aims to prepare teachers "to become independent, analytical, critical and creative thinkers who can readily apply their knowledge" (HKIEd, 2006, p. 5).

Hong Kong students are generally regarded to be passive learners (Watkins & Biggs, 1996), and thus the issue of how to promote innovative learning and teaching becomes critical. According to Morris (2003), the curriculum, as experienced by most students in Hong Kong schools, is "taught by transmission" and "[emphasizes] memory over understanding and reproduction over application to real problems" (pp. 51–52). Indeed Mok (2005) notes

> Traditionally, Hong Kong students are taught with a didactic approach. The teacher is the source of information and knowledge. Students listen and follow the instruction of the teacher. Feedback in this tradition carries a negative connotation and is usually in the form of the teacher telling students what they have done wrong ... My students and I were brought up in this tradition. (p. 185)

In order to change this style of learning and teaching, innovations in teaching approaches are necessary.

As teacher educators, we have learned that one of the key elements to success in teacher education programs is to make teaching a site for inquiry and learning.

R.T. Chiu-Ching (✉)
Department of Educational Psychology, The Hong Kong Institute of Education,
Counselling and Learning Needs, 10 Lo Ping Road, Tai Po, NT, Hong Kong
e-mail: tlchiu@ied.edu.hk

D.L. Tidwell et al. (eds.), *Research Methods for the Self-study of Practice*,
Self-Study of Teaching and Teacher Education Practices 9,
DOI 10.1007/978-1-4020-9514-6_2, © Springer Science+Business Media B.V. 2009

Similarly, other scholars (Clarke & Erickson, 2004a; Hamilton, Pinnegar, Russell, Loughran, & LaBoskey, 1998; Loughran & Northfield, 1996) assert that theories of teaching and learning in teacher education can be made explicit by systematic self-study of practice. Like Bullough (1997), inevitably we have to answer the question, "Why do we teach teachers the way we do?" This requires us to look deeply into our past experiences to see how they have influenced our beliefs and practice. This can be captured through the notion of reflection (Schön, 1983) and displayed through self-study (Russell & Loughran, 2007) via narrative inquiry (Clandinin & Connelly, 2000; Connelly & Clandinin, 1988, 1990). Wilcox, Watson, and Paterson (2004) stress that self-study is vital to professional practice as it encourages practitioners "to uncover, critique and celebrate the less explicit, yet significant, aspects of professional practice" (p. 307).

The Puzzles

As advocated by the HKIEd, one of the objectives of teacher education is to transform students into critical thinkers and reflective practitioners. As teacher educators, we have tried our best to fulfill this responsibility. However, due to the challenges of such traditions as didactic teaching and passive learning, we have not been as successful as we would wish. When we learned that narrative inquiry could be a viable means for us to achieve our aim, we began incorporating it into our teaching. The puzzles that intrigue us about this new pedagogy are

1. What are the implications of narrative inquiry for our own teaching practice?
2. What are the implications of narrative inquiry for student learning?

When teaching child development in different teacher education courses, instead of starting from the grand theories of child development, we share our family stories of our fathers with students. After sharing our stories, we invite students to reflect on the meaning of these stories and how they may resonate with their own stories. When students engage in reflection (Schön, 1983) and discover resonances (Conle, 1996), they become aware of the centrality of lived experiences and come to understand the intricate relationships among learning, teaching, and life. This allows us and our students a new way to tell and live our stories as part of the process of constructing knowledge about teaching and learning. Through working collaboratively with our students, we engage in a restorying of our experiences in teacher education.

Evolution of the Research Methodology

The evolution of our methodology is a story in itself. Although we are at the same institute, prior to 1998 we hardly knew each other, as Esther worked in the Department of Early Childhood Education, while Rosa taught in the Department of

Educational Psychology, Counselling, and Learning Needs. We only came to know each other well when we both enrolled in the same doctoral program at the Ontario Institute for Studies in Education at the University of Toronto (OISE/UT) in 1998. Since then, we have become "critical friends" (Schuck & Russell, 2005, p. 108) and colleagues who listen to and support each other in teaching and research. We ask each other provocative questions, help reframe events, and join in professional learning. We also serve as reflective sounding boards, critics, and evaluators of each other's work (McNiff, Lomax, & Whitehead, 1996). We share our classroom stories and teaching journals, and co-write papers for presentation at the American Educational Research Association annual meetings. We have developed a deep and shared interest in the role of narrative inquiry in teaching and learning. This interest was inspired by our thesis work with Michael Connelly into the transformative power of narrative. As we studied narrative inquiry with Connelly, we became intrigued by it as we engaged in active reflection on who we are, and why we are who we are today.

Connelly and Clandinin (1988) used narrative inquiry in the form of storytelling as a tool to help teachers reflect on their personal practical knowledge (Connelly & Clandinin, 1985). According to Clandinin and Connelly (1995), the notion of 'teacher knowledge' is related to teachers' personal history (the past) and expressed in the teachers' present classroom practices and their future actions. By examining our storied experiences, we can see our personal philosophy in action, leading us to understand how our views, values, and beliefs were formulated and now direct our actions in teaching.

Esther recalled the experience of the first time we tried self-study via narrative inquiry in our doctoral program. The course instructor advised each participant (all colleagues at HKIEd) to prepare a chronicle detailing critical events and persons that were thought to be influential in our lives. We then presented our autobiographical stories to all members. Esther was surprised that our colleagues' responses helped her reconstruct meaning from her past experience, and Rosa has clear recollections of her classmates' presentations of revealing life stories and their resonance with her own story. Besides enhancing learning about ourselves, we learned who our colleagues were and about their family background, school, developmental, and work experiences. As their narratives of experiences were situated within particular personal, social, professional, institutional, and cultural stories, we each came to know our colleagues more thoroughly as real persons rather than just people with whom we worked. We discovered that prior to taking the narrative course, we barely knew each other and our colleagues although we had all been working at HKIEd for quite some time. Since our initial foray into narrative inquiry, we have found it useful for learning about ourselves, or self-learning, and learning about each other. We were also delighted to discover that sharing experiential stories could be a way to conduct teaching, learning, and inquiry, something we have always been interested in but did not have a name for.

Although telling stories seems to be a simple task, we both find that the emotions released through the retelling of our experiences are complex. We cannot stop recalling the long-ago memories and the puzzles of how our teacher selves were shaped, and the explorations have let us look backward, tracing our lives from childhood to adulthood along temporal and social dimensions. Our earliest efforts in self-study were crucial as they led us to understand the importance of tracing our development and its contribution toward the shaping of our views of students and teaching. If we do the same for our students, it means that we value their life experiences and the connections between their tacit beliefs and their teaching practice.

This chapter documents our self-study (Loughran, 2004; Russell & Loughran, 2007) of how we make sense of our experiential stories through narrative inquiry (Connelly & Clandinin, 1988; Clandinin & Connelly, 2000) as a way to promote teaching in child development for ourselves and learning for our students.

Foundational Theoretical Frameworks

The Role of Self-Study

Self-study has been defined as "the study of one's self, one's actions, one's ideas, as well as the 'not self' " (Hamilton & Pinnegar, 1998, p. 236). Tidwell and Fitzgerald (2004) note that for teacher-researchers, self-study encapsulates a wealth of experience embodied by teachers and their understanding of what teaching is. It is through inquiry that teachers examine the self within the teaching environment and their practices in terms of roles, actions, and beliefs, in order to consider making changes for improvement. Most importantly, the inquiry can be made available for "public critique and dissemination, rather than solely residing in the mind of an individual" (Loughran, 2004, p. 26). Thus "self-study is important not only for what it shows about the self but because of its potential to reveal knowledge of the educational landscape" (Clandinin & Connelly, 2004, p. 597). We concur with the claim made by Clandinin and Connelly (2004) that "self-study holds the highest possible potential for improving education" (p. 597) and teacher education. In our self-study, we use narrative inquiry to tell experiential stories of our teaching that let us critically examine our practice in order to envision new possibilities in teacher education.

The Concept of Teacher Knowledge

Our view of teacher learning differs considerably from traditional views of teacher education. Indeed how teacher education is organized reflects different conceptions of teaching, learning, knowledge construction, and the curriculum. Traditionally, teacher educators are university-based researchers who transmit formal knowledge and theory (Cochran-Smith & Lytle, 1999) which is "developed at a distance through the use of systems of externally derived constructs or frameworks for understanding" the phenomena (Cole & Knowles, 2000, p. 10). Such 'knowledge for teachers' (Connelly & Clandinin, 2000a) or 'knowledge-for-practice' (Cochran-Smith & Lytle, 1999) is generally studied in teacher education programs. The assumption behind this organization of teacher education is a technical-rational

(Schön, 1983) or behavioristic one. It implies that teachers are empty vessels, passive knowledge receivers, and accumulators. Those who can implement what they have learned into practice will be able to teach effectively.

In recent decades, teacher knowledge has come to be viewed from a new vantage point. Beginning in the mid-1970s, research on teacher thinking, teaching, and teacher knowledge began to emerge (Cole & Knowles, 2000; Marland, 1998), leading to changes in various teacher education programs (e.g., Epanchin, Paul, & Smith, 1996). Research on new visions of learning and teacher knowledge has been prominent in the field of education (Cochran-Smith & Lytle, 1999; Putnam & Borko, 2000). This shift involves a growing realization that teachers generally do not rely on researchers as a source of knowledge for teaching. Instead they "draw heavily on another fund of knowledge which remains largely private and tacit" (Marland, 1998, p. 15). This knowledge arises from their personal experience as teachers and their own lived experiences.

Clandinin and Connelly (1995) argue that teacher knowledge is "that body of convictions and meanings, conscious or unconscious, that have arisen from experience (intimate, social, and traditional) and that are expressed in a person's practices" (p. 7). Other researchers have referred to it variously as 'practical knowledge' (Elbaz, 1983) or 'knowledge-in-practice' (Cochran-Smith & Lytle, 1999). Connelly and Clandinin (2000a) contend that teacher knowledge so generated is fundamentally personal, experiential, and practical. They coined the term, "personal practical knowledge" (Connelly & Clandinin, 1985, p. 190), to account for the tacit knowledge which can overshadow teachers' formal knowledge and prescribed policies in the education system. As teacher knowledge is always knowledge in context (Connelly & Clandinin, 2000a), it can be conveyed through a language of story that is "prototypical, relational among people, personal, contextual, subjective, temporal, historical, and specific" (Clandinin & Connelly, 1995, p. 14). Clandinin and Connelly (2004) suggest that "self-studies of teacher knowledge must somehow lie closer to practice, to be studies of practice, studies of what we call personal practical knowledge" (p. 582).

Narrative Inquiry

Our orientation in narrative is grounded in the study of experience, a philosophy of education put forward by Dewey (1938), Schwab (1973), Connelly and Clandinin (1988), and Eisner (1993). These authors assert that there are organic connections among experience, education, life and research, emphasizing that inquiries into human experience are experientially based, personal and social. As experience is rooted in the past, developed in the present and enacted in the future, it is embedded in temporality and context, and is ever-changing, fluid and dynamic. Following this line of thinking, we have grounded our research in narrative inquiry into how our stories of experience can prompt reflection and resonance, creating experiential and contextualized learning for ourselves and our students in teacher education programs.

According to Clandinin and Connelly (2000), "narrative is both the phenomenon and the method of the social sciences," and "the best way of representing and understanding experience" (p. 18). Experience is storied in nature and the phenomenon used in narrative inquiry is story (Connelly & Clandinin, 1990), and Connelly and Clandinin (2006) have identified "three commonplaces of narrative inquiry–temporality, sociality and place–which specify dimensions of an inquiry space" (p. 479). Temporality means that events and people have a past, present and future and are always in transition. Sociality takes into consideration the personal nature of experience (including feelings and moral dispositions) and the social context and conditions (including relationships) in which the events and people exist. Place involves the "physical and topological boundaries of place or sequence of places where the inquiry and events take place" (p. 480).

Our stories of experience reflect the commonplaces of temporality, sociality and place in action. We use our stories in teaching to stimulate our own reflection which in turn may inform our practice. We also anticipate that, through students' reflections on our stories and resonance with their own stories, our students will construct and revisit their teacher knowledge. In this way, we and our students can be acknowledged as 'knowers' (Fenstermacher, 1994) who are capable of producing teacher knowledge in teacher education programs. We anticipate that our inquiry will reflect our aim as follows:

> Narrative inquiries are shared in ways that help readers question their own stories, raise their own questions about practice and see in the narrative accounts stories of their own stories. The intent is to foster reflection, storying and restorying for readers. (Clandinin & Connelly, 1990, p. 20)

Narrative Inquiry, Story, and Self-Study

In our study, we adopt narrative as a form of inquiry and a method to understand and represent our experiences in teacher education as self-study. Clarke and Erickson (2004a) note that this is possible and they identify self-study as the "fifth commonplace" (p. 58), in addition to Schwab's (1973) 'four commonplaces' of the curriculum: the learner, teacher, milieu, and subject matter. They (Clarke & Erickson) indicate that self-study is indeed "the cornerstone to professional practice" (p. 59) because through it, professionals can "come to know, problematize, and improve their practice." Indeed various researchers have shown that it is possible to use narrative inquiry as a means of self-inquiry into teaching practice (see, for example, Conle, 2000; Miller Marsh, 2002; Ross, 2002).

We realized we had been unsuccessful in educating our students to become reflective practitioners when we taught child development primarily through the grand theories (e.g., Piaget, Vygotsky). We then began to explore alternate pedagogies that would enable students to make sense of our teaching and let them have more educative experiences. We started our inquiry with the initial puzzle of wondering how the teaching and learning of child development can be restoried and lived out. Stories are "the closest we can come to experience" (Clandinin & Connelly,

1994, p. 415), and thus we use storytelling as a springboard for building teacher knowledge. Instead of merely teaching the grand theories of child development and expecting students to apply them, we share our stories of our fathers. After hearing our stories, we encourage students to reflect on the meaning of our stories and how they may resonate with their own stories of their fathers. This enables us to examine our teaching of child development and students' construction of teacher knowledge.

Story as a Research Device

Eisner (1993) notes that different forms of representation can help convey the meaning of one's experiences. An artistic form of representation, such as narrative or story, is not simply a rhetorical device for expressing sentiments but a medium for understanding how people experience the world (Connelly & Clandinin, 1990; Van Manen, 1990). As teacher educators teaching child development, we use inquiry through narratives as a means to help us and our students attend to our lives closely so that we are in a good position to understand how our past experiences shaped our teacher selves. In addition, our inquiry helps us understand how culture affects our ways of thinking and behaving which also have implications for the way we develop our own personal perspectives on child development (Chan, 2004). The telling of family stories creates a space to bring our childhood memories forward in time as we think about who we are and where we came from. Buttignol (1999) reminds us not to undervalue the significance of stories which are essential expressions of self and personal creativity. Although the same story is heard, each of us may create a unique version in our minds. Barton (1999) also notes the importance of the stories that come to us from our families and culture and of the shapes and forms these stories often take. Indeed it is through narrative that cultures have been created and their worldviews expressed (Conle, 2000).

Story in Teaching and Teacher Education

The classroom is regarded "as a place where students and teachers tell stories to one another to make sense of where they have been and help them grow and develop in the future" (Connelly & Clandinin, 1988, xvi). If the best response to a story is to tell a story (Swartz, 1999), then the best response in the classroom is for us to tell stories of our own lives concerning how we make personal connections and recover meaning from our lived experiences and resonate with even more stories. Story is increasingly used in research about teaching and teacher education (Carter, 1993) as a medium of data representation and a guide in the development of methodologies (Conle, 2000). Although storytelling has long been regarded by students to be a relevant part of teacher education, its legitimacy is seldom acknowledged (Clandinin, 1992). Connelly and Clandinin (1988) advocate narrative inquiry in which storytelling is acknowledged as a powerful tool for reflection on the personal practical knowledge teachers hold and how such knowledge is formulated. Eisner (1988) and Carter (1993) stress that knowledge comes from experience, and teachers' stories are one of the most pervasive ways to represent their experience.

Connelly and Clandinin (2000b) point out that the stories that teacher narratives are built on are both personal and social since they reflect a person's life history and the professional contexts in which teachers live. When teachers share experiential stories, reflection and resonance can be fostered. As Schön puts it, the aim of reflection is to "lead the person to think differently in such a way that she might inquire differently or better on the next round of experience" (cited in Connelly & Clandinin, 1992, p. 5). Carter (1993) also supports the use of stories with teachers because these stories are closely linked to teachers' reflections in and on action. Conle (1996) indicates that resonance is "[a metaphor] for the human interactions ... a development of self through interaction with others at an intimate level. An intellectual understanding of this phenomenon in connection with narrative work in teacher education may help teachers become more aware of their knowledge processes" (p. 299).

As we reflect on our early experiences, we see human life as a long story along the temporal and social dimensions, and we are living in the midst of that long story. If we engage in telling and retelling our lived stories, we can better understand the development and changing aspects of ourselves and views. In our lived stories, we can find threads, patterns and narrative unity in our experiences. The puzzles that emerge from the stories lead us to search for themes and tensions that contribute to who we are and what we are like today. Our reflective journeys begin when we bring stories of our past experiences forward, examine how they interact with our present self and the social context, and reflect on the meanings we glean from these experiences. Clandinin and Connelly (1999) stress that narrative inquiry through storytelling is a reflective act during which "further inquiry takes place through their telling and through response to them" (p. 17). Glesne (1999) argues that "the beauty of a good story is its openness . . . .. It encourages you to compare its descriptions and analyses to your own experiences and to, perhaps, think differently about your own situation" (p. 196). Thus the lived stories of teachers and students can be central elements in research, teaching and teacher education (Connelly & Clandinin, 1994).

Stories of Experience with Family

Although we do not teach child development primarily through grand theories, we agree with Bronfenbrenner (1986) and Vygotsky (1962) who maintained that the earliest influences on a child usually come from the socialization provided by parents and family. Indeed, our parents, especially our fathers, have affected us deeply and in varied ways. In our inquiry process, we each developed our family stories, tracing experiences with our fathers ('father stories') and our memories of specific childhood episodes. We wrote our stories and shared them with students in class. We invited the students to reflect on the meaning of our stories, prepare their own father stories, and share these stories in class. We then discussed what we all learned. Below are our stories of our fathers and the stories (all used by permission) of four of our students (Annie, Nancy, Susan and Teresa, all pseudonyms). Annie and

Nancy were Rosa's students, while Susan and Teresa were Esther's students. As our medium of instruction was Cantonese Chinese, all stories have been translated into English by us, and we have attempted to maintain each individual storyteller's voice.

Rosa's Story of Her Father

I am the eldest daughter in a family of five children. Both of my parents were teachers. My father had been a primary school teacher for more than forty years. He had impressed me as being a very dedicated, responsible, diligent, straight but caring teacher who devoted much of his waking hours to his teaching and preparatory work. I still remember him returning home late from school after marking assignments, relaxing a bit before and after dinner, and going back to the nearby school to finish grading papers or preparing lessons until 10 or 11 p.m. As my father set a high standard for himself and the students, he always corrected their assignments so carefully that afterwards, there seemed to be more red marks on the papers than penciled Chinese characters. He was also a straight but caring disciplinarian who required students to abide by classroom rules.

I remember when I was young, my father used to tell me that one of the aims of education is to learn how to live as a human being. Although my father probably had not read Dewey, it is amazing that he shared similar views about education and life. From him, I learn that I should be dedicated to my students, establish cordial relationships with them, respect them, regard them as lifelong friends, and be devoted to teaching. I find that I resemble him for I usually stay up late to prepare lectures or meticulously grade assignments. My father provided me with a perfect model to follow. Probably these are some of the influences my father exerted on me. (Reflective journal, Fall term, 2000)

Esther's Story of Her Father

As a child, I always argued with my father and tried very hard to justify my behavior. He immediately stopped me and said, "I am the commander-in-chief, and you are my soldier. You have to follow my order no matter if it is right or wrong, or otherwise you would be executed." My eyes expressed my fearful yet skeptical feeling, but I dared not look at my father and asked him why.

There was another instance. "Come and pick up the tissue on the floor. Put it into the bin!" I was so concentrated on my study at that moment that I could hardly hear my father's voice. Instantly he yelled at me angrily, "Come and stand at the corner until I tell you to move!" I stood for an hour with a lot of grievances at heart. This incident taught me that I should respond quickly to his orders, and follow his instructions without delay. I was trained to be disciplined just like a soldier. I learned how to be "good" and obedient ever since I was a baby girl.

By living in the image of children as "soldiers" at home, I was totally terrified. Those experiences and feelings brought me negative effects that smothered my creativity and curiosity. Due to my father's coercive measures, I was threatened to behave properly, and an enormous gap thus grew between me and my father. (Reflective journal, Spring term, 2001)

Annie's Story of Her Father

I am the youngest daughter in a family of eight children. Both of my parents were from mainland China. My father came to Hong Kong when he was about 10 years old. For all of his life, my father worked as a coolie (an unskilled laborer hired to carry goods around the dock) *earning a meager salary. Due to some bad hobbies such as smoking, gambling, drinking, and prostituting, the financial situation of the family was very poor. The closest relationship I had with my father was established at times when I stayed up late not going to bed at the same time as my siblings. When he returned from work late at night, he would drink, smoke, eat bread with cheese, and peanuts. Although I enjoyed these intimate moments with him, I hated his bad habits of drinking and smoking as he would give me a drink made from alcohol and his pipe. As our financial circumstances were precarious, the other family members did not have the luxury to savour the expensive soft cheese, the bread and peanuts that my father consumed every night. All we could afford for meals were the skin of bread cooked with cane sugar. That is why to this day, I still hate those kinds of food that my father favoured. Due to his behaviour, my father left a very negative impression on the other family members. Nevertheless these were the only times that I could spend alone with him. Although I did not approve of his actions, this became the pattern of my relationship with him: communicating through drinking and smoking. I realized that it was not a normal father-and-daughter relationship because at all other times, there was not much exchange between us. I felt our relationship was in the dark.* (Reflective journal, Fall term, 2000)

Nancy's Story of Her Father

I am the third daughter in a family of four girls. My father had only attended junior secondary school. My impression is that we are not a rich family, and my parents have to work hard to make ends meet. Nevertheless I did not remember being hungry for any meal or without new clothes for the Chinese New Year. If my father had money, on Sundays, he would take us to a restaurant for steak or buy us things. I also remember when my father took me to the kindergarten, he would buy me a healthy drink. He would also carry me when going out. These are still in my memory today. I feel that it is not the material things but the company and the good parent–child relationships that matter.

My parents love me very much, and our family relationship is close. Although my parents were not well educated, they have influenced me much. If I know how to love the children I teach, I can attribute it to my parents. I remember once reading an article stating that the family environment will make a difference in a child's development. If the parents give the children more love, they will learn to love. I agree with what I have read. (Reflective journal, Fall term, 2000)

Susan's Story of Her Father

I was brought up in a family of eight children. My father was an authoritarian who considered obedience a virtue, and demanded us to accept all his decisions without question. We would immediately get scolded if we had a different opinion. I was always the first one to be punished which was probably due to the fact that I was the eldest. I dare not do anything but cry when he punished me. He always called me "stupid" and that made me become timid and shy.

My parents worked really hard to make ends meet. Therefore they hardly had time to communicate with us. During the day, we were told to keep silent in our house because my father worked overnight and needed to sleep in the morning. He would lose his temper and even throw a chair at us for any disturbances we made. My mother had to take us to another place in order to stay away from him. My parents looked upon me as a role model for my younger siblings, and they were asked to obey and respect my words because I was their "eldest sister." I was told to take care of all the housework as well as to look after my siblings. (Reflective journal, Spring term, 2001)

Teresa's Story of Her Father

I was brought up in a family of four children. My father was caring, fair and patient. He considered honesty as the most important virtue, and therefore telling lies was strictly prohibited. Whenever we were found to be dishonest, we would be seriously punished before he helped us understand the causes of the event. I can still remember there was an occasion that my younger brothers cut a soccer ball into two pieces. When my father found out and asked them why, they refused to tell him that they just wanted to examine what was inside. They got scolded and beaten for not telling the truth. My father's rearing style was authoritative, quite commanding and demanding, but always with good explanation. We therefore became his good followers and behaved properly. (Reflective journal, Spring term, 2001)

What We Have Learned

In discussing the significant characteristics of narrative practices as modes of inquiry and ways of knowing, Lyons and LaBoskey (2002) point out that narrative practices are intentional human actions, socially and contextually situated. Narrative engages participants in the interrogation of aspects of teaching and learning by 'storying' the experience, implicating the identities of the participants, and involving the construction of meaning and knowledge. We borrow these distinctive features of narrative practices to discuss the results of our stories of experience and to shed light on understanding how the teaching and learning of child development take place and how teacher knowledge can be constructed through narrative in teacher education programs.

All of the stories told above capture experiences which are socially and contextually situated along temporal dimensions in our families within the Chinese context of Hong Kong. It is apparent that most of us come from big Chinese families of four to eight children. This is not something extraordinary according to the old Chinese tradition. For our parents and their generation, big families with many children were symbols of expansion and prosperity. Times have changed; now there are usually two or in some cases at the most three or four children in Chinese families in Hong Kong. Nevertheless our stories reveal authentic childhood episodes in terms of how we experienced our relationship with our fathers, and the rearing practices and management of children.

Through retelling and reliving our stories of experience with our fathers, as teacher educators, we have a chance to look back and reflect upon how our fathers have influenced our development. This in turn shapes our views on students and the teaching of family influences on child development. Through interactions with our fathers, we learn the importance of love, care and discipline and their interrelationship in child development. We realize how our images of students are shaped through our own development. While recalling her father's diligence as a responsible teacher and his close relationship with students, Rosa sees him as a mentor. She finds that she takes after him, seeking to be a devoted teacher educator who regards her teaching seriously and looks upon students as lifelong friends. She remembers that at one time in a 7-year period, she had written three letters of recommendation for a former student for further studies. This student eventually acquired three degrees in education including a doctorate. In retrospect, she thinks that her long-time cordial relationship with students may have been a prime example of her father's legacy for her.

On the other hand, Esther sees herself living the image of "soldier" under her father's authoritarian management, and she admits that she is scared to communicate with him due to his style. Through interactions with her father, Esther knows she does not like to be treated that way. Although not an authoritarian type teacher herself, in tracking her experiences during the inquiry process, she gathers she must avoid adopting the "Do as I say!" attitude in working with her students. She admits that she usually keeps an open mind, allowing students to think democratically and acts accordingly so as not to repeat what she had undergone. We both find it helpful to look backward in our three-dimensional narrative inquiry space to examine our childhood experiences and explore their contribution toward our own development and the shaping of our teaching beliefs and attitudes. This indeed has implications for the way we interact with students at present and in the future as we understand the importance of adopting a genuine, concerned and democratic approach to teaching and building relationships. Through the inquiry process, we also come to realize that child development can be taught in an innovative approach by making connections to our own storied lived experiences. Not only are our experiences authentic and practical, the way we explore our development has been a very meaningful and an interesting way to conduct a self-study of our own teaching practice.

When our students reflect upon the meaning of our family stories, they revisit their family experiences and resonate with stories of their own fathers. We discover that, as with our storied experiences, they realize their fathers have greatly influenced them. As in the case of Rosa's father, Nancy and Teresa note that their fathers are caring, warm and supportive. Nancy and Rosa openly admit that if they know how to love their students, they attribute it to their loving parents and especially their fathers. Although Teresa considers her father to be authoritative and demanding, she considers him reasonable since he provides explanations for rules and discusses why certain behaviors are desirable or not. We experienced that when parents are warm and considerate, they tend to stimulate children more and scold less. We believe the love and concern our fathers showed us enable us to learn how to love the students we teach. Nancy, Teresa and Rosa all look upon their parents and especially their fathers as role models, and they seek to foster good family relationships and establish cordial rapport with the students they teach.

On the contrary, Esther and Susan admit that they have authoritarian and strict fathers who treat them like soldiers demanding complete compliance to orders. Esther remembers being terrified and having her curiosity and creativity smothered. Likewise, Susan becomes timid and shy as she has been labeled "stupid" by her father. Annie terms her relationship with her father as "strange" as they had to communicate through drinking and smoking, while at other times there was no exchange of communication. After sharing their stories of how they have been treated by their fathers, our students begin to realize the impact created by such experiences on their own development. Nevertheless Esther, Susan and Annie believe that their fathers' adoption of strict discipline and a strange way of communication were appropriate ways of teaching children at the time they were growing up within the context of Hong Kong. They understand that in those days, Chinese fathers were usually the primary bread-winners, emotionally reserved and viewed as the major authority within families. Thus their strict way of disciplining children was commensurate with the social practices of the time as it was thought that this would produce children with filial piety and obedience. In tracing these experiences, they realize that their fathers have influenced their development and their views of students. In their present roles as a teacher educator and teachers, Esther, Susan and Annie vow not to replicate what they have experienced with their students and own children. As the stories were shared in the class, Susan remarked that as she had been put down in the past, she now views her relationship with students and her parenting orientation along two dimensions: an authoritative style that is demanding but responsive, and a rational, democratic approach in which the rights of all parties including those of the students and the parents are respected. As teachers, instead of solely insisting on complete obedience, Esther, Susan and Annie realize that they should consider new ideas such as accepting students as unique beings, encouraging freedom of expression and respecting individual thinking.

Our students find that the inquiry process enables them to revisit their childhood experiences to make sense of learning child development in an experiential and practical approach. They report that they find this way of constructing teacher knowledge a practical and contextualized way of learning. They believe that inquiry through teacher stories had a greater impact on them than merely learning the grand theories of child development delivered in a didactic manner without much relevance to their personal experiences.

Conclusion

In our attempt to intertwine narrative inquiry with self-study, together with our students, we have discovered that child development can be taught and learned in an experiential and practical approach, and both we and our students have come to better understand our own development and our teaching beliefs. In essence, all of us have gained greater awareness of the impact our past experiences can have upon our views of students, our teacher knowledge and our teaching practice. This somehow has shifted our personal practical knowledge regarding the teaching and learning of child development. Indeed by using narrative inquiry as a form of self-study, we have experienced what Clarke and Erickson (2004b) called "the continuing quest to seek viable responses and appropriate actions to the questions of: . . . how to do it . . ." (p. 207).

References

Barton, B. (1999). The art of storytelling: Telling, retelling and listening. *Orbit: Story Matters*, *30*(3), 42–46.

Buttignol, M. (1999). We are our stories: Beginning with the personal in teacher education. *Orbit: Story Matters*, *30*(3), 38–41.

Bullough, R. V., Jr. (1997). Practicing theory and theorizing practice in teacher education. In J. J. Loughran & T. L. Russell (Eds.), *Teaching about teaching: Purpose, passion and pedagogy in teacher education* (pp. 13–31). London: Falmer.

Bronfenbrenner, U. (1986). Ecology of the family as a context for human development: Research perspectives. *Developmental Psychology*, *22*, 723–742.

Carter, K. (1993). The place of story in the study of teaching and teacher education. *Educational Researcher*, *22*(1), 12–15, 18.

Chan, Y. M. E. (2004). Narratives of experience: How culture matters to children's development. *Contemporary Issues in Early Childhood*, *5*, 145–159.

Clandinin, D. J. (1992). Narrative and story in teacher education. In T. Russell & H. Munby (Eds.), *Teachers and teaching: From classroom to reflection* (pp. 124–137). London: Falmer.

Clandinin, D. J., & Connelly, F. M. (1990). Narrative and story in practice and research. In D. Schön (Ed.), *The reflective turn: Case studies of reflective practice* (pp. 258–282). New York: Teachers College Press.

Clandinin, D. J., & Connelly, F. M. (1994). Personal experience methods. In N. K. Denzin & Y. S. Lincoln (Eds.), *Handbook of qualitative research* (1st ed., pp. 413–427). Thousand Oaks, CA: Sage.

Clandinin, D. J., & Connelly, F. M. (1995). *Teachers' professional knowledge landscapes.* New York: Teachers College Press.

Clandinin, D. J., & Connelly, F. M. (1999). Storying and restorying ourselves: Narrative and reflection. In A. Chen & J. Van Maanen (Eds.), *The reflective spin: Case studies of teachers in higher education transforming action* (pp. 15–24). Singapore: World Scientific.

Clandinin, D. J., & Connelly, F. M. (2000). *Narrative inquiry: Experience and story in qualitative research.* San Francisco, CA: Jossey-Bass.

Clandinin, D. J., & Connelly, F. M. (2004). Knowledge, narrative and self-study. In J. J. Loughran, M. L. Hamilton, V. K. LaBoskey, & T. Russell (Eds.), *International handbook of self-study of teaching and teacher education practices* (pp. 575–600). Dordrect: Kluwer.

Clarke, A., & Erickson, G. (2004a). The nature of teaching and learning in self-study. In J. J. Loughran, M. L. Hamilton, V. K. LaBoskey, & T. Russell (Eds.), *International handbook of self-study of teaching and teacher education practices* (pp. 41–67). Dordrecht: Kluwer.

Clarke, A., & Erickson, G. (2004b). Self-study: The fifth commonplace. *Australian Journal of Education, 48,* 199–211.

Cochran-Smith, M., & Lytle, S. L. (1999). Relationships of knowledge and practice: Teacher learning in communities. *Review of Research in Education, 24,* 249–305.

Cole, A. L., & Knowles, J. G. (2000). *Researching teaching: Exploring teacher development through reflexive inquiry.* Needham Heights, MA: Allyn & Bacon.

Conle, C. (1996). Resonance in preservice teacher inquiry. *American Educational Research Journal, 33,* 297–325.

Conle, C. (2000). Narrative inquiry: Research tool and medium for professional development. *European Journal of Teacher Education, 23*(1), 49–63.

Connelly, F. M., & Clandinin, D. J. (1985). Personal practical knowledge and the modes of knowing: Relevance for teaching and learning. In E. W. Eisner (Ed.), *Learning and teaching the ways of knowing. The eighty-fourth yearbook of the National Society for the Study of Education* (pp. 174–198). Chicago: University of Chicago Press.

Connelly, F. M., & Clandinin, D. J. (1988). *Teachers as curriculum planners: Narratives of experience.* New York: Teachers College Press.

Connelly, F. M., & Clandinin, D. J. (1990). Stories of experience and narrative inquiry. *Educational Researcher, 19*(5), 2–14.

Connelly, F. M., & Clandinin, D. J. (1992). An interview with Donald Schön. *Orbit: Story Matters, 23*(4), 2–5.

Connelly, F. M., & Clandinin, D. J. (1994). Telling teaching stories. *Teacher Education Quarterly, 21*(1), 145–158.

Connelly, F. M., & Clandinin, D. J. (2000a). Teacher education: A question of teacher knowledge. In A. Scott & J. Freeman-Moir (Eds.), *Tomorrow's teachers: International and critical perspectives on teacher education* (pp. 89–105). Christchurch, New Zealand: Canterbury University Press.

Connelly, F. M., & Clandinin, D. J. (2000b). Narrative understandings of teacher knowledge. *Journal of Curriculum and Supervision, 15,* 315–331.

Connelly, F. M., & Clandinin, D. J. (2006). Narrative inquiry. In J. L. Green, G. Camilli, & P. Elmore (Eds.), *Handbook of complementary methods in education research* (3rd ed., pp. 477–487). Mahwah, NJ: Erlbaum.

Dewey, J. (1938). *Experience and education.* New York: Touchstone.

Eisner, E. W. (1988). The primacy of experience and the politics of method. *Educational Researcher, 17*(5), 15–20.

Eisner, E. W. (1993). Forms of understanding and the future of educational research. *Educational Researcher, 22*(7), 5–11.

Elbaz, F. (1983). *Teacher thinking: A study of practical knowledge.* New York: Nicholls.

Epanchin, B. C., Paul, J. L., & Smith, R. L. (1996). The philosophical conundrum of teacher education in special education. *Teacher Education and Special Education, 19,* 119–132.

Fenstermacher, G. D. (1994). The knower and the known: The nature of knowledge in research on teaching. *Review of Research in Education, 20*, 3–56.

Glesne, C. (1999). *Becoming qualitative researchers: An introduction* (2nd ed.). New York: Longman.

Hamilton, M. L., Pinnegar, S., Russell, T., Loughran, J., & LaBoskey, V. (Eds.). (1998). *Reconceptualizing teaching practice: Self-study in teacher education.* London: Falmer.

Hamilton, M. L., & Pinnegar, S. (1998). Conclusion: The value and the promise of self-study. In M. L. Hamilton, S. Pinnegar, T. Russell, J. Loughran, & V K. LaBoskey (Eds.), *Reconceptualizing teaching practice: Self-study in teacher education* (pp. 235–246). London: Falmer.

Hong Kong Institute of Education. (2006). *Strategic plan 2006–2012.* Hong Kong: Author.

Hong Kong Institute of Education. (2007a). About HKIEd: A unique place for quality teacher education. Retrieved August 15, 2008, from http://www.ied.edu.hk/about´hkied/index.html

Hong Kong Institute of Education. (2007b). *Developmental blueprint: Becoming a university of education.* Hong Kong: Author.

Loughran, J. J. (2004). History and context of self-study of teaching. In J. J. Loughran, M. L. Hamilton, V. K. LaBoskey, & T. Russell (Eds.), *International handbook of self-study of teaching and teacher education practices* (pp. 7–40). Dordrect: Kluwer.

Loughran, J. J., & Northfield, J. R. (1996). *Opening the classroom door: Teacher, researcher, learner.* London: Falmer.

Lyons, N., & LaBoskey, V. K. (2002). Why narrative inquiry or exemplars for a scholarship of teaching? In N. Lyons & V. K. LaBoskey (Eds.), *Narrative inquiry in practice: Advancing the knowledge of teaching* (pp. 11–27). New York: Teachers College Press.

Marland, P. (1998). Teachers' practical theories: Implications for preservice teacher education. *Asia-Pacific Journal of Teacher Education & Development, 1*(2), 15–23.

McNiff, J., Lomax, P., & Whitehead, J. (1996). *You and your action research project.* London: Routledge.

Miller Marsh, M. (2002). Examining the discourses that shape our teacher identities. *Curriculum Inquiry, 32*, 453–467.

Mok, M. M. C. (2005). Assessment for learning: Its effect on the classroom and curriculum. In P. C. Miller (Ed.), *Narratives from the classroom: An introduction to teaching* (pp. 183–201). Thousand Oaks, CA: Sage.

Morris, P. (2003). School knowledge, the state and the market: An analysis of the Hong Kong secondary school curriculum. In P. Stimpson, P. Morris, Y. Fung, & R. Carr (Eds.), *Curriculum, learning and assessment: The Hong Kong experiences* (pp. 47–76). Hong Kong: Open University of Hong Kong Press.

Putnam, R. T., & Borko, H. (2000). What do new views of knowledge and thinking have to say about research on teacher learning? *Educational Researcher, 29*(1), 4–15.

Ross, V. D. (2002). *Living an elementary school curriculum: Rethinking reform through a narrative classroom inquiry with a teacher and her students into the learning of mathematics life lessons from Bay Street Community School.* Unpublished doctoral dissertation, University of Toronto, Canada.

Russell, T., & Loughran, J. (2007). *Enacting a pedagogy of teacher education.* New York: Routledge.

Schön, D. A. (1983). *The reflective practitioner: How professionals think in action.* New York: Basic Books.

Schuck, S., & Russell, T. (2005). Self-study, critical friendship, and the complexities of teacher education. *Studying Teacher Education, 1*, 107–121.

Schwab, J. J. (1973). The practical: Translation into curriculum. In I. Westbury & N. J. Wilk (Eds.), *Science, curriculum and liberal education: Selected essays* (pp. 365–383). Chicago: University of Chicago Press.

Swartz, L. (1999). The best response to a story is another story. *Orbit: Story Matters, 30*(3), 14–17.

Tidwell, D., & Fitzgerald, L. (2004). Self-study as teaching. In J. J. Loughran, M. L. Hamilton, V. K. LaBoskey, & T. Russell (Eds.), *International handbook of self-study of teaching and teacher education practices* (pp. 69–102). Dordrect: Kluwer.

Van Manen, M. (1990). *Researching lived experience: Human science for an action sensitive pedagogy*. Albany: State University of New York Press.

Watkins, D. A., & Biggs, J. B. (Eds.). (1996). *The Chinese learner: Cultural, psychological and contextual influences*. Hong Kong: Comparative Education Research Centre.

Wilcox, S., Watson, J., & Paterson, M. (2004). Self-study in professional practice. In J. J. Loughran, M. L. Hamilton, V. K. LaBoskey, & T. Russell (Eds.), *International handbook of self-study of teaching and teacher education practices* (pp. 273–312). Dordrect: Kluwer.

Vygotsky, L. S. (1962). *Thought and language*. Cambridge: Massachusetts Institute of Technology Press.

Passages: Improving Teacher Education Through Narrative Self-Study

Julian Kitchen

Narrative inquiry, the study of experience as story, is a methodology that can enhance our understanding of ourselves as teacher educators, our contexts and our practices. In the *International Handbook of Self-Study of Teaching and Teacher Education Practices*, Clandinin and Connelly (2004) stated, "Narrative inquiry is a multi-dimensional exploration of experience involving temporality (past, present and future), interaction (personal and social), and location (place)" (p. 576). Narrative self-study, they suggested, opens up "understandings about participant knowledge" (p. 575).

In this chapter, I trace my narrative self-study over 16 years in order to illustrate ways in which personal experience methods employed in narrative inquiry can contribute to deeper understandings of the personal and social dimensions of teaching and teacher education practices. Developing deeper understandings of our "personal practical knowledge" (Connelly & Clandinin, 1988) through narrative self-study can provide a solid foundation for improving our practices in the future.

Narrative inquiry has been central to my own development as a teacher, educational researcher and teacher educator. I first encountered narrative inquiry in 1992, well before I became a teacher educator in 1999 or encountered self-study in 2002. I began inquiring into my teacher education practices in order to understand how my stories of experience informed my practices and how well I was meeting the needs of teacher candidates in my classes. Today I continue to employ narrative inquiry to study myself in my practice setting.

When I was introduced to self-study, I discovered a community of teacher educators who share my interest in understanding the complexity of teacher education within its practice settings. Equally important, we share a commitment to researching practice in order to develop a more effective pedagogy for teacher education. We are pragmatic in our willingness to use a variety of research methods to understand and improve teacher education.

J. Kitchen (✉)
Brock University, Faculty of Education, 1842 King Street East, Hamilton, Ontario, L8K 1V7, Canada
e-mail: jkitchen@brocku.ca

D.L. Tidwell et al. (eds.), *Research Methods for the Self-study of Practice*,
Self-Study of Teaching and Teacher Education Practices 9,
DOI 10.1007/978-1-4020-9514-6_3, © Springer Science+Business Media B.V. 2009

Although an eclectic approach to practical inquiry is valuable, it is important that we as practitioner-researchers develop rich understandings of the methodologies from which we borrow and the particular methods we employ. Narrative methods of knowing help teachers understand their personal practical knowledge. Understanding ourselves as teachers is a crucial step toward improving our practices and better serving the students in our classrooms (Clandinin & Connelly, 2004). A fuller appreciation of narrative inquiry as a methodology and a means of interpreting phenomena can lead to deeper understandings of teacher education practices.

Research Questions

In this narrative self-study, I consider the following research questions:

- How have personal experience methods helped me to understand my experiences as a learner, teacher and teacher educator?
- How has narrative inquiry informed my practice as a teacher educator?
- How has narrative inquiry informed my understanding of others and the educational context?
- How has narrative self-study improved my teacher education practices?

In addressing these questions, I share my narrative as a means of showing, rather than telling, how narrative ways of knowing can contribute to the study and improvement of teacher education practices.

Methodology

Narrative inquiry is a methodology for understanding the personal dimension of teaching. I draw on a wide-range of personal reflections and narratives to consider how narrative knowing has informed my professional practice. These artifacts of experience are used to illustrate personal experience methods that can be utilized in narrative inquiry.

Teacher Knowledge

Narrative inquiry and self-study emerged as responses to the technical rational assumption that research knowledge can be applied to practical problems with little reference to people or context (Schön, 1983; Schwab, 1970). Drawing on John Dewey's view that educative experiences that lead to growth emerge when teachers are responsive to "the situations in which interaction takes place" (Dewey, 1938, p. 45), both explore ways in which the individual practitioner can make sense of the "complexity, uncertainty, instability, uniqueness and value-conflict" (p. 39) within a particular professional situation.

Russell (2004) argued that "our growing awareness of the importance of *self* in teacher education" was "not only necessary but also inevitable" (p. 1192) given the failure of the technical rational model to serve the needs of practitioners. Similarly, narrative inquiry stresses the importance of knowing oneself in order to understand and effectively teach students in classrooms (Connelly & Clandinin, 1988). In both, teachers and teacher educators are encouraged to draw on their own experiences as learners in order to adapt their practices to the needs of students and communities.

While self study and narrative inquiry begin with the self, attention to the self in self-study is always in the service of "better knowledge of their particular practice setting" (Loughran, 2004, p. 9) and "continually adapting, adjusting and altering their practice in response to the needs and concerns of *their* context" (p. 18). While narrative inquiries focus primarily on teacher knowledge, consideration is given to the social contexts within which teachers work and live (Clandinin & Connelly, 1995).

For Clandinin and Connelly (2004), "The boundary around what counts as self-studies of narrative teacher knowledge is a boundary that encircles the living of teacher knowledge in practice" (p. 582). Understanding and developing teachers' personal practical knowledge has been a crucial dimension of their work. Personal experience methods were promoted as a means to helping teachers understand themselves, their students, the curriculum and educational contexts. *Teachers as Curriculum Planners: Narratives of Experience* (Connelly & Clandinin, 1988) is a treasure trove of methods teacher educators can use to systematically study their stories and their teaching. The results of these inquiries into the personal dimension of experience can then inform our individual and collective teacher education practices in the future.

Narrative Inquiry

Narrative inquiry is more than "the study of stories or narratives or descriptions of a series of events" (Pinnegar & Daynes, 2007, p. 4). Narrative inquirers immerse themselves in experience as lived and told in stories. While there are several conceptions of narrative inquiry as phenomenon and methodology, I have chosen to focus on narrative inquiry as conceived by Connelly and Clandinin, who had the greatest influence on educational narrative inquiry and on narrative self-study. Also, as a student of Michael Connelly, I used this approach to inform my work as a doctoral student, educational researcher and teacher educator.

Narrative inquiry is the study of how people make meaning from experience. Telling or collecting stories is the beginning of the process, but it is through the multi-dimensional exploration of these stories that narrative knowledge emerges. For Clandinin and Connelly (2000), narrative inquiry is both the phenomenon under study and a method of researching oneself and others.

All inquiries, according to Clandinin and Connelly (2000), take place in a three-dimensional space: "Studies have temporal dimensions and address temporal matters; they focus on the personal and the social in a balance appropriate to the inquiry; and they occur in specific places or sequence of places" (p. 50). As all experiences simultaneously contain all these dimensions, narrative inquirers need to examine multiple dimensions in order to find meaning in their experiences. Narrative self-study, through the use of personal experience methods, offers ways in which teacher educators can inquire into the multiple dimensions that inform their practices.

The experiences of individuals, institutions and/or communities at any given moment in time need to be "contextualized within a longer-term historical narrative" (Clandinin & Connelly, 2000, p. 19). We also need to recognize that the interpretation of experience takes place in the present moment and anticipates plans for the future. Similarly, narrative inquiry situates the teacher within classrooms, schools and a range of other social spaces which influence their professional knowledge and practice (Clandinin & Connelly, 1995).

Narrative Self-Study

'Self-study' is the noun because the focus of narrative self-study is the improvement of practice by reflecting on oneself and one's practices as a teacher educator. 'Narrative,' the adjective, refers to the use of specific narrative inquiry methods to study ourselves and our practices in order to improve practice.

Clandinin and Connelly (2004) warned, "Self-study must somehow give an account of the living of teacher knowledge in action, rather than merely the verbal (whether written or spoken) accounts of action" (p. 582). Narrative inquiry can enhance the self-study of teacher education practices in two ways. As a methodology, narrative inquiry offers a range of methods for telling and retelling stories of our experiences, the experiences of others, and the dynamics in our teacher education classrooms. As a method for studying phenomena, narrative inquiry offers critical frames for making sense of these experiences, the personal practical knowledge underlying them and their social context.

In this study, I illustrate how narrative inquiry has helped me develop a deeper understanding of myself and my practices as a teacher and teacher educator. I focus primarily on "personal experience methods" (Connelly & Clandinin, 1988) that have helped me to critically examine the personal dimension of self-study. The temporal, social and spatial dimensions of experience, while critical aspects of experience, play a secondary role in this particular study.

Beginning with Ourselves: The Personal Dimension in Narrative Self-Study

Narrative inquiry is the study of experience as story and, in particular, how people shape their lives through the stories they tell and how they interpret their past through stories (Connelly & Clandinin, 2006). The personal experiences methods outlined below offer teacher educators a range of approaches to capturing experience in writing and studying these experiences as phenomena. By beginning with the personal dimension in narrative self-study, we as teacher educators can become more aware of the selves we bring to our work and how these inform our professional practices with students in classrooms.

The term 'personal history' is often used to refer to the examination of "formative, contextualized experiences that have influenced teachers' thinking about teaching and their own practice" (Samaras, Hicks, & Garvey Berger, 2004, p. 909). While all personal history writing has the potential to "transform our relationships to ourselves, to our students and to the curriculum" (Samaras et al., 2004, p. 933), the potential is more likely to be realized when practitioners engage in exercises that stimulate rigorous reflection and thinking. The personal experience methods presented in this chapter and the critical lenses employed in narrative inquiry constitute a rigorous methodology for interrogating and interpreting how experience is grounded in beliefs and practices.

Personal practical knowledge is respectful of teachers as "knowledgeable and knowing persons whose knowledge resides in their past experiences ... present mind and body, and ... future plans and actions" (Connelly & Clandinin, 1988, p. 25). This way of understanding narratives of experience also recognizes that "many of the most important educational experiences in our narratives occur outside of school" (p. 27). By addressing present concerns, we can see how past experiences inform present practice; the self-awareness that may emerge from the telling and retelling of stories of experience can then influence our intentions and actions in the future.

Teachers and teacher educators are often asked to reflect on their personal experiences without being taught effective methods for personal and professional inquiry. The personal experience methods contained in *Teachers as Curriculum Planners: Narratives of Experience* (Connelly & Clandinin, 1988) equip teachers and teacher educators to record, interrogate and interpret experience in an intentional and deliberate manner.

Narrative self-studies, and the personal experience methods employed in the process, can be arrayed along the personal-social continuum (Clandinin & Connelly, 2004). The most personal self-studies focus on how past experiences inform the personal practical knowledge of teacher educators. The first three personal experience methods below—storytelling, autobiography and metaphor are designed to help educators tell and interpret these stories of experience. Examples from my ongoing narrative self-study illustrate how educators might begin to tell stories of experience in order to understand our personal practical knowledge. Other self-studies may focus more on present practices as a means of improving future practice. Rules of practice, personal philosophies of teaching and reflective journals are three personal experience methods that can help educators examine their practices. The accounts from my self-study offer a glimpse into the ways in which these methods helped me to understand and improve my practices.

Although I have organized personal experience methods in a particular sequence, there is no right method or place to begin exploring your personal practical knowledge. Once you begin, persist in your efforts, and experiment with a variety of methods.

Storytelling

Storytelling involves the telling of a story about oneself as a learner or teacher. Writing stories, which generally contain characters, setting and a plot, is a powerful method for exploring critical events in one's life and work.

My first exposure to narrative inquiry was through telling stories about my past experiences as a learner while maintaining a journal about my present experiences for a graduate course in 1992. My first efforts were tentative, as I had difficulty shifting from persuasive to narrative writing, and from detachment to self-disclosure. I recalled 2 years later, "The fear of self-disclosure dissipated when I received feedback ... that was very sensitive and connected my story to literature on experience and education" (Kitchen, 1994). My breakthrough came when I began writing a story about my Grade 6 teacher.

A Tribute to Mr. Hunter

Mr. Hunter was a very influential figure. I was a shy, awkward underachiever in grade school. All my reports indicated that I was not motivated and needed to work harder. Ironically, outside class I was a voracious reader of history and literature. While I was in a low reading group, I was reading books well above my reading level at school. Mr. Hunter was the first teacher to bring me out of my shell. He called on me in class and forced me to make a contribution. ... More than a few times, I went home and cried to my mother that Mr. Hunter hated me and mistreated me. My mother, always supportive of teachers, assured me that he must like me to go to so much trouble. I soon realized that she was right and began to perform much better and to grow in his class.

As I look back at Mr. Hunter's class, I realize that he was a sensitive and special teacher. He did differentiate his program and involve us in group learning, much to my benefit. I spent lots of time in the library pursuing my fascination with the Aztecs and early explorers of the New World. I did lots of group work, including taking on leadership roles.

Once, towards the end of the year, I was in a group presenting on local geology. In retrospect, I realize that the members of the group were not strong students. We did not work very hard and our presentation was, at best, hastily thrown together. Mr. Hunter revealed his dissatisfaction through questions on aspects of the topic. I was upset at him, because I was always the last person asked a question and all the easy answers were taken. Thus, I looked like the least knowledgeable, which I was not. Now, I recognize that his expectations for me were higher and, perhaps, that he was disappointed in me for slipping to the group's level, rather than elevating it to mine.

Mr. Hunter was an important part of my life. He gave me opportunities and he rewarded me with praise and support. He always challenged me. Towards the end of the year, I saw real progress. The most striking example was when my score on the reading tests went up to the Grade 10 level.

I have remembered Mr. Hunter with great fondness, even love. Also, I am more aware now than before of how he achieved what he did. He cared enough *to tap my abilities, to challenge me and to reward me. This had to take time and commitment, as I was not easy to reach with my head hidden in the sand. I wish I could tell him how much he meant to me and that, as I write this, tears run down my cheeks. Would he be pleased that I am now trying to make an equally significant contribution to the lives of my students? How many students do you need to influence to have a successful career? How do you ever find out the results of your work? How many come back twenty years later to say, "Thank you, Sir"?* (Story, September 29, 1992)

Two years later, I reflected on the impact of writing this story and sharing it with others:

Once my memory was tapped, the matter-of-fact tone of the opening paragraphs is replaced by a more reflective and emotional tone. The tears mentioned in the second last paragraph indicate just how revealing and emotional the process of narrative was for me. Also, returning to the experience through writing helped me discover Mr. Hunter's significance for me and what made him a successful teacher. Telling this story to others in my class added to my awareness that such educational stories are universal and that sharing them enhances our awareness of what constitutes learning. I was now convinced of the value of narrative as a tool for structuring my experience. (Kitchen, 1994)

As I wrote about Mr. Hunter, specific classroom memories were vividly recalled, along with the accompanying emotions. In the process of recording the story, I began to retell the story by interpreting both its significance in my life and the significance of storytelling as a method for understanding my narrative of experience. The interpretation above, written 2 years later, demonstrates how we continually retell stories as a way of making sense of our lives at different points in time. The discovery or rediscovery of oneself and one's narrative is one of the great delights of storying experience!

Stories may involve classroom learning, family and learning beyond the school and classroom teaching experiences. By revisiting these stories individually and collectively, we can begin to story, re-story and reinterpret our narratives of experience. Connelly and Clandinin (1988) recommended that teachers begin with at least three stories, as three "seems to be a minimum number to examine for themes, threads, or patterns" (p. 48). It should be emphasized that these stories, or other narrative recollections, reveal our understanding of experience and are not necessarily objectively true.

Autobiography

Autobiographical writing is another personal experience method for understanding our narratives of experience. Connelly and Clandinin (1988) wrote:

We often begin our classes with having participants share brief autobiographical statements. It is helpful to follow up this brief oral presentation with longer written versions. We also ask our graduate students to begin their theses and dissertations with their own autobiographies. (p. 39)

In my first graduate course with Michael Connelly, participants began by drafting a brief chronicle of their learning and teaching experiences. These were then fleshed out as oral presentations to the class. When I presented in class, I divided my narrative into several time periods and identified three dialectical tensions as central to understanding my story. At the conclusion of the course in 1993, I wrote a 47-page autobiography titled "Becoming Whole: An Educational Life Story." Although almost two thirds of the paper concerned experiences before becoming a teacher, my central preoccupation was with improving as a teacher by better understanding myself and my interactions with others. My narrative was then retold as a Master's Research Paper (1994), as a chapter in my doctoral dissertation (2005c), and again as a narrative self-study of teacher education practices (2005a, 2005b).

Writing an autobiography, particularly an extended version, is not easy. It is, however, an excellent way of examining how one's personal history informs one's present practice and plans for the future. Stories that have been developed independently can be incorporated into the narrative or included as artifacts of experience to be examined. In addition, an autobiography can include consideration of current teaching practices as revealed through personal experience methods such as metaphors, rules and principles, personal philosophies and journals.

The following passage from a narrative self-study of teacher education practices illustrates the telling and retelling of stories through narrative inquiry. Events were first documented in a journal then re-examined 12 years later as part of a narrative self-study.

Looking Back on my Experiences as a Mentor Teacher

My experiences as a mentor teacher in a cohort-based program have also informed my understanding of teacher education. During my fourth year of teaching, I became involved in Secondary Program 1 (SP1)...In this secondary cohort, students spent one day per week in school sites while carrying a full course load compressed into four days. There was no formal evaluation of the additional day per week, so stress was reduced and opportunities for growth were increased. Student teachers observed classes, taught occasionally and asked many questions over the course of the academic year. Even when they were evaluated as part of their formal practice teaching session, more authentic apprentice-mentor relationships diminished pressure and enhanced growth opportunities.

The possibility of more authentic mentoring appealed to my emerging understanding of learning as personal and relational. In 1992, while taking a graduate course in teacher induction, I reflected on the advantages of SP1:

Observation is one of the most valuable aspects of the program and the one I most regret missing in my own teacher education and practice. The program co-ordinator, who also teaches a course in the option, provides them with things to look for, such as how selected students behave, how a lesson is organized and how discipline is handled. After class, I talk to my student teacher about what I did and why, answering any questions s/he may have. The student teacher develops a better understanding of a variety of teaching strategies, classroom procedures—something that is seldom taught—and the tacit knowledge underlying the teacher's actions. I also value the insights this offers for my own practice. Sometimes my successful adaptations to the situation are not even consciously made; sometimes my decisions were not the right ones.

The student teacher also teaches classes when s/he is ready. I have encouraged my students to teach at least one class before the first practice teaching session. ...Jeremy, my current student, claims that this has enabled him to be more relaxed and confident when teaching. Also, it allows him to take risks; indeed I encourage and, even, insist on this. The advice I offer also helps students modify and enhance their practice. As a result, they are more likely to internalize good new approaches...

The opportunity to work with one person over a period of time is another beneficial aspect. It gives student teachers the opportunity to grow over a period of time with a mentor to help them on the journey ...We discuss their practice teaching sessions, their courses and their problems juggling their program, since the program is more an "add-on" than an alternative. This genuine relationship with me as [a mentor] is complemented by a close relationship with the small group of students in the alternate program. (Course paper, December, 1992)

...Looking back on these experiences 12 years later reminds me that relational teacher development is grounded in how humans socially construct knowledge. The moment that best illustrates the advantages of meaningful relationships grounded in authentic school setting was a lunch I shared with Jeremy:

Over lunch, we had an excellent freewheeling discussion of educational philosophy and practice, which was of great value to both of us. We made connections between post-structural criticism and cognitive research, integrated practice and philosophy and redesigned teacher education. It was discussion at its best: not the exchange of ideas but the development of new ideas together and on our own. I came out of it with a clearer sense of what I am doing and what I could be doing. In particular, the barrier between philosophy and practice, which I have viewed as transparent, was demolished. As a mentor, my job is to give the trainee practical hands-on experience to complement his theoretical work at the faculty. Cognitive theorists have discovered, however, we cannot make artificial barriers between types of knowledge. This, however, is something that still happens in teacher education. An apprenticeship program under a mentor skilled in practice and theory would be a better approach. As he and I discussed education we made links back and forth. As his practical advisor, I am also becoming the main force in the theoretical side of his development, referring to current theories and authors, connecting them to my and his personal philosophies of education. (Journal, November 10, 1992)

The revelation that authentic relationships can lead to powerful learning opportunities has driven research and teacher education practice ever since.

This journal entry reflects a shift in my self-perception from passive mentor teacher to active mentor teacher and then to teacher educator. In my first year as a mentor teacher, I was simply offering a preservice teacher the opportunity to observe and teach. In my second year, I regarded myself as a mentor structuring learning opportunities and sharing my professional experiences with a colleague. With Jeremy, in my third year, I began to feel that I had become a field-based teacher educator who structured learning opportunities, shared professional experiences and connected practical experiences to the course work in order to make both more meaningful. This bridging of theory and practice led my student teacher to claim that he had learned more about the philosophy of teaching through our luncheon conversations than in a full term of classes. While it is common for preservice teachers to value field experiences more than their university classes, the significance here is the value Jeremy placed on our conversations as a bridge between the two worlds...

Reflection on subsequent experiences reinforced my perceptions and motivated me to seek the tools necessary to improve my practice as a teacher educator. As one always teaches the self, it is crucial that each teacher engage in a rigorous self-study process in order to develop greater self-awareness and a deeper understanding of education. Reflecting on this rigorous self-study process has led to increased understanding of the challenges faced by preservice teachers. This reflection has also motivated me to develop curriculum and establish classroom environments that foster collaboration and reflection on personal experiences in order to address the challenges of classroom teaching. (Kitchen, 2005b, pp. 21–23)

Metaphor

Lakoff and Johnson (1980), in *Metaphors We Live By*, argue that "metaphor is pervasive in everyday life, not just in language but in thought and action" (p. 3). By discovering the metaphors we live by we can gain greater insights into how our personal practical knowledge implicitly informs our practice.

I searched high and low for my metaphor when I began using personal experience methods to explore my narrative. I became exasperated before discovering the metaphor of teacher as tour guide. When I discovered this metaphor, it resonated with the ways in which I often spoke about life and learning as a quest.

As a Teacher I Am a Tour Guide
Learning is a journey of discovery. When we embark on such a journey, we are eager to see and appreciate many of the wonders of the world.

We begin life outside the womb as travellers transported into an alien land. The first years are spent identifying the landmarks in our immediate environment and adapting to the customs of the locals, particularly our parents. Everything is new and we soak up knowledge like sponges eager to make sense of the world's many delights. When students enter into the classroom, they generally come with an explorer's sense of wonder and discovery.

As a teacher, I see myself as a tour guide for my students. The tour guide, like the good teacher in Dewey's work, constructs events so that the educative potential of the experiences is maximized for his charges. Indeed, both spend a great deal of time researching and preparing tours so that they are rewarding and flow smoothly. Each must practice their craft to become more effective. Each must engage the group as a whole and have it work as a unit. Each must also get to know the individuals and try to connect the new discoveries back to the knowledge and interests of the followers. Also, both are servants who seek to maximize the benefits to the clients.

Both the guide and the teacher, however, also have a commitment to the territory being explored. They both seek to make their clients aware of the landmarks of the communities visited. A teacher teaches Shakespeare because it is important to our heritage, even if it is less accessible to many. He then tries to make it more interesting for the students. So too, the tour guide sometimes tells us things we should know, even if we are not keenly interested in those facts or experiences. Some may find the Rembrandt museum dull, but a visit to Amsterdam is not complete without it; some anecdotes, however, may spice it up.

The guide and teacher are also experts eager to share their knowledge with the group and should be eager to answer questions or suggest other sights to see. After all, both would be pleased if the client spent a free day looking at more paintings or reading another Shakespeare play. Even better, they would both be pleased if the desire to travel further along the path was enhanced by their guidance. Will the tourist want to see more of Holland or want to travel again soon? Will the student become a lifelong reader of literature? Both hope so.

Being a guide or a teacher is not without its drawbacks. First, while both try to make the journey rewarding for each individual, the nature of the group limits opportunities to individualize activities, although both may create options, such as giving them free time in different galleries in a museum. Also, in the case of a tour guide or teacher of students, the parent and the public are paying for the trip, so one is accountable to them and must adapt to their agendas too. Also, in a classroom or on a class trip, the teacher or guide has power over the explorers we are leading. We tell them what to do or take them in directions they do not want to go. Also, as teachers, we evaluate what they learn from the trip, using our criteria not theirs. Holidays would not be fun if there were a quiz after a visit to each sight or–even worse–a comprehensive examination upon returning home! (Kitchen, 1994)

Understanding how this image informed my practice made me a better guide, while being aware of the limits of this metaphor helped me develop compensatory strategies to ensure that my students had rich experiences while on tour.

After I became a teacher educator, and my practice focussed increasingly on helping teacher candidates better understand their personal practical knowledge, I continued to see myself as a guide though I no longer envisioned myself as conducting a tour. Other images that often creep into my conversations about education are teacher as juggler and the classroom as a garden.

Rules and Practical Principles

"Personal philosophy is a way one thinks about oneself in teaching situations," wrote Connelly and Clandinin (1988, p. 66). Understanding a teacher's personal philosophy statement entails probing beneath beliefs and values in order to reconstruct meaning as contained in the teacher's actions and narrative of experience. While rules, practical principles and personal philosophies are informed by past experiences, they are situated within the present moment and the social context of the classroom.

Before one can articulate a personal philosophy of teaching, it is useful to begin modestly by examining rules and practical principles. A rule of practice is a brief, well-formulated statement of what to do in common teaching situations. For example, when I began to examine my personal practical knowledge, my rules included

- I will try to build community in the classroom and beyond;
- I will try to balance individual and group learning;
- I will model listening skills.

A practical principle "embodies purposes in a deliberate and reflective manner" (Connelly & Clandinin, 1988, p. 65); it emerges from a process of reflection and deliberation on a problem. Principles I developed included

- By creating a safe environment, I will encourage student learning;
- If I want students to work hard, I must work hard to provide them with excellent lessons and feedback;
- By modelling my values, I will help students to behave appropriately and respect each other. Too often, teachers are insensitive while demanding respect from students.

The development of rules and practical principles is an effective way to examine one's philosophy of education as practiced in the classroom. For this exercise to be meaningful, however, teachers need to consider the connection between words and practices. In writing out my rules and practical principles, however, was I accurately representing my practice? Making these rules and principles explicit forced me to ask questions about my practice. Did I live out these values in my day-to-day practice? Were these rules and principles evident to my students? Were there ways in which I could have changed my practices to be truer to the beliefs and values embodied in these statements?

Heston and East (2004) adopted a similar approach when they identified the tacit 'private rules' that often guided their classroom practice. Having identified their private rules, these were then made explicit in the hope that preservice teachers might benefit from identifying and examining their own rules. Two ways I addressed these issues were to regularly collect feedback from students and to make my philosophy of teaching explicit to my teacher education classes.

Personal Philosophy of Teaching

A personal philosophy of teaching, a more elaborate working out of rules or principles, should be equally grounded in the realities of practice. An introductory letter I shared with students in the cohort I coordinated illustrates how narrative knowing informed my understanding of myself, my students and teaching context and my teacher education practices. In the excerpt below, I articulate why I believe that personal reflection is critical to becoming an effective teacher.

My Personal Philosophy: Letter to Preservice Teachers (excerpt)
Teaching is a complex act involving thousands of decisions and judgments each day. You need to master an array of strategies as well as understand the curriculum. You will face 150 students per year from a wide array of backgrounds, with a range of abilities and special needs. You will need to work with colleagues and parents as well as be familiar with the community/communities in which you work. An education sufficiently sophisticated to prepare you for this career should be four years in length!

What can I offer? It is likely that each of you has amassed approximately 15,000 hours of classroom experiences! One way to succeed as a teacher is to draw upon those experiences in a meaningful manner. In this course, you will be asked to reflect on these narratives of experience in order to prepare yourself for teaching. Whether you reflect on these experiences or not, they will shape your approach to teaching. When a situation occurs in a classroom, you may respond acerbically, as one of your teachers did. Is that the best approach? A student's challenge to you in class or quiet refusal to become involved may irritate you. Can you recognize yourself in that student? How might a teacher have reached you?

Draw on this deep well of personal experiences to help you sort through your teaching experiences. An instance in your classroom may occur for the first time, but recalling similar experiences may help you discover effective strategies.

Some incidents in the teacher education program or in schools may "press your buttons". Write about these. Why are they pressing your buttons? To which past experiences do they relate? Are there better ways to cope?

You enter the profession carrying tremendous baggage. Most of it is a cargo of immense value; revisiting these stories of experience will enhance your understanding of education and make you a better teacher. Some stories of experience are negative or miseducative; these too need to be re-examined in order to learn new lessons and more effectively work with students. Not confronting these experiences could result in them influencing your work in unintended ways.

In this course, you will also write stories about critical incidents during the school year. For these critical incidents, consider what happened and how your prior experiences informed your feelings and actions at the time.

Your experiences tend to form patterns. Often, these life experiences can be summarized in metaphors. For example, I see my life as a journey and my professional role as that of a guide.

Understanding how this image informs my practice as a teacher educator makes me a better guide. Being aware of the limits of this metaphor helps me develop compensatory strategies. You will be writing and explaining your metaphors in this class.

Each of you is a unique individual with your own philosophy of teaching. I will not attempt to force my philosophy on you. Rather, I want you to articulate your philosophy and consider the most effective manner in which to bring it to life in the classroom.

Yet you also need knowledge and skills to make informed choices in your class and bring your approach to life in the classroom. In this course, we will discuss assessment, instruction, diversity and special education. You will be challenged to incorporate such theoretical and practical knowledge into your work as teachers. Also, I will use a range of strategies in the hope of modeling their application.

Classrooms are extremely complex and dynamic environments in which teachers, students, curriculum and milieu intersect. As teachers, you play the pivotal role in negotiating this complexity to ensure meaningful learning for your students. Since "we enter new experience through the portal of prior experience" (Connelly, 2001), knowing and examining your stories of experience is crucial to your first year of teaching. Ongoing reflection is vital to continual development as a teacher over the years.

I have enormous respect for each of you and the unique qualities you bring to the teaching profession. My class will be a place in which your uniqueness will always be respected. I am committed to fostering a safe environment in which you can make meaning of your experiences and in which you can build strong bonds with your classmates. I am honored to be working with you this year. I will do all I can to ensure that you have an enriching year!

While it is impossible to teach you how to teach in nine months, I think that we can provide you with useful knowledge and skills which, when combined with your rich set of experiences, will enable you to effectively begin a long and rewarding career! (Kitchen, 2005a, pp. 197–198)

The writing of stories of experience was a cognitive process through which I tried "to make sense of life as lived" (Clandinin & Connelly, 2000, p. 77) by untangling the complex narrative threads that have contributed to my identity, knowledge and practice. By "retelling stories that allow for growth and change" (Clandinin & Connelly, 2000, p. 71), I made my teaching practices more authentic and relational. In retelling my story to teacher candidates, I hoped it would resonate with their stories as learners and beginning teachers so that they would be more open to growth and change as they examined their personal practical knowledge as teachers.

This letter is an example of a philosophy of practice written in order for teacher candidates to understand me, my pedagogy and how they can develop their personal practical knowledge of teaching and learning. By sharing it with them, I was holding myself accountable to the standards I set for myself.

Reflective Journals

Keeping a journal is a useful method for recording and reflecting on practice. The process of journal writing on an ongoing basis helps educators describe experiences as lived at the time and reflect on their actions. Journals are also valuable as artifacts for retrospectively interpreting patterns in experience in order to develop deeper insights into one's practice. This excerpt from a self-study article illustrates both how I employed journal writing on an ongoing basis and the ways in which I used journal entries to inform a broader understanding of my teacher education practices.

> Harnessing the Power of Reflective Portfolios
>
> *Rory saw me this morning. He sent me an email regarding his reflection. It began with a statement of gratitude then a comment that suggested he was upset that I thought he was not reflective. I immediately sent a note to apologize if that was how it came across. I was suggesting that reflection was not present in his writing, though I had no doubt he reflected. I offered to meet and talk. He emailed me back to say that he took no offence but was not good at being reflective in writing. He agreed to meet and we set a time. At our meeting we chatted about his practicum, which he was very pleased with. His love of teaching and of students was evident! I then made some suggestions about how to reflect effectively, to which he was most receptive. One comment that seemed to help was my recounting of my difficulty moving from the certainty of undergraduate essays to reflection and puzzling.* (Teacher Education Journal, November 30, 2001)
>
> Rory, a student in my elective course, lacked positive experiences with reflective writing in his core courses. The combination of offering feedback and making a personal connection afterwards enhanced both the quality of his writing and deepened the level of his reflection. Our engagement over his writing was a powerful educative moment that enhanced his learning in the course. Recognizing that the reluctance of preservice teachers to reflect meaningfully was partly due to the lack of instruction and modeling they received, I sought to address this more effectively in my classes.
>
> Indeed, I had already learnt that the time I spent replying to reflections helped preservice teachers make important connections, while enabling me to be responsive as a teacher educator...
>
> My engagement with their personal and professional reflections was generally appreciated because they demonstrated a genuine commitment to their personal professional growth, modeled reflection as a rigorous process and helped them notice patterns in their experiences. By responding mindfully to my students, I was putting into practice the lessons that I learned through my collaborative experiences. (Kitchen, 2005b, pp. 24–26)

Temporal, Social and Spatial Dimensions in Narrative Self-Study

Autobiographical writing involves struggling to understand how one's past, present and anticipated future shape our actions. Although the examples above focus on the personal dimension of experience, it is critical that we see ourselves not as islands unto ourselves but as individual teacher educators situated within contexts with temporal, social and spatial dimensions.

The temporal dimension is tightly interwoven with the personal dimension of the experiences recounted in this chapter. In looking back at the sources of my personal practical knowledge, I was standing in the present moment in order to understand how my past informs my present understanding. The story of Mr. Hunter enabled me understand what mattered to me as a learner and, in doing so, inspired me to establish authentic relationships with students as the guiding principle in my teaching at the time and in the future. Similarly, by writing practical principles and a personal philosophy of teaching, I was both identifying that my priorities at the time were informed by past experiences and moving forward to revise future practices.

The social dimension is equally important. Clandinin and Connelly (2004) stressed giving "a complex historical and social/relational account of the teacher knowledge under study" (p. 589). Including rich contextual detail in accounts of experience allows one to stand back from oneself to notice the social relationships, the wider context and the implications for the students with whom we work. The details in my journal account of being a mentor teacher helped me to probe more deeply as I interpreted entries at a later date. Standing at a distance helped me situate specific experiences within the wider context of practice teaching and to draw lessons about the needs of preservice teachers more generally.

The spatial dimension, which Clandinin and Connelly (1995) refer to as the professional knowledge landscape, is a critical yet often unexamined dimension of experience. My classroom work with students in classrooms cannot be separated from the wider professional landscape which informs my practice. As a teacher I navigate, for example, the tensions between my commitment to constructivist learning with the curriculum standards imposed by my school and regulatory bodies. In the letter outlining my personal philosophy to preservice teachers, I stressed the importance of adapting one's practice to the realities of the communities in which we work.

While the focus of this chapter has been narrative methods for examining the personal dimension of our experiences as teacher educators, the personal is constantly interacting with the temporal, social and spatial dimensions of experience.

Final Words: Continuing My Narrative Self-Study

The examples of personal experience methods in this chapter emerged from my discovery of narrative inquiry as a classroom teacher and my exposure to self-study as a new teacher educator. I selected these artifacts in order to illustrate how accessible and meaningful narrative self-study can be for educators making their first forays into this kind of practitioner inquiry.

Recently, as a new tenure-track professor, I returned to narrative self-study to help navigate through major changes in the temporal, social and spatial dimensions of my work. By revisiting my stories of experience and the ways in which I had previously interpreted them helped me to adapt to these changes while remaining true to my core educational values.

Teaching a course on education law proved to be a source of considerable personal tension. There were considerable differences between the constructivist general methods teaching course I had previously taught and the positivistic education law curriculum I was asked to teach. As I negotiated these tensions in my first year, I recalled stories of experience in order to construct meaning:

Education law can be a very dry subject. I vaguely recall studying law as part of my Bachelor of Education program over twenty years ago: dull lectures, laws decontextualized from experience, and excerpts from the Education Act to be memorized for the final examination. Worse, this information did little to prepare me for the ethical and legal dimensions of teaching. For example, in my first year of teaching, a girl sprained her ankle during soccer practice. The next morning, as I collected my mail, I casually mentioned this to the vice-principal. Until then, I had no idea that I needed to complete an incident report and failed to realize that an injury could lead to a negligence lawsuit. Fortunately, like most teachers, I was able to avoid ethical and legal problems due to a combination of good sense and good luck. (Journal, November 13, 2006)

These stories of experience reinforced my sense that education law needed to be more connected to the ethical dilemmas and practical realities of teaching. Along with my ongoing observations and the feedback collected from students, this narrative retelling of experience prompted me to modify my practices in an effort to better serve the needs of students and to advocate for major changes to the course of study.

Another source of tension concerned the balance between teaching and scholarship. I wrote:

Once I was on the tenure-track, however, I was torn between fidelity to teacher education and the call of scholarship. Should I maintain a singular commitment to teacher education? Should I heed the seductive eyes and sighs of scholarship? Could I be faithful to both? (Journal, April 17, 2008)

As part of my efforts to find a suitable balance between the two, I reviewed my stories of experience in order to remind myself of my core values as a teacher educator. Thinking narratively about these experiences prompted critical questions about what mattered to me as a teacher educator. These questions helped me reposition myself as a professor of education committed to improving teacher education while pursuing a broader program of research. I am currently writing an education law textbook that is more consistent with my core beliefs as a teacher educator.

Narrative inquiry continues to be an important dimension of my ongoing self-study work as a teacher educator. Examining stories of experience helps me to remain grounded in my personal practical knowledge as an educator while helping me to situate myself in a new context.

While there are many methodologies that are complementary with self-study, narrative inquiry is particularly helpful in exploring and critically examining the self in the self-study of teacher education. The personal experience methods presented and illustrated in this chapter are practical tools for unlocking stories of experience and finding meaning in these stories. Examining the personal dimension of experience through narrative inquiry also helps us make sense of the temporal, social and spatial dimensions of the contexts in which we work as teacher educators. By helping us better understanding ourselves and our context, narrative inquiry may assist self-study practitioners in developing more effective practices.

References

Clandinin, D. J., & Connelly, F. M. (Eds.). (1995). *Teachers' professional knowledge landscapes.* New York: Teachers College Press.

Clandinin, D. J., & Connelly, F. M. (2000). *Narrative inquiry: Experience and story in qualitative research.* San Francisco: Jossey-Bass.

Clandinin, D. J., & Connelly, F. M. (2004). Knowledge, narrative and self-study. In J. J. Loughran, M. L. Hamilton, V. K. LaBoskey, & T. Russell (Eds.), *International handbook of self-study of teaching and teacher education practices* (pp. 575–600). Dordrecht: Kluwer.

Connelly, F. M. (2001). Reverberations. *Journal of Critical Inquiry into Curriculum and Instruction, 3*(3), 58.

Connelly, F. M., & Clandinin, D. J. (1988). *Teachers as curriculum planners: Narratives of experience.* Toronto: OISE Press.

Connelly, F. M., & Clandinin, D. J. (2006). Narrative inquiry. In J. L. Green, G. Camalli, & P. B. Elmore (Eds.), *Handbook of complementary methods in education research.* Washington, DC: American Educational Research Association.

Dewey, J. (1938). *Experience and education.* New York: Collier Books.

Heston, M. L., & East, K. (2004). You're wrong and I'm not! Private rules and classroom community in the presence of diversity. In D. L. Tidwell, L. M. Fitzgerald, & M. L. Heston (Eds.), *Journeys of hope: Risking self-study in a diverse world. Proceedings of the Fifth International Conference on the Self-Study of Teacher Education Practices, Herstmonceux Castle, East Sussex, England* (pp. 145–148). Cedar Falls, IA: University of Northern Iowa.

Kitchen, J. (1994). *A journey within: A quest narrative.* Unpublished masters and qualifying research paper, Ontario Institute for Studies in Education of the University of Toronto, Toronto, Ontario, Canada.

Kitchen, J. (2005a). Conveying respect and empathy: Becoming a relational teacher educator. *Studying Teacher Education, 1*(2), 194–207.

Kitchen, J. (2005b). Looking backwards, moving forward: Understanding my narrative as a teacher educator. *Studying Teacher Education, 1*(1), 17–30.

Kitchen, J. (2005c). *Relational teacher development: A quest for meaning in the garden of teacher experience.* Unpublished doctoral dissertation, Ontario Institute for Studies in Education, University of Toronto, Toronto, Ontario, Canada.

Lakoff, G., & Johnson, M. (1980). *Metaphors we live by.* Chicago: University of Chicago Press.

Loughran, J. (2004). Learning through self-study. In J. J. Loughran, M. L. Hamilton, V. K. LaBoskey, & T. Russell (Eds.), *International handbook of self-study of teaching and teacher education practice* (pp. 151–192). Dordrecht: Kluwer.

Pinnegar, S., & Daynes, J. G. (2007). Locating narrative inquiry historically: Thematics in the turn to narrative. In D. J. Clandinin (Ed.), *Handbook of narrative inquiry: Mapping a methodology* (pp. 3–34). Thousand Oaks, CA: Sage.

Russell, T. (2004). Tracking the development of self-study in teacher education research and practice. In J. J. Loughran, M. L. Hamilton, V. K. LaBoskey, & T. Russell (Eds.), *International handbook of self-study of teaching and teacher education practices* (pp. 1191–1210). Dordrecht: Kluwer.

Samaras, A. P., Hicks, M. A., & Garvey Berger, J. (2004). Self-study through personal history. In J. J. Loughran, M. L. Hamilton, V. K. LaBoskey, & T. Russell (Eds.), *International handbook of self-study of teaching and teacher education practice* (pp. 905–942). Dordrecht: Kluwer.

Schön, D. (1983). *The reflective practitioner.* New York: Bantam Books.

Schwab, J. J. (1970). The practical: A language for curriculum. *School Review, 78,* 1–23.

Part II
Self-Study Through Discourse and Dialogue

Talking Teaching and Learning: Using Dialogue in Self-Study

Katheryn East, Linda M. Fitzgerald and Melissa L. Heston

Beginnings: Catching Currents, Merging Streams

Two of the great North American rivers, the Mississippi and the Missouri, form the east and west borders of our state, and all of the nine tributary river systems within its borders were flooding at historic levels at the time we were writing this chapter. Since metaphor is one hallmark of our self-study method, river and tributary imagery lent themselves to a description of the origins of our method.

Our entry into self-study was rather accidental, being the confluence of three distinct experiences: (a) a bi-weekly seminar in 1994–95, facilitated by the university's teaching enhancement center to help new faculty be intentional about instructional choices as they began their careers; (b) regular meetings of the team of faculty members teaching sections of a foundations development course for beginning preservice teachers, some members of which were also new faculty; and (c) a partnership between Melissa (a member of the latter group) and Deborah Tidwell, as they prepared to attend the first international meeting of the Self-Study of Teacher Education Practices special interest group. Members in these overlapping groups recognized common interests and proposed a weekly lunch meeting in the spring of 1995. The primary purpose of these early meetings was collegial support and sharing teaching tips and tricks. Group discussions focused on the various trials and tribulations common to most new faculty: managing a 9-hour teaching load while pursuing scholarly work and responding to service demands; making sense of instructor evaluations; coping with challenging students; coming to terms with the nature of the students in our particular context (well-schooled passive learners); and negotiating our relationships with the tenured faculty within our departments.

Initially, none of us saw these meetings in terms of collaborative scholarship on teaching. However, as Melissa began the self-study that she would present at the first Castle Conference (Tidwell & Heston, 1996, 1998), she suggested that we use Fenstermacher's (1994) practical argument technique to focus our group's inquiry

K. East (✉)
University of Northern Iowa, 617 Schindler Education Center, Cedar Falls, IA 50614-0607, USA
e-mail: katheryn.east@uni.edu

D.L. Tidwell et al. (eds.), *Research Methods for the Self-study of Practice*,
Self-Study of Teaching and Teacher Education Practices 9,
DOI 10.1007/978-1-4020-9514-6_4, © Springer Science+Business Media B.V. 2009

into more effective teaching. At that time, we and two other colleagues (Robert Boody and Annette Iverson) began meeting regularly and calling ourselves the Talking Teaching group. A small grant to support transcriptions of audiotapes of our discussions launched us into the first of what would be many collaborative self-studies carried out with dialogue among teacher educators and other college instructors. In the winter of 1997, after a year of this work together, we crafted our first collaboratively written paper for presentation at the national conference of the Association of Teacher Educators (Heston, East, Fitzgerald, Boody, & Iverson, 1997), later published in the association's journal (Boody, East, Fitzgerald, Heston, & Iverson, 1998).

While at that conference, we met with Christine Canning, another UNI teacher educator whose primary assignment was supervising student teachers in San Antonio, Texas. We asked her to lend us her expertise in community-building techniques (see Canning, 1993) when she returned to our Iowa campus later that spring. In May 1997, she and Melissa organized a 3-day faculty workshop on community building. This particular workshop was employed regularly with our program's student teachers and used an experiential approach emphasizing the development of and reflections on a wide variety of skills for working effectively with others. Authentic communication and specific techniques for facilitating such communication formed the foundation of the workshop. Although advertised as an all-campus event, the workshop drew only nine faculty (all women) willing to participate for the full 3 days. Despite – or perhaps because of – the small group size and some chaos creating events (two men who began the workshop chose not to come back after the first day, and another man appeared unexpectedly on the second day and was not allowed to stay) six of the nine participants decided, after the conclusion of the workshop, to meet regularly on Saturday mornings for 2 hours to talk about teaching and learning, in the context of the community the group had established. The workshop provided us with some foundational notions for our dialogue process and we used this group to practice what became our primary self-study tools. It was in these Saturday sessions that we first developed and used a set of mutually agreed upon ground rules designed to assist with group function (see *Appendix* for one early set of these ground rules).

From these separate sources our collaborative work in self-study began to flow. All three of us participated in the lunch group meetings, the community building workshop, and the Saturday morning meetings. The ideas and skills we learned through the new faculty seminar and the community building workshop and ensuing group, together with the beginnings of self-study theories and methods to which Melissa introduced us on her return from the 1996 Castle Conference led us into self-study proper. Our self-study work has always been collaborative, and we have always used dialogue as our primary data generation, and analysis tool. While the three of us have been continuously involved in self-study since 1996, the main channel as it were, the membership in our actual working group ebbs and flows. Some groups have been interdisciplinary while others have been strictly teacher educators. Past and current participants have included faculty (tenured, tenure track, and adjunct) in classroom assessment and research methods, educational psychology and motivation, early childhood and special education, early literacy education, graphic design, metal sculpture, computer science education, mathematics education, higher mathematics, English and humanities, and communication studies. In addition, individuals and subsets of our various groups have pursued specific self-study projects outside of the larger collaborative groups.

Our way of developing and using dialogue in self-study is the primary focus of this chapter. We will describe how we start our groups and what we believe is necessary for these groups to productively use dialogue as a method. We will talk specifically about what we consider 'recalibration points' in our work together, providing specific examples from our collaborative work over the years. Finally, we will discuss the realities of self-study using dialogue, for we have found that, although any group can talk together, it is far more difficult to create the kind of dialogue that leads to recalibration or transformative recalibration points.

Dialogue as Self-Study Methodology

Before describing our dialogue process and how we engage in it, we need to clarify what we mean by dialogue as method. For us, dialogue goes beyond carrying on a conversation or even having an academic discussion. More people than just a dyad can, and usually do, participate in our self-study dialogues. The participants most often are face-to-face, but as we describe below, sometimes a participant can be present in a published text.

We use dialogue as a method in two senses. First, dialogue is a method through which we examine our practice in our self-study work for the purpose of improving our teaching. Our dialogues afford immediate catalysts for changing classroom practice when we discover what we call a recalibration point, which we describe in detail below. Briefly, our dialogue takes us to a point at which we recalibrate our understanding of a topic or of our practices. We have found this to be true whether the dialogue is stimulated by text or classroom incidents. Second, our use of dialogue as method is the way we carry out collaborative self-study with attention to content and to process; that is, we critically analyze our self-study process itself, and we do so through dialogue. Transcripts of dialogue in meetings, meeting notes, journal entries, writing assignments for meetings, drafts of collaborative papers, our professional presentations and publications, and most importantly the continued use and refining of dialogue as a method over an extended period have all provided data for improving the collaborative process that we use. While we draw upon a number of our past studies in this chapter, we pay particular attention to the most recent in the current series of self-studies using our data to improve our self-study practice itself (East, 2005a; East & Fitzgerald, 2006; East, Fitzgerald, & Manke, 2008).

Although some of us have been informed by discourse analysis (e.g., Silverstein & Urban, 1996) and by dialogic analysis (e.g., Wortham, 2001), we do not apply these analytic methods to the text of our collaborative self-study dialogue data, nor do we use thematic analysis. While we have sometimes used traditional qualitative methods to analyze our transcripts (East, 2005a; East & Fitzgerald, 2006; East et al., 2008), we more often use the dialogues themselves as the analysis tool. That is, we focus upon our insights-in-the-moment as they arise spontaneously in the actual dialogue process. What we are identifying as dialogue can take place internally as we write reflections, as well as in actual meetings. This is akin to what Gordon Wells (1999) described in his book, *Dialogic Inquiry*:

> More specifically, by contributing to the joint meaning making with and for others, one also makes meaning for oneself and, in the process, extends one's own understanding. At the same time, the "utterance" viewed from the perspective of what is said, is a knowledge artifact that potentially contributes to the collaborative knowledge building of all those who are co-participants in the activity. (p. 108)

Starting the Dialogue Process

Essentially, when we begin a self-study project, we identify a specific focus for our dialogue. Some of our work has been centered on our own reflections regarding a particular aspect of our teaching. For example, early in our practical argument group (Boody et al., 1998) we gave ourselves an assignment to write a brief response to the question, "What do you think learning is and how does that belief influence your teaching?" Initially we audiotaped every dialogue for transcription and assumed that the transcriptions would be our data. While we have found those data useful when developing a paper, over time we realized that it was the dialogue process itself that changed our thinking about our practice. Sometimes that change could be quite dramatic, and those were the recalibration points that we harkened back to, rather than the transcriptions.

In other cases we have used articles, chapters, and books as prompts for our dialogues. Sometimes, we simply came to a dialogue meeting with the reading completed, while in other cases we wrote and exchanged reflections in advance and focused the dialogue upon these reflections. We have used a wide variety of texts as prompts: Brookfield (1995), Bullough and Gitlin (1995), Clandinin and Connelly (1996), Duckworth (1996), Fishman and McCarthy (1998), LaBoskey (2004), and Palmer (1993, 1998). When we have been able to truly grapple well with a text, it has been as if we were actually in a direct dialogue with the author(s) as well as with each other (East, 2005b; East & Heston, 2004; Heston, East, & Farstad, 2000).

On occasion, a particular text suggested a specific activity which we would try, write about, and then discuss together. For example, along with colleagues Catherine Miller and Tamara Veenstra (Miller, East, Fitzgerald, Heston, & Veenstra, 2002), we used a suggestion from Palmer's (1998) *The Courage to Teach* to identify and examine our personal metaphors for when we were teaching at our best. In this work, we also employed dialogue techniques based on the "clearness committees" used by Quakers and adapted by Palmer (1998, pp. 152–156). We began by preparing individual written descriptive reflections on our own teaching metaphor. Then during each session, one person and her metaphor would serve as the focal point. Other members of the group prepared for the meeting by reading her descriptive reflection and generating authentic, open-ended questions about various aspects of the metaphor and its relationship to her teaching. During each meeting, we used a set of ground rules to facilitate the dialogue process:

1) ask only questions about which one is genuinely curious;
2) draw conclusions only about one's own practices and metaphor, and
3) maintain absolute confidentiality about what others share. (Miller et al., 2002, p. 82)

Based on the clearness committee process members were encouraged to ask "open, honest question(s)" (Palmer, 1998, p. 153) and could "not offer advice or refer to expert authority" (Miller et al., 2002, p. 83).

Ground Rules: Essentials for a Robust, Productive Dialogue

While quite varied across our groups, our use of ground rules has been critical to our process of using dialogue in self-study. Our intention has always been that a group would develop a shared set of ground rules using our initial list as a starting point. Not set in stone, ground rules were to be revisited and revised throughout the group's lifetime as the group felt necessary. In reality, not all groups have been willing to engage in that process. A group's adaptation or resistance to the use of ground rules has resulted in what we consider to be a less than ideal process for creating dialogue that can be used for genuine self-study.

Ground rules often seem restrictive or unnecessary to new members. As one of our previous group members stated, it seemed "stupid that adults would need rules like kindergarten... [discourse communities] don't have to talk about process...they get right to the good stuff...I just wanted to talk about teaching." Ironically, this statement illustrates the presence of a tacit personal ground rule about what should and should not happen within the group; since the rule was tacit, it could not be examined nor adopted by the group as a whole, and thus violations created interpersonal conflicts within this group that could not be directly addressed. This phenomenon of treating private rules as if they are shared group rules was actually examined by Melissa and Katheryn (East, 2006; Heston & East, 2004) within the context of their classroom practice, yet we did not realize this could also happen within a group of colleagues who all shared the goal of improving practice. We have found that, in the absence of explicit and collaboratively created ground rules, a group's dialogue can easily take on other, less productive conversational forms, such as the way some professors "take advantage of others to make their point via academic discourse" (East & Fitzgerald, 2006, p. 74).

Even when the group as a whole does not use the ground rules, we continue, in a fashion, to use those rules we consider most essential, and thus model their use for colleagues who may be resistant to developing a set of overt rules. This tacit enactment of ground rules seems to create a protective space in which all participants feel free to talk about their teaching in ways that they cannot do as easily in other university settings. For instance, even though confidentiality was not explicitly discussed in every group, we found that the participants in these groups did maintain the confidentiality of the group. Unfortunately, because we have had neither the consistency nor energy to actively push every group through the ground rule process, we do not know how much more productive some of our less effective groups might have been had we made our tacit use of ground rules more explicit.

Recalibration Points

During our dialogues, we pay particular attention to what we have come to think of as recalibration points, which are in some cases similar to nodal moments (Tidwell, 2006). A recalibration point is a place within the dialogue at which an understanding is captured in the dialogue as it emerges. Sometimes a word or phrase crystallizes the understanding, and it is recognized with an "a-ha!" from others around the table. Other times there is a more gradual recognition of an idea that has recalibrated our thinking about practice. And sometimes, the recalibration occurs solely within an individual. Rather than use the term 'reframing,' we have chosen to call these recalibrations; rather than being major transformations of our thinking about our practice they are smaller in scale and more like fine-tuning in our awareness and understanding of our teacher education practices. These recalibrations hold our history and help us frame current issues in our practice. When one of us invokes the statement of a recalibration point, much more than the moment is produced.

Our first example of a group recalibration point also underscores one of the outcomes of our close collaboration. Linda realized that

> Just as I bring my class with me into our weekly discussions, I bring our discussion group with me into my classroom. Far from the image of the teacher isolated behind a closed door, I feel that I am assisted by my team of Critical (but friendly) Others as I take risks in changing my practice. (Boody et al., 1998, p. 98)

Another example of an important recalibration point in this particular group is captured through a spontaneously and collectively developed metaphor, one we call 'the brain in the middle of the table.' In early 1997 when we first identified this moment we did not have the language of recalibration point, and we described it like this: "The thinking in our group meetings does not go on inside our individual heads but in the open space in the middle of the group" (Boody et al., 1998, p. 91). This shared collective brain image captures our experience that in dialogue there are instances when something that none of us could create alone is created in the middle of the group as it were. Indeed, we are more than the sum of our parts when it comes to thinking deeply about our practice. When brought to mind, this past moment reminds us that we really do need each other if we are to fully examine our individual practices. However, as we have studied our own group processes over time, we have come to realize that not everyone we identify as thinkers who use that brain in the middle of the table actually experienced the initial recalibration point (see Canning, Fitzgerald, Miller, & Johnson, 2007), nor do they necessarily experience moments of thinking together in the same way that we do.

In our metaphor group, which we feel best illustrates our use of dialogue method, our process resulted in numerous recalibration points that we have continued to use in studying our practice. In this group, about half way through our 14 years of collaboration, Melissa came up with this description of our process: "In essence, I tell my story for me and you hear it for you" (Miller et al., 2002, p. 82). This statement captures our realization that an important part of our dialogue method is the creation of space for honoring each person's story of practice. In the process, by listening well we also learn about our own practice and how we think about it. When invoked, this recalibration point can call us to that kind of deep listening, reminding us of how we want to be with each other, and that we are not present to fix the speaker but to honor a teaching experience as she or he understands it. This statement also reminds us that dialogue is most productive as self-study when we suspend judgment and hear with open-minded curiosity what others have to share.

We identified the recalibration point of "professional intimacy" (Fitzgerald, East, Heston, & Miller, 2002, p. 77) when we began writing about the group from which this recalibration point ("I tell my story") was derived.

> [Professional intimacy] means we have created a community where we can...speak about our teaching lives..., sharing how we fail and what we struggle with in teaching. In this place, we are able to be wholehearted because it is not required that we censor certain ideas or topics nor posture for validation as we are often compelled to do in our other working contexts. (Fitzgerald et al., 2002, p. 77)

When one of us recalls this recalibration point, we become more authentic in assessing how well the process is working in the existing group. Are we moving toward such intimacy or are we merely skating on the surface and therefore needing to change our approach? If we decide we are engaged in superficial skating, then we can ask what we need to do to develop relationships that will allow us to speak more openly and authentically about our practice.

"Wanderfahring" (Miller et al., 2002, p. 83) is a word of recalibration that we coined to describe seemingly off-topic digressions that ended up being generative and refreshing. When we wanderfahr we let the process move us forward rather than pushing toward a specific goal. When invoked, this moment gives us permission to allow joy and laughter to become part of our work. We realize that being serious and task oriented is not necessarily the same as being productive. When we forget to laugh we find our intimacy and productivity reduced. In a counter-intuitive way, what might seem like a digression can often become a short cut that provides routes to deeper analysis and understanding. Our hypothesis is that these topics are in some non-linear and non-conscious way related to the topic immediately preceding our wanderfahring and thus provide dialogue opportunities that might not otherwise be available.

The last recalibration point we will discuss here was contributed by an author in one of our text-based dialogues. Although Parker Palmer actually did join us on our campus in a session sponsored by our campus center for the enhancement of teaching, and elaborated on this concept at that time, he first was present to us through a study group focused on his 1998 book, *The Courage to Teach*. We had been grappling with dilemmas in our teaching in which there were no clear solutions, but rather each apparent solution seemed to be less than satisfactory because it required some kind of trade-off we would prefer not to make. We were justified and energized when we encountered this passage in Palmer's book:

> Paradox is another name for that tension, a way of holding opposites together that creates an electric charge that keeps us awake. Not all good teachers use the same technique, but whatever technique they use, good teachers always find ways to induce this creative tension. (1998, p. 74)

Since then, all we have to say is "both/and, not either/or" to give ourselves permission to hold off from resolving a dilemma too quickly, to keep the benefits of each contradictory side in mind so that a dialogue can develop without premature closure. This position gives us faith in our process and its products. For example, because of this recalibration point we were able to argue with a reviewer who found collaborative self-study, or selves-study, to be a contradiction that had to be edited one way or the other. In the end we prevailed with both self-study and selves-study.

Effects of Recalibration Points on Teacher Education Practices

Melissa

During the Boody et al. (1998) study, I was teaching an advanced child development course in which I asked students majoring in early childhood education to engage with content in mathematics (bases) and science (the moon's phases and density) in ways that students often resisted (e.g., Duckworth, 1996). In discussing my frustration with the students' resistance, I realized how important it was to me for these students to overcome their fear of mathematics and science, learn to play with ideas, and become more comfortable with (and even intoxicated by) the challenges of figuring something out and being in a place of not knowing. One of the group members, Annette Iverson, wondered if these were not rather grand goals for a one-semester class that met twice a week for only 16 weeks, and whether these were actually reasonable expectations for me to hold either for myself or for the students. Annette went on to speculate that perhaps what I was attempting to do was somewhat akin to the process of psychoanalysis where a therapist works with a client to restructure long standing and deeply held beliefs. Although the true legitimacy of this possible parallel can be challenged, the analogy did help me realize that I was indeed attempting to undo the learning patterns that many students had developed over 12 or more years. This analogy, which arose spontaneously through dialogue, helped me think more clearly about how deeply ingrained both fears and learning patterns could be for many students. This analogy also helped reduce my sense of incompetence when students did not undergo the transformations I was seeking and enabled me to respond a good bit more empathetically to student frustrations. Insight into both my goals and the broader context in which I was pursuing those goals actually happened within a single meeting during the Boody et al. (1998) self-study, and I began to make greater efforts to explain to students why I was teaching as I was, and to be more open to students' expressions of concern and frustration.

Katheryn

One of the biggest effects of a recalibration point on my practice centers on the brain in the middle. After we had that experience, I realized that this was an experience that I wanted to create for my students if at all possible. To that end I have developed my classes around students working together. This approach is not about cooperative learning, but about students in groups working on intellectually challenging tasks. The tasks engage them in a wide variety of activities that require a variety of products ranging from written responses to drawings of their understanding. Success on the task is dependent on every student contributing.

I am uncertain whether students have had the experience of the brain. I do, however, have evidence that I occasionally provide them with tasks that may provide that experience. It is not at all unusual for students to comment that their heads hurt from thinking in my class. Moreover, students sometimes become so excited about their work that they call me over to see what they have done, and occasionally they will work past the end of the class period and even ask to take work with them because they are so engaged in the project. Just as with our process, this does not happen every class period or even every class, so I have had to bring other recalibrations about time, persistence, and commitment into my work, too. These moments of deep student engagement do happen often enough that I have some sense that they may have experienced or come close to experiencing the brain. Along with that perhaps they have begun to know a level of professional intimacy, to realize that the thinking of others can be carried with you wherever you go, and to understand that it is possible to learn from dialogue whether it be dialogue with a peer or with a text.

Linda

One recalibration point that continues to send waves through my teaching is the paradoxical tension of making room for both silence and speech. Like many teachers, I have a hard time waiting for a response beyond a few moments of awkward silence and have often rushed to fill the void with my own comment or even answer. I have been working hard to listen actively, to put my own interpretation on hold while asking questions in order to draw out the thinking of the student. At the same time I also have tried to directly teach these techniques to my preservice teachers to use with children and parents in their classroom-based field experiences and practica. The documentation that my preservice teachers have been doing demonstrates increasing use of active listening as a strategy they use to guide young children's behavior, and increasingly effective use of productive questions as pedagogical technique.

Using Metaphor to Recalibrate Our Process

In addition to the spontaneous or emergent recalibration points, we also have deliberately undertaken to recalibrate the alignment of our beliefs and our teaching practices through dialogue. For this purpose, metaphor has served as a powerful engine for understanding and for change (Heston, East, & Fitzgerald, 1998; Miller et al., 2002). As we began working together on this chapter, it was natural to generate a metaphor to help us decide to what in our process we needed to give closer examination if we were going to describe it for others. Metaphors help us to surface what we know deeply (Lakoff & Johnson, 1980) – as we say, knowing not just with our heads but also with our hearts, really knowing. During this process we played with a metaphor of wild yeast to describe what seems to us to be a very organic process and grappled with explanations for the failure of some of our talking teaching and learning groups to engage in dialogue that was recognizable as self-study. As an example of an extended metaphor, and as an alternative way to summarize this section and transition to a section about the weaknesses of our process, we offer our Wild Yeast Metaphor.

Here are some facts about wild yeast that will provide a helpful foundation as you read about our capturing our practice in that image. Perhaps you are familiar with dried, packaged yeast, stored on your shelf or in your refrigerator, ready, and waiting for moments of inspired baking? Or maybe you are acquainted with its earlier counterpart of compressed living yeast, which was more difficult to store, but when properly stored, was just as useful for those baking projects. Before such yeast was available, bakers relied entirely on the wild yeast. Growing wild yeast is a longer, less certain, and definitely less familiar process now than using dried or compressed yeasts with their nearly foolproof rising capabilities. The payoff for the extra effort is that it can produce a complexity of taste such as can be found in good sour dough or artisan breads.

Using wild yeast requires only two ingredients, but for a successful process those ingredients must be of high quality: freshly ground, preservative-free flour and pure water. To start the process the baker mixes equal parts of the water and flour, covers the mixture with a cloth and lets it sit at 70° F (i.e., room temperature). Each day some of the mixture needs to be removed and new flour and water added. After several days, though the process is proceeding well, the mixture will not smell or look all that appetizing. Frothing and an alcoholic smell rises from the work of the non-yeast microbes. They are harmless, but necessary for creating an environment suitable for the growth of the yeast. There can, however, be microbes that are harmful and bring sudden death to the wild yeast. Despite the mixture's smell and appearance, the baker sticks with it and continues feeding, and one day opens the cover to reveal starter, a slightly yellow, creamy mixture suitable for rising bread. While the starter can be used immediately, its flavor develops more fully during storage with continued feeding. Untended, the starter quickly dies and becomes an unpleasant mess.

For us this image captures the balances necessary for the method of dialogue to work as self-study. Like wild yeast, dialogue cannot be forced, but must instead be nurtured. A group desiring to engage in this method can increase the chances of the method being productive by using the quality ingredients we have described above, such as texts and ground rules; by adding professional intimacy to the group to feed it; by providing time for the group to develop or to wanderfahr, not expecting or attempting to force recalibration points but rather letting them surface; and by tending to and keeping alive the stories that have given the group meaning. Using dialogue effectively for self-study is a longer and less certain process than other research methods, yet one that is suitable for the depth needed in self-study.

Although no one of the conditions we have identified as important to our process is sufficient in itself, we have identified a set of requirements necessary for moving forward together in self-study. As we made one-to-one connections between the description of wild yeast and the data from our collaborative self-study dialogue groups, we realized we needed to talk about some of the ways in which the process can fail. We asked, what in our dialogue method corresponds to the less positive characteristics of the metaphor such as the medium that is removed and disposed of each day so the starter can continue to grow, the non-yeast microbes that can take over and ruin a starter, or the untended starter that eventually dies? And so we add some cautionary tales from our experiences in the less successful dialogue groups.

Cautionary Tales

We have described above our collaborative dialogue process when it worked well, but there have certainly been times when it did not work. This is very much like our knowing about best teaching practice and not always being able to enact those practices in our classroom. Just so, despite our successes with dialogue as method we sometimes fall short in our own process. We make mistakes or fail to take our own advice, sometimes because we forget and sometimes because a context makes it difficult to do what we know will lead to what we consider productive dialogue. For instance, why did we continue attending and supporting groups that were not nurturing productive dialogue for months before they dried up and died naturally? We certainly knew that process was important if a dialogue method was to be used, and yet we could not or would not insist on such a process in those groups. It is, however, from times that our process did not work that we have learned where challenges to the process can arise. To return to the metaphor with which we opened this chapter, we envision our process as the main channel of our river of work together. The channel always exists but there are also sandbars which strand us and backwaters into which we drift and lose our way. Without describing those, we are not accurately presenting our process. In addition, there are cases when one or more of the characteristics we have identified were missing and the dialogue process slowed or stopped altogether.

Time investment is a first prerequisite. We recognized this in the self-study group that identified professional intimacy:

> The process that brought us to this point was long in both time and effort. Preceding this meeting we had worked together for a year in sessions from one to four hours long. These were large time commitments from busy schedules. Significant time together, however, was a crucial part of what allowed us to develop professional intimacy. How we designed and spent this time together were equally important. (Fitzgerald et al., 2002, p. 77)

One ground rule to which the three of us have been strongly committed is that we will give priority to participating regularly in our various groups, choosing our self-study dialogue sessions over most other commitments when we encounter conflicts in our schedules. For a meeting to be productive it is also crucial that members invest the necessary time in preparing, such as reading the text for the week or writing the reflective piece to share. Along with Palmer (1993) we believe that by investing in time together we get to know each other and that yields new understandings and allows the rest to happen.

However, we also know that other members of some of our groups have experienced contradictions around our use of time. Having made a commitment of valuable time, they sometimes are dismayed when "time has to be treated as a fluid resource" (East & Fitzgerald, 2006, p. 73). Taking the time to support wanderfahring and/or less linear ways of reaching a session's goals, or addressing problems with process can seem a waste of time to these colleagues. Moreover, sometimes colleagues are impatient for a peak experience, having heard or read about some of the amazing sessions we have had, such as those which yielded productive and powerful recalibration points. They come to our process without understanding the long-range view we have embraced because we have repeatedly seen what dialogue method can produce when it is working optimally. The concept of "flow" accurately describes the cadence of experience in our process: "When high challenges are matched with high skills, then the deep involvement that sets flow apart from ordinary life is likely to occur" (Csikszentmihalyi, 1997, p. 30). Yet, there are as many if not more times when flow is only a distant memory. The time and effort required to develop professional intimacy and the process skills needed for productive dialogue about challenging teaching situations, and thus creating an opportunity for a flow experience, demand an investment of time that occasional and/or casual engagement in a discussion group does not support.

Persistence is another crucial characteristic of successful dialogue-based self-study. Members need to trust in the long-term value of the work, suspending judgment about what might not seem to be particularly productive at any one time. Staying with a process that does not yield immediate results all the time can try one's patience. We have found that in the long run, when we stick with the process and the community even when they are not meeting our individual needs at the moment, more often than not the process and community come back around to serve us even better. For instance, we have found that some members need to tell their story over and over again. Actively listening through multiple tellings is challenging, but often doing so reveals subtle shifts in the details of the story that signal the teller is beginning to either reframe or let go of the story. When we allow group members to do what they need to do, they often become more productive members of the group, and even to return the favor when we try their patience at a later date.

Related to persistence is the more general disposition of commitment – to the group, to each other, even through times of chaos within the group (Peck, 1987). Our self-study dialogue is not for the impatient, those who are uncomfortable with a nonlinear process, or those who need an immediate pay-off or at least clear progress toward a tangible product (e.g., a presentation, publication, or dramatically better teaching evaluations). While we have data that support our claim that self-study dialogue has made us better teachers, we know that our improvements have been hard won through a process that cannot be forced or shortened. The specific goals of our self-study dialogue groups have been varied, but they have shared an overall focus on continual improvement rather than the discovery of nomothetic solutions to teaching conundrums.

Genuine vulnerability is also essential in dialogue-based self-study. Even with careful attention to conditions that nourish trust (e.g., ground rules, confidentiality), participants in the dialogue still have to be willing to become vulnerable through the sharing of their own conundrums and challenges in teaching. Group members whose narratives repeatedly blame students or administrators often resist the deep reflection necessary to reveal their own role in difficult situations. We have wondered sometimes whether or not some people are constitutionally incapable of the kind of reflection and vulnerability required by self-study. However, analysis of longitudinal data across our groups (East et al., 2008) revealed that, when they continue to commit time and energy to dialogue within our groups, some resisters slowly become more willing to be vulnerable and to engage in honest reflection, thus joining with us in the self-study process.

Some members have joined us in hopes of fixing problems identified by evaluators for tenure and promotion. What is valued by the institution for professional advancement may or may not relate positively to best practices for the improvement of teacher education. The pressing needs of untenured colleagues can bring them to self-study dialogue, but they may not stay due to a lack of time to invest, a narrow focus on specific goals (such as improving student instructor evaluations by a certain time or with quick tricks), or a need to complain while avoiding reflection or taking ownership of their own contribution to difficult teaching situations. Our approach to self-study is not especially conducive to the easy achievement of tenure and promotion. Our approach to self-study requires time; while highly productive over the long term, it can be several years before that productivity becomes clearly evident. In addition, while evaluators who place higher value on quantitative research may be puzzled by self-study methods and often express skepticism, even evaluators from qualitative research backgrounds may not fully recognize work that does not adhere to standards of the methods with which they are most familiar (e.g., constant-comparative method, ethnographic methods, discourse analysis techniques). Finally, what is valued by an institution changes over time, so the institutional legitimacy that a self-study may have in one case may not generalize to the next case.

Though we have consistently found our use of dialogue to be a productive self-study method, we have also found that the process does not always work. To use the language of our wild yeast metaphor, unfriendly microbes may take over the medium, a lack of quality ingredients may stymie its growth, or a lack of tending may cause it to die. How do we decide that a group will not ever become sufficiently productive or professionally enriching and thus terminate our involvement, thereby perhaps killing the group? How long do we persevere in the face of resistance and unwillingness to enter into authentic dialogue that may lead to worthwhile recalibration points and ultimately to important and positive changes in our practice? We have no answers to these questions and in all honesty, we have been unwilling to abandon any group. Some of our uncertainty about these questions is due to some exclusionary choices that we made in an early group, which we regretted almost immediately (e.g., when we refused to let a latecomer join the community building group described in the first section of this paper). Since that time, we have put explicit value on welcoming the stranger and providing support for whomever commits to the group, even when that person contributes little or perhaps actually makes our work in the group more difficult. For example, in one group we honored a member's objections to going through the ground rule process and we put explicit invocation of ground rules aside. The group later faltered and we in hindsight realized that our accommodation was a poor decision, however much at the time we thought this would allow the group to move forward. We also keep in mind the fact that we were once beginners in self-study and more experienced members of the self-study community readily welcomed and mentored us. We do not see how we can do any less. In the process of writing this chapter, however, we have come to see that we may have sacrificed our collaborative work together for the sake of supporting others whose interests in teaching and learning are not connected to self-study.

Because of issues in our larger groups, the disciplined self-study work we have done lately has been in pairs or partnerships with colleagues other than each other, not in our larger Talking Teaching and Learning group which continues to exist and which we all attend. However, the commitment to our dialogue method that would allow earlier groups to engage in productive self-study has diminished, and the resistance to our suggestions for activities that have supported self-study in the past has seemingly increased. Unwilling to turn away colleagues who desire to improve their teaching but resist using self-study methods to do so, we have kept the larger group going. As we met to work together to prepare this chapter, we were confronted with the realization that our inclusiveness and willingness to accommodate colleagues has cost us the time and energy needed for the dialogue process collaborative self-study that we have done and desire to continue doing.

Looking Back and Looking Forward

In this chapter we have described our use of dialogue in collaborative self-study over the past 14 years. For us this work has been highly productive, providing professional enrichment while allowing us to examine and transform our teacher educator practices. We believe our dialogue method is an effective tool in self-study because it can lead to positive changes in practice and because it is a process that can be used by others to create a community where such changes may become more likely. The process is different from other dialogue processes we know because, instead of capturing and analyzing the dialogue as an artifact, for us the data and the analysis reside in the dialogue as a process. While this leads to a method that is productive, it is neither easily established nor maintained.

We have demonstrated the concept of recalibration points in practice by providing examples of such instances that arose in our groups. Recalibration can occur at the individual or group level and it is these moments of crystallized understanding that have a significant positive impact on our practice and push us to describe and share the process through which we create recalibration points. We have each provided a personal example of a recalibration point that has transformed our thinking about practice and in turn resulted in changes in our practice. We have identified a set of characteristics, none of which is sufficient for creating the process in and of itself, but all of which we find contribute to a dialogue in which recalibration points can occur. These include time (both investing it as a resource and treating it in a session as if it were plentiful and fluid), persistence, commitment, willingness to be vulnerable, and flow. Finally, we described some of the difficulties that we have faced when attempting to welcome others into this kind of self-study work. In the process, we have discovered losses and developed a new awareness of how our own values may sometimes undermine the work we most enjoy. We will not give up using dialogue in our self-study work. That said, if we do wish to continue along this path, we will need to find better ways to balance our desire to be inclusive and open with our recognition that our form of self-study can only occur when we pay close attention to ensure that all the necessary ingredients are present and tended to consistently over time.

Appendix: Ground Rules

Document created on September 27, 1997 by the three co-authors and six other colleagues in the Saturday Community Building discussion group. We wrote, "It is intended to be a flexible document and was designed to guide our process as we work together in our group."
Communication is expected to be honest and authentic.

- Talk to the person who is involved
- No stuffing, deal with it here

- Stay in the here and now
- Speak from your experience
- Focus on those who are here.

Membership means commitment to consistent contribution and being willing to both get and give.

One person speaks at a time; no side conversations.

Monitor your own behavior and communication style.

Meetings will begin with a go-round and end with a go-round with go-rounds interspersed throughout the meeting.

What's said here stays here.

Everyone has the right to pass and to call time.

No put downs. Everyone is responsible for identifying put downs and defining their personal boundaries regarding what feels like a put down.

Agendas will be set by the group for the coming meeting. People may request to be on the agenda at the beginning of a given meeting.

Meetings will start and finish on time.

A volunteer timekeeper will assist the group in keeping to the established agenda.

New members will be oriented to the group ground rules before joining the group.

References

Boody, R., East, K., Fitzgerald, L. M., Heston, M. L., & Iverson, A. (1998). Talking teaching and learning: Using practical argument to make reflective thinking audible. *Action in Teacher Education, 19*, 88–101.

Brookfield, S. (1995). *Becoming a critically reflective teacher.* San Francisco: Jossey-Bass.

Bullough, R. V., Jr., & Gitlin, A. (1995). *Becoming a student of teaching: Methodologies for exploring self and school context.* New York: Garland.

Canning, C. (1993). Preparing for diversity: A social technology for multicultural community building. *Educational Forum, 57*, 371–385.

Canning, C., Fitzgerald, L. M., Miller, C., & Johnson, J. (2007, April). *Take two – Meaningful collaboration that is not consensus or even consensus-seeking: A self-study of professional learning.* Paper presented at the annual meeting of the American Educational Research Association, Chicago.

Clandinin, D. J., & Connelly, F. M. (1996). Teachers' professional knowledge landscapes: Teacher stories—stories of teachers—school stories—stories of schools. *Educational Researcher, 25*(3), 24–30.

Csikszentmihalyi, M. (1997). *Finding flow: The psychology of engagement with everyday life.* New York: Basic Books.

Duckworth, E. (1996). *"The having of wonderful ideas" and other essays on teaching and learning* (2nd ed.). New York: Teachers College Press.

East, K. (2005a, April). *Collaborative inquiry: Whose voice counts?* Paper presented at the annual meeting of the American Educational Research Association, Montreal, Canada.

East, K. (2005b, April). *Text-based collaboration.* Paper presented at the annual meeting of the American Educational Research Association, Montreal, Canada.

East, K. (2006). diversity: One teacher educator's journey. In D. L. Tidwell & L. Fitzgerald (Eds.), *Self-study and diversity* (pp. 153–172). Rotterdam: Sense.

East, K., & Fitzgerald, L. M. (2006). Collaboration and community over the long term. In L. M. Fitzgerald, M. L. Heston, & D. L. Tidwell (Eds.), *Collaboration and community: Pushing boundaries through self-study. Proceedings of the Sixth International Conference on Self-Study of Teacher Education Practices, Herstmonceux Castle, East Sussex, England* (pp. 72–75). Cedar Falls, IA: University of Northern Iowa.

East, K., Fitzgerald, L. M., & Manke, M. (2008). Same forest: Different path. In M. L. Heston, D. L. Tidwell, K. East, & L. M. Fitzgerald (Eds.), *Pathways to change in teacher education: Dialogue, diversity and self-study. Proceedings of the Seventh International Conference on Self-Study of Teacher Education Practices, Herstmonceux Castle, East Sussex, England* (pp. 103–108). Cedar Falls, IA: University of Northern Iowa.

East, K., & Heston, M. L. (2004). Talking with those not present: Conversations with John Dewey about our educational practices. In D. L. Tidwell, L. M. Fitzgerald, & M. L. Heston (Eds.), *Journeys of hope: Risking self-study in a diverse world. Proceedings of the Fifth International Conference on Self-Study of Teacher Education Practices, Herstmonceux Castle, East Sussex, England* (pp. 94–98). Cedar Falls, IA: University of Northern Iowa.

Fenstermacher, G. D. (1994). The place of practical argument in the education of teachers. In V. Richardson (Ed.), *Teacher change and the staff development process* (pp. 23-42). New York: Teachers College Press.

Fishman, S. M., & McCarthy, L. (1998). *John Dewey and the challenge of classroom practice.* New York: Teachers College Press.

Fitzgerald, L. M., East, K., Heston, M. L., & Miller, C. (2002). Professional intimacy: Transforming communities of practice. In C. Kosnik, A. Freese, & A. P. Samaras (Eds.), *Making a difference in teacher education through self-study. Proceedings of the Fourth International Conference on Self-study of Teacher Education Practices, Herstmonceux Castle, East Sussex, England* (Vol. 1, pp. 77–80). Toronto, Canada: OISE, University of Toronto.

Heston, M. L., & East, K. (2004). You're wrong and I'm not! Private rules and classroom community in the presence of diversity. In D. L. Tidwell, L. M. Fitzgerald, & M. L. Heston, (Eds). *Journeys of hope: Risking self-study in a diverse world. Proceedings of the Fifth International Conference on Self-Study of Teacher Education Practices* (pp. 145–148). Cedar Falls, IA: University of Northern Iowa.

Heston, M. L., East, K., & Farstad, J. (2000). *A waltz with Eleanor, a polka with Parker: Using text as a tool for self-study.* Paper given at the annual meeting of the American Educational Research Association, New Orleans, LA.

Heston, M. L., East, K., & Fitzgerald, L. M. (1998). Using practical argument to create communities of conversation. In A. Cole & S. Finley (Eds.), *Conversations in community. Proceedings of the Second International Conference on Self-Study of Teacher Education Practices, Herstmonceux Castle, East Sussex, England* (pp. 195–199). Kingston, Ontario: Queen's University.

Heston, M. L., East, K., Fitzgerald, L. M., Boody, R., & Iverson, A. (1997, February). *Talking teaching and learning: Using practical argument to make reflective thinking audible.* Paper presented at the annual conference of the Association of Teacher Educators, Washington, DC.

LaBoskey, V. K. (2004). The methodology of self-study and its theoretical underpinnings. In J. J. Loughran, M. L. Hamilton, V. K. LaBoskey, & T. Russell (Eds.), *International handbook of self-study of teaching and teacher education practices* (pp. 743–784). Dordrecht: Kluwer.

Lakoff, G., & Johnson, M. (1980). *Metaphors we live by.* Chicago: University of Chicago Press.

Miller, C., East, K., Fitzgerald, L. M., Heston, M. L., & Veenstra, T. (2002). Visions of self in the act of teaching: Using personal metaphors in collaborative selves study of teaching practices. *The Journal of Natural Inquiry and Reflective Practice, 16*(3), 81–93.

Palmer, P. J. (1993). *To know as we are known: Education as a spiritual journey.* San Francisco: Harper.

Palmer, P. J. (1998). *The courage to teach: Exploring the inner landscape of a teacher's life.* San Francisco: Jossey-Bass.

Peck, M. S. (1987). *The different drum: Community making and peace.* New York: Touchstone.

Silverstein, M., & Urban, G. (Eds.). (1996). *Natural histories of discourse.* Chicago: University of Chicago Press.

Tidwell, D. L. (2006). Nodal moments as a context for meaning. In D. Tidwell & L. Fitzgerald (Eds.), *Self-study and diversity* (pp. 267–285). Rotterdam: Sense.

Tidwell, D. L., & Heston, M. L. (1996). Self-reflection through practical argument: Getting the hows and whys out of the what. In J. Richards & T. Russell (Eds.), *Empowering our future in teacher education. Proceedings of the First International Conference on Self-Study of Teacher Education Practices, Herstmonceux Castle, East Sussex, England* (pp. 183–186). Toronto, Canada: OISE, University of Toronto.

Tidwell, D. L., & Heston, M. L. (1998). Self-study through the use of practical argument. In M. L. Hamilton, with S. Pinnegar, T. Russell, J. Loughran, & V. K. LaBoskey (Eds.), *Reconceptualizing teaching practice: Self-study in teacher education* (pp. 45–66). London: Routledge-Falmer.

Wells, G. (1999). *Dialogic inquiry: Toward a sociocultural practice and theory of education.* Cambridge: Cambridge University Press.

Wortham, S. (2001). *Narratives in action: A strategy for research and analysis.* New York: Teachers College Press.

"Name It and Claim It": The Methodology of Self-Study as Social Justice Teacher Education

Vicki Kubler LaBoskey

Naming the Context

The teacher education program in which I work has long had a commitment to the goals of equity and social justice. Our stated aim is to prepare our candidates to become urban teachers who engage in practice that will enhance the possibility that their students will "live in a more equitable and just society" (Kroll et al., 2005, p. 2). The conceptual framework that both undergirds this agenda and informs our enactment of it is embodied in our notion of "principled practice." In essence, this means that teaching for social justice is too complex and necessarily context specific to be reduced to a set of competencies, standards, or interventions. It is instead an active, decision-making praxis that is informed by a set of well-grounded dynamic principles that can guide and interpret interventions and outcomes in relationship to the goals of equity and social justice, like those we currently utilize at our institution:

- Teaching is a moral act founded on an ethic of care.
- Teaching is an act of inquiry and reflection.
- Learning is a constructivist/developmental process.
- The acquisition of subject matter and content knowledge is essential.
- Teaching is a collegial act and requires collaboration.
- Teaching is essentially a political act.

These inform every aspect of our work from our program design and implementation to our individual assignments and interactions.

We have a fifth-year graduate program that results in a teaching credential and a master's degree in education serving approximately 60 students per year, half of whom are seeking an elementary teaching credential and half secondary. They all teach students in the mornings and take courses at the college in the afternoons, so that there is constant interaction between the theory and the practice of social justice teaching and learning.

V.K. LaBoskey (✉)
Mills College, Education 219, Oakland, CA 94613, USA
e-mail: vickikl@mills.edu

D.L. Tidwell et al. (eds.), *Research Methods for the Self-study of Practice*,
Self-Study of Teaching and Teacher Education Practices 9,
DOI 10.1007/978-1-4020-9514-6_5, © Springer Science+Business Media B.V. 2009

Naming the Questions

Agreeing with Griffiths (2003) that social justice education is dynamic and never fully accomplished, my colleagues and I embrace the notion that ongoing investigation and self-study are a necessary aspect of this agenda. Therefore, we ask hard questions of ourselves with regularity. We seek out disconfirming evidence, indicators of a need for the transformation or enhancement of particular program aspects.

Most recently, our search seemed to suggest that we should give more attention to how we were dealing with issues of race and racism in our curriculum. Many of our student teachers, for instance, were still uncomfortable with discussions of race and racism. Our graduates were increasingly disturbed by the narrowing of the curriculum for their urban students of color, as a result of the No Child Left Behind Act, and unclear about appropriate pedagogical responses. An external study of our program revealed a weakness with regard to the preparation of our students for teaching African-American children (McDonald, 2005). And finally, the demographics of the state of California, where over 70% of the K-12 population are students of color, seemed to demand it. Consequently, we decided to focus our self-study on the question, What does it take to prepare teachers to teach each child well in a racist nation?

Each of us then designed an individual investigation we felt would enhance our personal practice and understandings, as well as contribute to the larger question. I decided to experiment with an assignment I give in my yearlong course, "Curriculum and Instruction in the Elementary School," taken by all elementary credential candidates. It was an assignment I had already used quite successfully for several years (LaBoskey & Cline, 2000), which addressed teacher identity development. I speculated that if I added a requirement for them to focus on their attitudes and understandings of race and racism, it might contribute to their acceptance of and ability to engage effectively in this aspect of their teaching. It is a 3-week project that involves their collection of data including daily journals, supervisor observations and debriefings, and a videotape of teaching. Drawing upon this evidence and the course readings, they explore, in a written case on self, an issue of interest to them in the development of their teacher identities.

The adaptations I made to the assignment for the purposes of this investigation were to change the title from "Case on Self as Teacher" to "Case on Self as Teacher for Equity and Social Justice," to require that the issue they chose to study had to do with race/racism, and to substitute for the making of a videotape, data collection from their students on their focus topic. The first two changes were intended to insure that the students would be addressing our self-study issue of race/racism. The latter was made because the literature suggests that student teachers, especially those from the dominant culture, may not even recognize "the salience of race, class, and culture in students' experiences" (Darling-Hammond, 2003, p. 207). So they need to be helped "[t]o 'see' students in another way, [by learning] to look and listen carefully and nonjudgmentally in order to understand who students really are, what they think, and how they make decisions about how they behave" (p. 210).

My study was thus designed to answer these questions: What can student teachers learn from an assignment like the 'Case on Self as Teacher for Equity and Social Justice' about issues of race and racism in classrooms? How can their explorations contribute to our understanding of the meaning, implementation, and assessment of social justice teacher education and the specific role that self-study might play in that? Such an investigation seemed to be well justified not only by our particular self-study agenda but also by the broader educational context.

Naming the Methodology

The overall methodology I employed in this research is self-study because it is "a methodology for studying professional practice settings" (LaBoskey, 2004a, p. 817) (see also Pinnegar, 1998) and thus is appropriate for the examination of efforts like this in a social justice teacher education program. I designed the study, therefore, to be consistent with the five primary characteristics of self-study I have previously identified (LaBoskey, 2004a). First, it was, from the outset, self-initiated and focused; I chose to do this study on my own practice. Second, it was improvement aimed; I wanted to enhance my and my program's ability to support student teacher learning with regard to the educational social justice issues of race and racism.

Third, it was interactive at several stages of the process and with several relevant constituencies. The student teachers engaged in these projects interacted with their supervisors, cooperating teachers, students, one another, and me in order to check understandings and push the boundaries of their thinking. In addition, to do the same for myself, the researcher, I interacted with my students during and long after the assignment; I interacted with my colleagues at Mills about the design and the results before, during, and after the actual intervention; and I interacted with my AERA symposium colleagues, where this work was originally presented, and with the AERA audience, that is, with other teacher educators at other institutions.

Fourth, it included multiple, mainly qualitative methods. I collected and analyzed all 32 cases written by the students in the course during that year. The cases were accompanied by a freewrite reflection on their reactions to the assignment, which were also collected and analyzed. I took journal notes on my experiences of constructing, implementing, and evaluating this project, which included feedback from both my Mills and AERA colleagues.

Fifth, defining validity as a validation process based in trustworthiness, I assumed that validation of the potential value added to social justice teacher education by an assignment like this case on self cannot be determined within the confines of this particular self-study. What I am doing instead is offering an exemplar of practice to the relevant scholarly community, others in the field concerned with social justice teacher education, for their examination and future testing. According to Mishler (1990), who articulated this notion of exemplar-based validation quite thoroughly, "the assessment of the validity of a single study must remain provisional.

The trustworthiness of an approach or a finding needs to be tested repeatedly within a field and can thereby gain in strength over time" (LaBoskey, 2004a, p. 853).

The analysis of the data presented in the next section was intended, first and foremost, to inform my own understandings and practice. I will continue this investigation in subsequent years and thereby contribute to the validation process myself. Second, it was to provide others with sufficient information for them to determine its trustworthiness and thus, in part, its validity. In Mishler's (1990) view, validation is accomplished when "the results of a study come to be viewed as sufficiently trustworthy for other investigators to rely upon for their own work" (p. 429).

But my intention was not simply to employ, in a static manner, self-study methodology for these research ends. I was also interested in investigating the relationship between social justice education and the methodology of self-study and how those interactions might be enhanced. I have previously proposed (LaBoskey, 2004b) that self-study needs to fully embrace a social justice agenda and capitalize more on its "strengths that reside in its personal and interpersonal nature—in its acknowledgement of the humanity of the teaching/learning endeavor—and the need for us as teachers and teacher educators to take responsibility for our actions" (pp. 1180–1181).

As Brown (2004) has pointed out, "Self-study is uniquely suited to contribute to an understanding of race and social class issues in education [because]...self-study is a research paradigm that promotes educators' identification of the problems of practice that emerge in their work and fosters an examination of the values, beliefs, and assumptions that inform their educative decisions and actions" (p. 520). Other forms of research, in her view, even action research or teacher research, can keep these issues opaque and at a distance—it is about them or about that structure and not about me. But despite that potential, she too feels that this investigation arena has yet to be fully capitalized upon by the field of self-study and joins with me and others in encouraging us to do so. This study was intended to follow that advice.

Naming the Results

I analyzed all cases and accompanying freewrites, as well as my notes on the process, looking for evidence of transforming student teacher understandings and attitudes regarding the role of race/racism in social justice education. First, and most fundamentally, I looked for an acknowledgment of the existence of racial issues in their classrooms. Second, I looked for particular transformations in their thinking and/or practice with regard to race/racism in social justice education. This process was iterative in that I framed the analysis with broad categories that included the dispositions, pedagogies, and curricular orientations generally advocated by the literature on social justice and culturally relevant pedagogy (e.g., Cochran-Smith, 2004; Ladson-Billings, 1994). As the specifics emerged from the data, I then reapplied them to the whole. In this study those were (a) recognizing the importance of hearing their students' voices concerning the issues of race/racism; (b) understanding the need to include an explicit equity curriculum; and (c) embracing an inquiry orientation toward their practice, what Cochran-Smith (2004) refers to as "inquiry as stance" (p. 14).

Furthermore, I looked for indicators of how my self-study process may have helped or hindered these outcomes. I will discuss each results category separately, before considering their joint implications.

Student Teacher Outcomes

Overall

The operative term for describing the general reaction to the process would be resistant. From the moment the assignment was distributed until completion, many students complained about the focus on race. At the end of every class period, for instance, one or two would come up to me to request a waiver from that requirement and the primary reason cited was that there were "no issues of race" in their classrooms—this despite the fact that most were student teaching in classrooms with many if not all students of color. The following quote from one of the freewrite reflections is representative of this struggle (note that all names are pseudonyms):

> *I found it challenging to conduct this study through the lens of racial issues. This could be because of my discomfort when talking about these issues or perhaps because of my own inability to see the presence of race issues in this environment. I also feel that, although race is a vital issue for teachers for equity and social justice, there are other issues of inequity that are just as vital and present. I wonder a little about why I do not feel prepared to address issues of race, however, and am concerned that I have missed something in the coursework at Mills, which would have better prepared me for this process.* (Kendra, freewrite)

I shared her concern. At this point in time we were part way through the second semester of this two-semester credential year. Race had been an explicit target issue from day one—at our student retreat prior to the start of the program we focused many of our activities on a discussion of racism in schools, using as our central text for the summer reading, *Why Are All the Black Kids Sitting Together in the Cafeteria?* (Tatum, 1997). During the first semester, one of their required courses was called "Leadership for Equity," which was explicitly concerned with explorations of their personal experiences with race and with the undoing of their own racism. They also had a course entitled "Introduction to the Profession of Teaching Diverse Learners" that was continuing in the second semester. In addition, all faculty members were stressing the issue of race in their courses even more so than usual because of our self-study focus for the year. If student teachers in this context are still resistant about addressing issues of race and racism, then the challenge is clear—but so is the mandate.

Kendra's resistance was so strong that she did not address race in her case. The encouraging news is that she was one of only three out of the 32 student teachers in the class to avoid the topic of race/racism altogether. One of the others, a student teacher of color, claimed to be addressing the issue of race, but in fact remained resistant and concluded in the end that race was irrelevant to her teaching. Another, a white student teacher, tried to address the racial issues she was clear existed in her classroom, but was unable to make any progress in that regard, concluding instead that white teachers like her probably did not have the ability to teach students of color well.

All of the other 29 student teachers (90%) chose to explore an issue having to do with race/racism very directly, sometimes in connection with other equity issues like gender, language, or socioeconomic status. As previously emphasized by Darling-Hammond (2003), the transformational process must begin with a recognition of the salience of race in students' lives and school experiences. These student teachers not only took that critical first step, they also made, to varying degrees, important transformations in their thinking and/or practice in ways consistent with current definitions of teaching for social justice.

Hearing Students' Voices

Many of these student teachers acknowledged the importance of hearing their students' voices with regard to issues of race and racism. Often this was noted as a key factor in helping them to make the transformations that they did. Catherine, for instance, had given her class of seventh graders an anonymous questionnaire where she asked them several direct questions about race in school, e.g., "Do you think about your race a lot? Do you think teachers judge you upon your race?" She was amazed to discover that virtually all of the students answered "yes" to the first question and in her follow up, "How much?" some of the students of color said, "Every hour." She was particularly impressed by responses to the question, "Do you think teachers judge you upon your race?" like these: *Yes, because maybe if your [sic] Latino they would think that they only think about soccer and not school* (Latino male); *Yes, one of my teachers expects me to be a good girl all the time just because I'm white* (White female). This questionnaire triggered a classroom discussion initiated by the students that gave Catherine even greater insight: *My students have made me realize that I had to face the issue of race and racism because most importantly it concerned them.*

Several not only saw the value in the moment, they also made a commitment to continuing these interchanges in the future. In addition to noting the importance of this information to their teaching and personal development, they recognized the curricular value for students.

Explicit Equity Curriculum

Many of these student teachers expressed the desire to use the hearing of their students' voices as a starting place, as a part of a curricular focus on equity and social justice. In addition to helping their students become powerful knowers of the traditional curriculum, as would be essential in any definition of social justice teacher education, they wanted to engage in more explicit teaching of "inequity, power, and activism" (Cochran-Smith, 2004, p. 77):

> *As a teacher for equity and social justice, I must embrace contemporary dilemmas related to race and racism as instructional content. . .. I don't want to deny my students the opportunity to think in sophisticated ways about how their world is ordered and how their lives are defined; I want them to make sense of what they're inheriting and know that they can influence it, that it's theirs.* (Laura, case)

Laura concluded her case by setting the stage for her own subsequent and continual growth:

> *If I believe this deeply and apply it to my teaching, then I think I will have some basis upon which to evaluate my future work as I try to teach each child well in a racist nation. Acknowledging the challenge of this task, I can interrogate my actions and my work deeply and critically, and ask myself to what extent I'm meeting the challenge.* (Laura, case)

All 29 student teachers in this group acknowledged the need for this kind of ongoing investigation and development. Seeing this assignment as only a beginning, they wholeheartedly embraced the inquiry orientation so central to our notion of social justice education.

Inquiry as Stance

These student teachers recognized the merits of engaging in investigations like this case on self, admitted that even with regard to the issue they had been investigating, they had much more to learn, and committed to continuing the process in the future, as is apparent in these statements: *I am still working on this project. The assignment itself is done but the thinking and processing is definitely just beginning* (Katie, freewrite).

> *I now feel as if I know what I need to do to identify my prejudices: keeping the mirror upon myself, engaging in daily self-reflection, taking time to connect and communicate with ALL my students, examining my actions and my practice, and asking others for help so that I can continue to improve—both as a teacher, and as a human being.* (Sharon, freewrite)

These student teachers seemed to understand the need to take an inquiry orientation to their practice, in some cases, with more clarity than they had prior to this project. Such declarations were one indication of the value added by this particular assignment and by the self-study in which I was engaged, which related to my second research question.

Role of Self-Study

Student teacher comments in the cases and accompanying freewrites suggested that they learned things about social justice education from this experience that they had not learned elsewhere in the program. Furthermore, they identified what aspects of the endeavor most contributed to that outcome. The following quote is representative:

This type of assignment is invaluable. I have never really examined in detail these issues of race or gender in my own teaching. . ..These three things, my extensive reflection in journal writing, discussions with colleagues, and examination of my students' feelings, were crucial in this case on self. These were invaluable tools and were important when analyzing one's own teaching. They helped to cement and make obvious what needed to be changed and how this can happen. In this way, I was able to learn that teachers need to relate what we are teaching to our students and constantly think about them, and how what we are doing affects them. (Jen, freewrite)

The specific features mentioned by Jen, when compared with those identified by the others, revealed some consistencies in this data.

Four qualities of the assignment seemed to be most beneficial to this group of student teachers. First was its personal focus—the need for them to examine themselves and their developing teacher identities, and this is key, in relationship to their actual teaching efforts with diverse student populations. Several talked about how, even though we had been examining issues of race in classes throughout the year, it did not sink in until they had to study it in their own practice.

Second, they found particular value in the interactive requirements of the project. Especially beneficial were the interchanges they had with their students about their experiences with race and racism. This input seldom triggered any defensiveness, even if some of it had to do with them. Indeed quite the opposite; if they gathered information that was poignant and compelling, they became energized for change. Also of importance were interactions with supervisors, which will be discussed further below.

Third, different student teachers found value in different aspects of the assignment. For instance, several felt that it was the writing of the paper that really made the difference, whereas at least one felt that the paper was unnecessary and should be replaced by more worthwhile conversations like those she had had with her supervisor. So, in a sense, it was the package—the inclusion of multiple ways to both gather and make sense of their data—that made widespread benefit more possible. There was something in it for just about everyone.

Fourth was the overall framing of the assignment as an inquiry project. Many found value in the opportunity to ask and investigate their own questions. Even more importantly, they felt they had not only gained insights into the particular issues they were investigating, they had acquired a system that could guide their future deliberations and decision making. They understood more completely what it meant to engage in reflective practice with a social justice agenda.

"Name It and Claim It"

What is striking in these data is how well these results map on to the characteristics of self-study: "it is self-initiated and focused; it is improvement-aimed; it is interactive; it includes multiple, mainly qualitative, methods; and, it defines validity as a validation process based in trustworthiness" (on-going investigations over time) (LaBoskey, 2004a, p. 817). Thus, I concluded that the positive impact of this case assignment could, in part at least, be attributed to the self-study methodology I was employing. But not entirely; there were important additions that derived more from the explicit social justice intention of the process than from the self-study structure itself.

Most particularly, my insistence on the topic of race and racism despite the considerable resistance to it was critical to the outcome. Likewise, direct interventions, pushes from the supervisors, often made the difference in whether or not the student teachers made substantive transformations to their thinking and/or practice, as is apparent in this statement from one of the students whom I was supervising:

> *The second important part of the process was my conversation with Vicki, in which we looked at my journal entries together in an initial attempt to come up with a focus for the study. During that conversation, Vicki both highlighted threads of continuity she saw running through my journals, and also called attention to the categorical assumptions underlying many of my questions and concerns. . ... Our conversation served as a jumping off point, for me, in moving deeper and examining the mental frameworks giving shape to my journaled concerns. Without Vicki's willingness to call me out, so to speak, on my underlying assumptions, and to give me an initial lens through which to view them, I do not think this project would have resulted in much growth.* (Beth, freewrite)

But there were also missed opportunities—situations where I, or one of the other supervisors, did not intervene when we should have, sometimes resulting in maintained misconceptions and diminished growth. Only when we were bold enough and direct enough to "call them out," were we able to promote the growth we were looking for, which is a message we would do well to heed.

The results of my investigation support the conclusion that there is great compatibility between self-study methodology and social justice teacher education, but the connection is not automatic. To maximize this natural association, the social justice agenda must be given explicit attention throughout the self-study process. If we are to realize the power of self-study to "promote substantive changes in teacher education and support democratic, transformative efforts to provide a quality education for all students" (Brown, 2004, p. 543), we must ask the hard questions about equity of ourselves, our programs, and our students. For the methodology of self-study to truly serve as social justice education, we must "name it to claim it."

References

Brown, E. (2004). The significance of race and social class for self-study and the professional knowledge base of teacher education. In J. J. Loughran, M. L. Hamilton, V. K. LaBoskey, & T. Russell (Eds.), *International handbook of self-study of teaching and teacher education practices* (pp. 517–574). Dordrecht: Kluwer.

Cochran-Smith, M. (2004). *Walking the road: Race, diversity, and social justice in teacher education.* New York: Teachers College Press.

Darling-Hammond, L. (2003). Educating a profession for equitable practice. In. L. Darling-Hammond, J. French, & S. P. Garcia-Lopez (Eds.), *Learning to teach for social justice* (pp. 201–216). New York: Teachers College Press.

Griffiths, M. (2003). *Action for social justice in education: Fairly different.* Maidenhead, England: Open University Press.

Kroll, L., Cossey, R., Donahue, D., Galguera, T., LaBoskey, V. K., Richert, A. E., et al. (2005). *Teaching as principled practice*. Thousand Oaks, CA: Sage.

LaBoskey, V. K. (2004a). The methodology of self-study and its theoretical underpinnings. In J. J. Loughran, M. L. Hamilton, V. K. LaBoskey, & T. Russell (Eds.), *International handbook of self-study of teaching and teacher education practices* (pp. 817–869). Dordrecht: Kluwer.

LaBoskey, V. K. (2004b). Moving the methods of self-study research and practice forward: Challenges and opportunities. In J. J. Loughran, M. L. Hamilton, V. K. LaBoskey, & T. Russell (Eds.), *International handbook of self-study of teaching and teacher education practices* (pp. 1169–1184). Dordrecht: Kluwer.

LaBoskey, V. K., & Cline, S. (2000). Behind the mirror: Inquiry-based storying in teacher education. *Reflective Practice, 1*(3), 359-375.

Ladson-Billings, G. (1994). *The dreamkeepers: Successful teachers of African American children*. San Francisco: Jossey-Bass.

McDonald, M. A. (2005). The integration of social justice in teacher education. *Journal of Teacher Education, 56*(5), 418-435.

Mishler, E. (1990). Validation in inquiry-guided research: The role of exemplars in narrative studies. *Harvard Educational Review, 60*(4), 415–442.

Pinnegar, S. (1998). Introduction to Part II: Methodological perspectives. In M. L. Hamilton, S. Pinnegar, T. Russell, J. Loughran, & V. K. LaBoskey (Eds.), *Reconceptualizing teaching practice: Self-Study in teacher education* (pp. 31–33). London: Falmer.

Tatum, B. D. (1997). *"Why are all the black kids sitting together in the cafeteria?" and other conversations about race*. New York: Basic Books.

Many Miles and Many Emails: Using Electronic Technologies in Self-Study to Think About, Refine and Reframe Practice

Amanda Berry and Alicia R. Crowe

Introduction: Finding a Place to Start

We met several years before our professional collaboration began. Both of us are experienced teacher educators, although we work in different countries (Mandi in Australia and Alicia in the USA), and in different discipline areas (Mandi in biology and Alicia in social studies). From our first meeting we knew that we had a lot to talk about, that we were able to communicate well with one another and that we would love to work as collaborators. But what were we to do with our locations on different continents and at least 10,000 miles between us? After a few years of once yearly meetings at the American Educational Research Association (AERA) conference and as our collegial friendship grew, we began to realize that we had a lot to gain as teacher educators by working together. So, Alicia sent the following invitation to Mandi:

> Hi Mandy. I hope you are doing well. I have thought of you several times this summer but have been away a lot. Have you finished your PhD?
> How did it go? How's the family doing?
> Professionally I would love to get started on a dialogue and try to do something together this year. (August 16, 2005) (Editor's note: All email excerpts are verbatim and the typical notation (sic) of any errors in spelling, grammar, and so on has not been used so as to better maintain the voices of the authors, and more clearly illustrate the natural use of ICTs.)

On August 17, 2005, Mandi replied,

> Hey Alicia,
> Great to hear from you. I took my PhD thesis to the bindery today. . . bit scary!
> Family ok. Max (son) has had glandular fever for last 7 weeks.... So we are all living life a little differently...On other matters I would really love to have a conversation about our work; lots of good reasons for that. My students are out on practicum at the moment and when they come back have 6 weeks before they finish their teacher ed program... How shall

A. Berry (✉)
Monash University, Wellington Road, Clayton, Victoria 3800, Australia
e-mail: amanda.berry@education.monash.edu.au

D.L. Tidwell et al. (eds.), *Research Methods for the Self-study of Practice*,
Self-Study of Teaching and Teacher Education Practices 9,
DOI 10.1007/978-1-4020-9514-6_6, © Springer Science+Business Media B.V. 2009

*we start? Are you about to start the year? What are you teaching? Are you going to study
part of your practice?
I'm ready to talk!*

On August 18, 2005, Alicia responded,

*I am about to begin classes and always have loads of teacher ed stuff on my mind and no
one who likes to study it to discuss things with. We begin classes on the 29th. I haven't made
a decision on what to study yet. Ideas? :-) ...I think we should just start a regular email
dialogue. That would also provide a great set of data for us to analyze later – not to mention
just being able to share our struggles and triumphs with someone who has similar interests.*

And so it began. Our email collaboration, starting in 2005, evolved from these
enthusiastic but tentative first steps into a productive, continuing research program.
Despite our physical separation, we have developed and sustained strong personal
and pedagogical connections that have supported each of us in our work as self-
study researchers and teacher educators.

We found that we shared similar concerns and experiences and it was these sim-
ilarities and experiences that helped us begin our conversations. However, even
though our overall focus was the same, that is, the education of prospective teachers, our immediate focal points were different given our different locations, different discipline areas and different timing of the academic year (for example, Alicia
is beginning a semester when Mandi is halfway through). Nevertheless, we found
that we could offer each other ideas and insights from our work that were useful
and that carried our collective thinking forward into bigger issues that were located
underneath our initial questions.

Over the past 3 years our questions have developed into research agendas and
our research agendas into a research program, resulting in stronger understandings
of our purposes and frameworks as teacher educators, as well as tangible products such as conference presentations and publications. Interestingly, what also has
emerged over time is a recognition that the process of working together to better
understand practice is a messy one – and one that does not become less messy over
time. Although we have developed more complex understandings of our work and
have worked out more organized ways of articulating our ideas, we find that our
thinking continues to develop in non-linear and recursive ways. The complexity of
our conversations is reflective of the complex nature of teaching and learning and
teasing out this complexity through discussion is what we feel we are better at now
and more confident to do.

In this chapter we describe and discuss our collaboration in terms of three particular aspects: (1) the development of our critical friendship; (2) the development of
our understanding of teaching about teaching; and (3) our evolving understanding of
the ways in which information and communication technologies (ICTs) can be used
as tools for self-study research. Through this chapter we explore the nature of our
critical friendship as we have built a shared research program across the miles for
the development of our knowledge of practice and ourselves as teacher educators.
We begin by examining some of the literature relevant to our work.

Self-Study as Tool for Researching Practice

Self-Study as a Methodology

Self-study offers a framework for inquiry into one's beliefs and practices as an educator with a focus on better understanding the interaction between beliefs and practices for the improvement of teaching and learning. Self-study as a methodology draws on a range of methods for the study of professional practice settings (Pinnegar, 1998) that is driven largely by the concerns of teaching, the development of knowledge of teaching and the development of learning (LaBoskey, 2004). Bullough and Pinnegar (2001) identify narrative methods, such as autobiography and correspondence as predominant choices among self-study researchers as these forms of representation tend to best capture concerns with 'self.'

Self-Study as Collaboration

Traditional views of collaboration in educational research position the researchers as "looking outward together at the same data set" (LaBoskey, 1998, p. 151). Typically in this form of collaboration, the researchers are interacting around an external data set, with their ultimate goal being to reach consensus on a final product, usually prepared as a univocal text. On the other hand, collaboration in self-study research actively seeks interaction between the researchers that both promotes diversity of opinion around the data set and makes the researchers' interactions "the data set, or at least a part of it" (LaBoskey, 1998, p. 151).

Collaboration is a defining characteristic of self-study (Lighthall, 2004). Enlisting colleagues to collaborate in studies of teaching practice offers insights into experience that are not possible when working alone (Brookfield, 1995). When colleagues share critical conversations about practice, new possibilities for practice can emerge, as well as new ways to analyze and respond to problems. At the same time, professional knowledge and expertise can be developed and shared as collaborators learn to articulate their insights and reframe their conceptions of practice. This is particularly important in the field of teacher education where the professional knowledge base of teaching about teaching has only recently begun to develop (Berry, 2004; Korthagen, Loughran, & Lunenberg, 2005).

Collaboration in self-study draws together different groups of people (e.g., colleague/colleague, teacher(s)/student(s)) and makes use of a range of interactive modes (e.g., face to face, on-line) depending on the purpose of the study and the location of those engaged in the research. Collaboration can be "contrived" (Hargreaves & Dawe, 1990, p. 227), in which participants are brought together through some external, formalized structure, such as mandated meetings, or self-selected, emerging naturally from participants' needs and interests. One mode of collaboration is that which aims to bring together self-study researchers separated by geographical distance. Examples of long-distance collaboration among self-study scholars include colleagues working within their own country (e.g., Guilfoyle, Hamilton, Pinnegar, & Placier, 1995) and those working internationally (e.g., Dalmau & Guðjónsdóttir, 2000; Freese, Kosnik, & LaBoskey, 2000; Russell & Schuck, 2005). The long-distance collaborative relationship described in this chapter has emerged through mutual recognition of our shared concerns about how to better understand and develop our pedagogy as teacher educators and improve the quality of the learning-to-teach experience of prospective teachers in our respective classes.

We view our collaborative relationship as a partnered practice of critical reflection; that is, one in which partners engage each other in ways that promote the critical reflection of each. For us, critical reflection involves deeply questioning, analyzing and reconsidering experience within the broader contexts of our work. Similarly, Loughran (2004) notes that accessing a critical friend can lead to a reframing of one's thinking through opportunities to reconceptualize new approaches to practice and new possibilities for students' learning. We believe that our critical friendship leads us to challenge our taken-for-granted assumptions, and in so doing, build both our individual and collective knowledge of practice.

Our collaboration is not only long distance but also long-term. East and Fitzgerald (2006) emphasize the importance of collaborators cultivating appropriate conditions if a long-term self-study partnership is to work successfully. These conditions include allowing time for the collaboration to develop (East and Fitzgerald suggest that the establishment of a productive relationship takes about 1 year) and collaborator vulnerability (that is, the preparedness of collaborators to think of themselves in new ways, even when those ways may be unpleasant or uncomfortable). Many examples of long-term self-study collaborations can be found in the literature (e.g., Berry & Loughran, 2002, 2005; East & Fitzgerald, 2006; Guilfoyle et al., 1995, 2004; Kosnik & Beck, 2005, 2006; Russell & Bullock, 1999); this is not surprising given the personal nature of the work, and the ongoing, developmental nature of the learning involved. However, a substantive challenge for long-term collaborators is finding ways of maintaining a research program that keeps the motivation to pursue research into practice fresh and stimulating and continues to push new boundaries in pursuing deeper understandings of practice.

ICTs as Tools for Self-Study

Information and communication technologies (ICTs) offer self-study researchers an array of tools and practices that can be used to facilitate both the sharing of experience and the construction of knowledge of practice. In particular, Hoban considers the use of ICTs as a means of "representing, accessing, analysing, retrieving, sharing, communicating and editing data" (2004, p. 1039) to be quite important in self-study. Electronic communication technologies can work in either a synchronous or an asynchronous manner. Synchronous communication involves users interacting in real time as they are on-line at the same time (e.g., through instant messaging technologies such as iChat or Skype). In asynchronous interaction, users are not on-line at the same time and interactions are usually conducted in text format (e.g., discussion forums and blogs). Email is an example of an ICT that can be used both synchronously and asynchronously depending on the location and availability of the users. Email is the electronic tool of choice for many self-study researchers since it offers a means of both representing experience for others and reflecting on experience through storing and revisiting email communications. Hence email functions as a tool for both framing and reframing practice (Barnes, 1992; Schön, 1983).

For self-study researchers, ICTs can both limit and enhance their work. A limitation is that since both sender and receiver may be selective in what they choose to communicate or respond to, the level of researcher vulnerability so important in self-study can be reduced. We see this as different from a face-to-face situation because in working over a distance researchers do not have access to direct observation of each other's daily practices and interactions with students. One's personal agenda could limit the range of ways in which one reflects on practice since the other is not there to draw from the same set of shared experiences. On the other hand, an enhancing aspect of ICTs is that in communicating with another, particularly through text, users are forced to articulate their thinking, and through sharing make their thinking public, an essential component of self-study (Hoban, 2004).

In our collaborative self-study work, we have engaged in both synchronous and asynchronous interactions. Initially, our predominant means of communication was via email, although we have experimented with a range of tools, depending on the purpose of our communication and as we have become better informed about the range of possible technologies. (We discuss the evolution of our communication processes in more detail later in the chapter.) A unique aspect of our collaboration is that our partnership has been sustained mostly through electronic communication. We rarely interact face to face as our schedules and personal situations make it thus far extremely difficult.

A Story of a Long-Distance Self-Study in Perpetual Motion

Our long-term self-study collaboration has resulted in developing our understandings of our critical friendship, of teaching about teaching and of the ways in which ICTs can be useful tools for self-study researchers. The process of our collaboration, as with any such process, is complex and recursive. In this section, we address the first two aspects of our learning journey using narrative to illustrate the evolving nature of our critical friendship and our learning about teaching about teaching.

The Beginning

As highlighted in the introduction to this chapter, turning our collegial friendship into research took a few years. As we began, one of the first challenges we faced was deciding how to focus our inquiry. Our initial emails provided an avenue to both share our ideas and keep a record of our emerging relationship and interests. Initially our impetus for collaboration was conceptualized around the broad frame offered by self-study: How do I improve my practice? How do I help my students improve the quality of their learning about teaching? We wondered if we should begin with a more narrow focus or just write to each other and see what happened. In the end we just began to write. Our email exchanges helped us identify questions about practice that we wished to address in our self-study. These questions emerged from our experiences of teaching student teachers.

At first, we shared questions and experiences that allowed us to begin to understand each other's thinking. Interestingly, the questions or problems we shared in those initial exchanges did not become the foundation for our collaborative research; rather they seemed to act as the means for us to become acquainted with each other pedagogically. For instance,

> *Here's one possible idea....just to start??? When my students start back I am concerned about how do I re-engage them with thinking about teaching and learning? They have finished their last practicum and while there is still 6 weeks of uni, they feel like it is over for them and they are teachers now. I have some interesting things to do with them but I know that getting their minds on to pedagogy will be really hard work. Does this happen for you? What do you do? What will be issues for the group you are starting with?* (Mandi, August 21, 2005)

> *That is definitely a problem. Mine are like that when they come back from their fall practicum and still have a five week course before their full-time spring placement. . .I have been trying to figure out what to focus on this year, I am interested in how my students come to understand themselves as teachers (social studies in particular) as they go through our course and I am always wondering how being in my course impacts that. I always feel as if there is something happening but I haven't captured it before. . .* (Alicia, August 24, 2005)

We found that despite the fact that email can feel confining as a form of communication, writing emails forced us to articulate our ideas more clearly so that the other person could understand our intended meaning.

Emergence of a Focus

After several correspondences we began to engage in a process of framing and reframing what we shared. For instance, through posing a question about how she might capture and document the nature of her students' learning experiences, Alicia was prompted to consider a deeper issue related to the way in which we, as teacher educators, shape the context for our students' learning, and which could serve as a frame for our research approach.

> *. . .. My students are really growing. We have been grappling with critical thinking. . .They were making connections that I had hoped for but didn't think would happen this early. How do I document this stuff? The dialogue in the groups is amazing but capturing it is difficult – there is so much going on I can't be taking notes while I'm facilitating. I just had a thought, what about thinking about ways that we construct "methods" courses – this is fuzzy – . . . a conversation, analysis, etc. of what we do to construct the environments we want to help the students learn?* (Alicia, October 4, 2005)

As our dialogue continued, we began to see common questions surfacing and a possible new frame for consideration of these questions emerged, as illustrated in the exchange below.

As I prepare for spring I've been thinking about what challenges me most and I think one thing is getting students, future teachers, to begin to think more and more like teachers. Sounds simple but it is a constant issue... I would like to know about what help[s] them begin to move to a more 'teacher thinking' place. How do I get them to get past classroom management and into student learning, how to get them to think about lessons as conceptual wholes instead of a bunch of activities? That is actually something I've been grappling with a lot for the last couple years. (Alicia, January 12, 2006)

[In your emails] I could see these questions (amongst others) popping out:

1. *How do I help my students think more like teachers?*
2. *How can I help student teachers think/move beyond survival and more about their students' learning?*
3. *How can prospective teachers think more about lessons as conceptual 'wholes' and less like a (mostly disconnected) bunch of activities'?*
4. *How can I help student teachers develop a conceptual thread through their teaching, to promote student learning?*

Then I realised that these were the same kinds of questions that I was asking myself, too, and that linked with the frame ...[of] seeing the work of teacher educators conceptualised as a series of tensions. I saw the ideas of the tension between 'telling and growth' really strongly here. I'll explain a bit more about what I mean and hopefully this will make a bit more sense (?!!?). (Mandi, February 9, 2006)

Through the process of articulating our questions, particular facets of our thinking became highlighted that related well to a particular tension experienced by teacher educators, identified in earlier self-study research by Mandi (Berry, 2004), between the notions of "telling and growth." This tension relates to the experience of teacher educators wanting to help their student teachers learn about teaching without perpetuating a transmission model of education. The notion of telling is most commonly experienced as an attempt to transfer propositional knowledge from the teacher to the student (a practice deeply embedded in the culture of education). We believe that a pedagogy of 'telling' rarely carries sufficient understanding to the learner to be personally useful. Teacher educators who attempt to alter this deeply embedded teaching style need to find new ways to support student teachers to learn what teacher educators intend. In this case, Alicia wanted to encourage her students to "think more like teachers," yet she could not achieve this simply by telling them to do so, or offering her experiences of teaching as vicarious teaching experiences for her students. By beginning to conceptualize our practice through this tension, both of us also recognized an important shared assumption about the need for student teachers to develop their own personally meaningful understandings of practice rather than learning to reproduce the teacher educator's teaching approach. This view was one not necessarily shared by their colleagues, as Alicia explained in an email to Mandi:

You wrote [previous email]: *"Learning to teach does not mean learning to teach like me. Being an effective teacher educator means that I need to develop ways of working that*

are responsive to and encourage the strengths, interests and concerns of individual student
teachers rather than their learning to reproduce my approach."

    Yes, yes. I had this talk with my two social studies colleagues at Kent and they were
surprised that I don't tell more stories. I explained that I don't usually, especially in the
beginning because I feel that it sets them up to think that I am the master and they the clone.
(February 10, 2006)

Alicia explained to Mandi how she deliberately withdrew her "authority of experience" (Munby & Russell, 1994), that is, stopped telling stories in order to facilitate her students' development of their own authority as teachers. Her view led her to plan alternative ways to teach. For example, she identified that helping student teachers draw upon knowledge developed through their own experiences and making explicit to student teachers her thinking about the purposes for various activities is an important part of her approach. However a difficulty she confronts is that despite her chosen approach, students often still struggle to accept and take on their own forms of authority.

From an Emerging Focus to Principles of Practice

Through our emails we began to focus our work, and our conversations turned more intently to developing and articulating our thinking about teaching preservice teachers into 'principles of practice' (Loughran, 2006). During this process, we found that we needed a format that allowed us to think together more easily, as up until this point our correspondence had been via email alone. Thus, we began experimenting with various forms of ICTs but found it frustratingly difficult to find a program that matched our needs (an aspect we return to later in the chapter). Fortunately, our yearly meeting at AERA occurred around this time and we were able to get together face to face. This meeting let us collaboratively construct an initial framework from which we could continue to work. When we left the conference and returned to our long-distance situation we had a more tightly defined focus for our work, with the outcome being the articulation of a set of five principles of practice related to teaching our prospective teachers to "think like a teacher":

- Principle One: Thinking like a teacher involves learning to see teaching from the viewpoint of the learner. Experiencing the role of learner is an important means of developing an understanding of the learner viewpoint.
- Principle Two: Prospective teachers need opportunities to 'see into' the thinking like a teacher of experienced others.
- Principle Three: Prospective teachers need opportunities to try out thinking like a teacher in order to develop their thinking as a teacher.
- Principle Four: Prospective teachers need scaffolding (guidelines, questions, structures) as they begin thinking like a teacher to support them in the process.
- Principle Five: Developing responsive relationships is at the heart of learning to think like a teacher and at the heart of supporting our students (relational support) (Crowe & Berry, 2007, p. 33).

Moving Beyond the Articulation of Principles

After we had articulated these principles, we were fortunate to be able to meet again in the same year, this time at the Castle Conference (a biennial self-study conference held at Herstmonceux Castle, East Sussex, England). At this conference we presented and discussed with colleagues our initial ideas about our principles. Making our thinking more public in this way provided us with further insights and refinement of our set of principles. Our principles of practice were subsequently developed into a book chapter (Crowe & Berry, 2007) and through publishing our work, our confidence in our ideas grew and we began to look for how we might push the ideas further. Our thoughts then turned to moving beyond simply naming our principles and into studying them in action. Below is a short series of email messages that help illustrate the change in our focus.

Mandi: *Now maybe we have to talk soon about how we are using the POPs [Principles of Practice] to look into practice? Have your students started yet??* (August 23, 2006)

Alicia: *I begin next week. I want to begin a study of how we use them. Ideas? I would need to begin with class on Tuesday, right?*
           Is our main question – how do we use our PoPs in practice?
           How do we change as we think about these in practice?
           How do our students (a sample) respond to our PoPs in practice?
           What do you think? (August 24, 2006)

Mandi: *Yes, I like these questions and somehow I have to be able to help critique your practice with you from a distance ... .* (August 24, 2006)

As Alicia began teaching her class, Mandi sent some questions and more conversation ensued.

Mandi: *Hi there, I have been wondering how things went on your first day of classes? Did you think about the POPs as you were teaching? How did your classes compare with the vignette we constructed for the chapter? Did what we write at all influence what you did/said/thought about?? As you can see I am hungry for your experiences!!!!* (August 29, 2006)

Alicia: *I have been wanting to chat about it. I did think about them as I taught. I was very conscious of what I was saying – at times I wondered if I was messing up my flow by thinking of them at the same time. Sounds odd I know, but in the debrief I was doing I was thinking of the learner one and the teacher one at the same time...*
           I thought about the vignette [from our chapter] a lot as I went through the first day. As I lived it again, I realized the vignette was very close to what I experienced once again. I realized I thought a lot about the relationship principle (5). Almost all was that but a little of thinking about what I did and why. I did video tape the class b/c I thought the first day would be an important one to revisit. I'm going to have my grad assistant transfer it to dvd and see if that is a way we can exchange. We'll see.

I've attached my lesson plan with edits – maybe this can help convey some of what happened. Boy I'm busy this week. :-) (August 30, 2006)

And so our focus shifted again. We began to consider how to document and understand how our students experienced these principles, how they understood them, how we struggled to teach in ways that reflect these principles and what these principles looked like in different circumstances.

Since then we have been interested in several questions: How have we changed as teacher educators since we articulated our principles of practice? How does each of us implement our principles and what challenges/insights have we encountered in the process of their enactment? How does our enactment of our principles influence our students' learning about teaching? Do we have any evidence of how our students have changed? What do we count as evidence? How do our students experience our principles in action? How is our critical friendship supporting and challenging our understandings and experiences of change? How is our critical friendship itself changing? We have spent the last year and a half focusing on these questions in various ways and email has taken a variety of forms depending on where we are in the process.

Summary

Although from an outside observer's point of view, our practice may not look considerably different since we began our collaboration, developing and having these principles of practice as a frame for understanding our work as teacher educators has helped each of us to become more purposeful and focused in the way we work. What we have learned is that we have developed stronger understandings of our teaching and our ability to articulate why we do what we do. For instance, we can now discuss our work together using a common language that is more specific to our goals (through the principles of practice), and as each of us works we are more aware of which principles are more or less visible in our work. By examining our principles in action and by continually discussing these we have adjusted smaller activities and assignments from each of our courses. For example, this year, after one of our conversations Mandi began a blog to highlight her thinking about her practice for her teacher education students to see (http://edf4113mandi.blogspot.com/). This is an example of our second principle in action.

The Use of ICT in Self-Study

The collaborative self-study work that we have undertaken has been possible through the use of electronic technologies. Therefore, besides learning about teaching teachers and ourselves as teacher educators, we have also learned a great deal about the advantages and disadvantages of using various ICTs, in particular email, as tools for collaboration and analysis in self-study research. Finding and learning how to use the kinds of tools that could help us connect in ways that matched our needs has proven both a challenge and an opportunity in the development of our critical friendship and our research. In this section of the chapter, we offer some insights into the challenges and opportunities that we have encountered, using Hoban's (2004) categories of research processes facilitated by ICTs as an organizing frame, that is, representing, accessing, analyzing, retrieving, sharing, communicating and editing data. We have grouped and discussed the processes identified by Hoban according to the way in which we have encountered them in our work.

Representing and Sharing Data

One of our first tasks was to find ways of representing our experiences and our thinking for each other in order to learn about each other's work and identify connections that could direct our research. While in our occasional face-to-face conversations this was relatively easy to achieve because we could see each other's nonverbal expressions and build on each other's ideas immediately or ask for clarification on the spot, in our email conversations we struggled at times to find words to convey our ideas without these other supports. In the 'slowed down' environment of email we had to be much more explicit about expressing our thinking through text alone. Our shared struggles to articulate our thinking and our openness to confessing the sense of frustration and struggle each of us experienced acted both as an apology for a lack of clarity in our emails and as evidence to ourselves that we needed to add more detail and refine our statements to each other. For example, during the time in which we were developing a shared frame for our research we exchanged numerous comments about the difficulties associated with writing and finding the right words to convey the intended meaning. An excerpt from an exchange between us at the beginning of October in our first year (2005) illustrates this point. Alicia wrote, *I wish I could beam my brain to you to make the thought clear – ok try again… I'll have to work on this.* The following day Mandi replied, *I wish I could 'brain beam' too! It is often so hard to get all the thoughts out in the way I want.*

Issues with communicating in text alone also linked to the notion of writing as a formal act and hence brought expectations from each of us about the quality of the writing that we shared. For instance, Alicia noted,

> *I know exactly how you feel. A conversation over coffee would be so much easier. Do you think it could be because it is text and asynchronous? I just misspelled asynchronous and had to stop to fix it– that could be a problem too? Knowing that our conversation is written takes it into the realm of the formal. That's definitely something to overcome as well since it feels like it should be profound to be written.* (November 7, 2005)

Finding time for sharing was also a difficulty we encountered. No matter how well intentioned, it was hard for each of us to find time and energy to write to each other. This was particularly so in the beginning of our relationship because of our lack of familiarity with each other's work context. We needed to spend time initially setting the scene for each other so that we could better understand each other's experiences, questions and motivations. We have since come to recognize this mutual scene setting as an important aspect of our learning that applies equally to the ways in which we work with students to support their learning about practice.

As we learned more about each other's teaching and thinking, we found we wanted to think together in ways that email did not allow. Sharing via email was not fast enough for certain activities; we wanted a tool that we could think together with, something synchronous versus the delayed response effect of emailing each other ideas, then reading, responding, waiting for a response, responding and so on. We tried instant messaging technology (IMs) – technologies that allow two or more users to communicate via text, in real time, for example, iChat. This seemed to work for briefer communications or decisions, but we quickly learned that this format could not accommodate or keep up with and reflect the dialogic twists and turns that we needed for more in-depth conversations. As we experimented with IM, we found that there was too much mismatch in our conversation; we ended up with too many loose ends or confusing moments, particularly if our sequencing was off-balance, which meant that sometimes we were having conversations about several different ideas at once, as each of us waited for a response from a previous comment. In one particularly frustrating session Alicia described the technology as being *"too linear for the way we talk and think."* The ideas did not flow well and the subsequent documentation of those ideas did not make sense when we retrieved them later.

We longed for something more synchronous that would allow us to think together – basically replicating a face-to-face experience. When we next met in person we sought technical assistance at a computer store and learned how to use video conferencing. (We were fortunate to be using the same computer platform, so this helped with decisions about which software to use!) However, when it came to using a camera we found that seeing each other actually distracted us more than it added to our conversation because of slight delays in seeing an image and hearing our voices. We discovered that by using the audio component alone of iChat (an IM technology) we could hear each other clearly, which allowed us to talk as if we were together while being miles apart. Being able to talk 'ear-to-ear' in this way helped us share experience in ways that we were unable to via text. We found that hearing the voice of the other was very much like having her there – in a hands-free environment – which also meant that we could type as we talked when moments of inspiration occurred. We found that our conversations rarely lasted more than one hour, due to the intensity of the talk we engaged in and because the time difference meant that one of us was preparing to go to work while the other was preparing to go to bed!

Our developing competence with the technologies grew hand in hand with refining our understandings of practice, so that as we understood more clearly what we needed to talk about, we could select and combine our use of different technologies and software tools to meet our developing communication and collaboration needs. For instance, we used iChat to send documents, paragraphs, sentences and so on, to each other as we communicated by voice, to further explain and add to each other's writing, rather than sending email summaries of our thinking at the end of an audio conversation. We also found email a wonderful tool that allowed us to quickly and easily share artifacts of our teaching (e.g., PowerPoint presentations, lesson plans) as well as sharing data gathered from surveys, interviews and focus groups with our students.

Retrieving, Accessing and Analyzing Data

Having a repository of stored data in digital format meant that we could each easily retrieve and revisit what we had written as needed. We did this in various ways, including preliminary searches of our exchanges so as to surface themes and through initial analyses of data for later discussion in an audio chat. An example of how this worked is documented earlier in the chapter as our beginning questions about our practice were revisited and organized into preliminary themes for our research; these themes later became our principles of practice. Later still, for instance in the preparation of this chapter, we have been able to search the data in order to trace both the frequency patterns of our interactions and the types of concerns that have most preoccupied us over time.

In hindsight, our richest data sources were our emails since their content was more detailed and organized, compared with notes taken during audio chats or exchanges through IMs. Emails provided artifacts that gave us something to analyze and helped us recognize more clearly the sequence of ideas that we were developing about our work. Similar to others who have engaged in email collaboration (e.g., Freese et al., 2000), we have gained insight into our beliefs and practices through visiting and revisiting our communications over time.

Communicating and Editing Data

Our ability to communicate personal insights initially to each other, then later through text-based publications or conference presentations, has been facilitated by the various electronic technologies we have used. Through the process of developing more formal representations of our work we have been able to communicate the knowledge developed to the wider academic community. Interestingly, as we prepare such work, we have encountered few difficulties or disagreements about what to write or how to express particular ideas. Perhaps knowing each other well as writers has helped us to be able to overcome what can be a stumbling block for some collaborators as they write and edit each other's work. Throughout, we have maintained a view of shared authorship whereby we alternate taking lead authorship in order to satisfy institutional demands for publication achievements, an approach similar to that used by other collaborative self-study researchers (e.g., Guilfoyle et al., 1995).

What Have We Learned? What Does It Mean?

As we consider the development of our collaboration, we recognize that our interaction tends to move in and out of particular phases – from the initial sharing of ideas and pushing each other to articulate our thinking, to analyzing and conceptualizing, and then writing and editing – and that as we move through these different phases, we experience different needs. The range of technologies available to us can support us in various ways depending on where we are in the process. Hoban (2004, p. 1066) notes the reciprocal influence of on-line technologies and self-study research "as an iterative process with one informing the other. In short technology should inform our self-study purposes and vice versa. . .[and] as new technologies are developed, then new opportunities for teaching and self-study are developed." This observation aligns with our experiences, and we anticipate that we will continue to find new ways to support our working together. For instance, although we have experimented with making videos of our classes and exchanging them, the different DVD formats we work in have made this very difficult. In the future, we hope to learn how to load and share video via the web.

We also recognize the possibilities for delusion and deception in the use of electronic technologies in self-study research. Since we do not see each other's classes and do not have access to colleague conversations it is possible to present a particular view of ourselves to each other. Furthermore, as we develop our collaboration it is seductive to simply affirm each other's work through what we choose to research and how we choose to report it. From the outset, we have discussed these issues and how we might work to address them to promote honesty and quality in our work. To this end, we have looked for disconfirming examples of what we are seeking to do, for instance when students tell us that what we intend in our practice is not what they experience, and we tell each other when we struggle to enact the principles that we see as guiding and supporting our work. We bring to the surface our struggles and frustrations as much as (or perhaps more than?) our successes, anticipating that pursuing these challenges may well be more fruitful to our attempts to uncover new understandings of our practice and our students' learning.

References

Barnes, D. (1992). The significance of teachers' frames for teaching. In T. Russell & H. Munby (Eds.), *Teachers and teaching: From classroom to reflection* (pp. 9–32). London: Falmer.

Berry, A. (2004). Self-study in teaching about teaching. In J. J. Loughran, M. L. Hamilton, V. K. LaBoskey, & T. Russell (Eds.), *International handbook of self-study of teaching and teacher education practices* (pp. 1295–1332). Dordrecht: Kluwer.

Berry, A., & Loughran, J. J. (2002). Developing an understanding of learning to teach in teacher education. In J. Loughran & T. Russell (Eds.), *Improving teacher education practices through self-study* (pp. 13–29). London: Routledge.

Berry, A., & Loughran, J. (2005). Teaching about teaching: The role of self-study. In C. Mitchell, S. Weber, & K. O'Reilly-Scanlon (Eds.), *Just who do we think we are? Methodologies for autobiography and self-study in teaching* (pp. 168–180). London and New York: Routledge Falmer.

Brookfield, S. D. (1995). *Becoming a critically reflective teacher* (1st ed.). San Francisco: Jossey-Bass.

Bullough, R. V., Jr., & Pinnegar, S. (2001). Guidelines for quality in auto-biographical forms of self-study. *Educational Researcher, 30*(3), 13–22.

Crowe, A., & Berry, A. (2007). Teaching prospective teachers about learning to think like a teacher: Articulating our principles of practice. In T. Russell & J. J. Loughran (Eds.), *Enacting a pedagogy of teacher education: Values, relationships and practices* (pp. 31–44). London: Routledge.

Dalmau, M. C., & Guðjónsdóttir, H. (2000). Framing professional discourse with teachers: Professional working theory. In J. Loughran & T. Russell (Eds.), *Exploring myths and legends of teacher education. Proceedings of the Third International Conference of the Self-Study of Teacher Education Practices, Herstmonceux Castle, East Sussex, England* (Vol. 1, pp. 45–49). Kingston, Ontario: Queen's University.

East, K., & Fitzgerald, L. M. (2006). Collaboration over the Long Term. In L. M. Fitzgerald, M. L. Heston, & D. L. Tidwell, (Eds.), *Collaboration and community: Pushing boundaries through self-study. Proceedings of the Sixth International Conference on Self-Study of Teacher Education Practices, Herstmonceux Castle, East Sussex, England* (pp. 72–75). Cedar Falls, IA: University of Northern Iowa.

Freese, A., Kosnik, C., & LaBoskey, V. (2000). Three teacher educators explore their understandings and practices of self-study through narrative. In J. Loughran & T. Russell (Eds.), *Exploring myths and legends of teacher education. Proceedings of the Third International Conference of the Self-Study of Teacher Education Practices, Herstmonceux Castle, East Sussex, England* (Vol. 1, pp. 75–79). Kingston, Ontario: Queen's University.

Guilfoyle, K., Hamilton, M. L., Pinnegar, S., & Placier, M. (1995). Becoming teachers of teachers: The paths of four beginners. In T. Russell & F. Korthagen (Eds.), *Teachers who teach teachers* (pp. 35–55). London: Falmer.

Guilfoyle, K., Hamilton, M. L., Pinnegar, S., & Placier, M. (2004). Epistemological dimensions and dynamics of professional dialogue in self-study. In J.J. Loughran, M.L. Hamilton, V. K. LaBoskey, & T. Russell (Eds.), *International handbook of self-study of teaching and teacher education practices* (pp. 1109–1167). Dordrecht: Kluwer.

Hargreaves, A., & Dawe, R. (1990). Paths of professional development: Contrived collegiality, collaborative culture, and the case of peer coaching. *Teaching and Teacher Education, 6*, 227–241.

Hoban, G. F. (2004). Using information and communication technologies for the self-study of teaching. In J. J. Loughran, M. L. Hamilton, V. K. LaBoskey, & T. Russell (Eds.), *International handbook of self-study of teaching and teacher education practices* (pp. 1039–1072). Dordrecht: Kluwer.

Korthagen, F., Loughran, J., & Lunenberg, M., (2005). Teaching teachers – studies into the expertise of teacher educators: An introduction to this theme issue. *Teaching and Teacher Education, 21*, 107–115.

Kosnik, C., & Beck, C. (2005). Community-building and program development go hand-in-hand: Teacher educators working collaboratively. In G. Hoban (Ed.), *The missing links in teacher education: Innovative approaches to designing teacher education programs* (pp. 209–230). Dordecht: Kluwer.

Kosnik, C., & Beck, C. (2006). The impact of a preservice teacher education program on language arts teaching practices: A study of second-year teachers. In C. Kosnik, A. Freese, A. Samaras, & C. Beck (Eds.), *Making a difference in teacher education through self-study: Personal, professional, and program renewal* (pp. 243–259). Dordrecht: Springer.

LaBoskey, V. K. (1998). Introduction: Case studies of collaborative self-study. In M. L. Hamilton, with S. Pinnegar, T. Russell, J. Loughran, & V. K. LaBoskey (Eds.), *Reconceptualizing teaching practice: Self-study in teacher education* (pp. 151–153). London: Falmer.

LaBoskey, V. K. (2004). The methodology of self-study and its theoretical underpinnings. In J. J. Loughran, M. L. Hamilton, V. K. LaBoskey, & T. Russell (Eds.), *International handbook of self-study of teaching and teacher education practices* (pp. 817–869). Dordrecht: Kluwer.

Lighthall, F. F. (2004). Fundamental features and approaches of the s-step enterprise. In J. J. Loughran, M. L. Hamilton, V. K. LaBoskey, & T. Russell (Eds.), *International handbook of self-study of teaching and teacher education practices* (pp. 193–246). Dordrecht: Kluwer.

Loughran, J. J. (2004). A history and context of self-study of teaching and teacher education practices. In J. J. Loughran, M. L. Hamilton, V. K. LaBoskey, & T. Russell (Eds.), *International handbook of self-study of teaching and teacher education practices* (pp. 7–39). Dordrecht: Kluwer.

Loughran, J. J. (2006). *Developing a pedagogy of teacher education.* London: Routledge.

Munby, H., & Russell, T. (1994). The authority of experience in learning to teach: Messages from a physics method class. *Journal of Teacher Education, 45,* 86–95.

Pinnegar, S. (1998). Introduction to Part II: Methodological perspectives. In M. L. Hamilton, with S. Pinnegar, T. Russell, J. Loughran, & V. K. LaBoskey (Eds.), *Reconceptualising teaching practice: Self-study in teacher education* (pp. 30–33). London: Falmer.

Russell, T., & Bullock, S. (1999). Discovering our professional knowledge as teachers: Critical dialogues about learning from experience. In J. Loughran (Ed.), *Researching teaching: Methodologies and practices for understanding pedagogy* (pp. 132–151). London: Falmer.

Russell, T., & Schuck, S. (2005). Self-study, critical friendship and the complexities of teacher education. *Studying Teacher Education, 1,* 107–122.

Schön, D. A. (1983). *The reflective practitioner: How professionals think in action.* New York: Basic Books.

Part III
Self-Study Through Visual Representation

Faces and Spaces and Doing Research

Morwenna Griffiths, Heather Malcolm and Zoè Williamson

Introduction

Where do teacher educators find spaces and places for research, especially given their increasingly busy lives and all the competing demands on their time? This was the question that five of us, all working in a teacher education department, asked of ourselves at the outset of our self-study.

The study used visual methods. This was largely because one of us, Morwenna, had been so impressed by what she had learnt from using such methods in two earlier self-studies. While working in Nottingham, England, she had participated in collaborative self-studies using visual methods in 2004 and again in 2006. At the end of 2006 she moved to a new job in Edinburgh, Scotland, where, in 2007, she instigated a third visually based self-study, which is reported here.

In this chapter, we explain how we set about doing the Edinburgh self-study, drawing on and developing the methods used in the two Nottingham studies. We remark how the process was affected by the specific context: the place, the people and their reasons for doing research. The chapter has drawn on the work of many people, some of whom have written about this work elsewhere (Griffiths, Poursanidou, Simms, & Windle, 2006; Griffiths, Windle, & Simms, 2006; Simms, 2007) and some of whom may decide to write about it in the future. This chapter is written by three of the five participants in the Edinburgh study (Morwenna, Heather and Zoè) in consultation with the other two (Rosemary and Amanda).

All three studies share an overarching set of ethical and epistemological principles. The specific methods and processes varied, including variation in the use of the visual at different stages of the research. In this chapter we give a brief overview of the overarching principles. We then go on to summarize how the Nottingham studies were carried out and show how the Edinburgh study was influenced by them in articulating the research question. In the main body of the paper we go on to report

M. Griffiths (✉)
The Moray House School of Education, University of Edinburgh, Hollyrood Road,
Edinburgh Scotland EH8 8AQ, UL
e-mail: morwenna.griffiths@ed.ac.uk

D.L. Tidwell et al. (eds.), *Research Methods for the Self-study of Practice*,
Self-Study of Teaching and Teacher Education Practices 9,
DOI 10.1007/978-1-4020-9514-6_7, © Springer Science+Business Media B.V. 2009

on the Edinburgh study. We discuss the methods used to gather evidence and ways in which the evidence was analysed in order to draw conclusions. At the end of the chapter we bring out how our own practice has been affected. We suggest how readers might use a similar visual methodology in their own self-studies.

Methodology: Epistemology and Social Justice

A set of principles underlies the methodologies of all three self-studies. The principles relate to epistemology and to social justice. Morwenna has discussed social justice and epistemology in some detail elsewhere (e.g. Griffiths, 1998, 2003; Griffiths, Bass, Johnston, & Perselli, 2004). Here we just summarize the main issues for the visual self-studies reported in this chapter. First, the view is taken that the kind of educational knowledge constructed and created in a self-study is (and ought to be) wisdom rather than information. This is knowledge as praxis. Praxis entails the growth of wisdom (or 'professional knowledge') by reflection on specifics while remaining ever mindful of wider social and political contexts (Griffiths, 2006; Hamilton, 2004). In other words, it is knowledge which is context dependent and revisable: an epistemology of the unique and particular (Cavarero, 2002: Griffiths & Macleod, 2008). Second, the study is concerned with active knowledge which is constructed by human beings as social beings engaged in symbolizing and understanding their world. This implies, as John Dewey noted nearly a century ago, a sense of purpose and enjoyment, and the deployment of a range of symbolization and expression (Dewey, 1916). Third, this is research which is underpinned by a concern for social justice. So it was important in all the studies to respect and value individual selves, to seek out diversity through partnership and consultation, and to aim to make a difference through individual and collective action (Griffiths 2003, p. 60).

The ethical and epistemological principles governing the research are consistent with those which are central to the methodologies of self-study, as exemplified in self-study research over the last two decades (found at http://sstep.soe.ku.edu/), and helpfully drawn together in contributions to the *International Handbook of Self-Study of Teaching and Teacher Education*(Loughran, Hamilton, LaBoskey, & Russell, 2004; especially LaBoskey, 2004; Lighthall, 2004). The methodologies of the studies focus on ourselves as teachers and researchers in our own specific contexts. They focus on trying to change those contexts, by changing both ourselves and the constraints we experience. Our studies are collaborative. They self-consciously try to include participants from different social and/or professional positions. They are intended to be inclusive and democratic. We try to use methods which are engaging: fun, motivating and serious. We are trying 'to make the familiar strange' in such a way that it delights and intrigues us and provokes us into both reflection and action.

Our conceptual framework is based on the view that when human beings try to understand their world and act in it, they use both visual and verbal means. Learning theory tells us that babies and young children express and communicate their perceptions using gestures, words and pictures – and that all three modes continue to be significant. The philosopher Michele Le Doueff (1989) argues that both images and words continue to play a key role in even the most abstract of thought. She analyses works by philosophers like Kant and Descartes showing how images are inextricably bound up with their thinking from initial conceptions to final formulations. The methodology we follow allows for the research to be informed by both visual and verbal expression at every stage of the research, from the formulation of the questions, through data collection and analysis, to presentation and dissemination, though not, as yet, in explorations of the issue through literature.

Our research draws on and contributes to the growing tradition of using visual and visualizing methods in self-study. Useful overviews are found in Weber and Mitchell (2004) and Mitchell, Weber, and O'Reilly-Scanlon (2005). (Also see chapters *Facing the Public: Using Photography for Self-Study and Social Action, Making Meaning of Practice Through Visual Metaphor, Creating Representations: Using Collage in Self-Study* and *How Do I Influence the Generation of Living Educational Theories for Personal and Social Accountability in Improving Practice? Using a Living Theory Methodology in Improving Educational Practice* in this volume.) Self-studies vary in the stages of research in which the visual is used and also in what kind of visual material they use. Mostly, visual and visualizing self-studies use images as data though some have also used it in analysis. Indeed, visual or visualizing methods outwith self-study also appear largely to be confined to the data collection stage, in which images are used as simple depictions of reality or as a way of understanding how the makers of the images have (re)constructed reality (Van Leeuwen & Jewitt, 2001).

Self-studies have used pictures which depict a reality. This may be in the form of photographs (Griffiths, Poursanidou, et al., 2006; Mitchell & Weber, 1999) or in the form of three-dimensional artefacts (Allender & Manke, 2002). They may also be in the form of drawings, for instance of an ideal teacher or of a nodal moment in class, or of symbols which represent an understanding of a situation such as a metaphorical representation of teacher (Derry, 2005; Diamond & van Halen-Faber, 2005; Tidwell, 2006; Tidwell & Tincu, 2004). The pictures and images need not be physical depictions; they may be memories of images, such as of school photographs (Mitchell & Weber, 1999; Weber & Mitchell, 2004). Alternatively they may be metaphors which are highly visual but which are described in words (Griffiths & Tann, 1992; Magee, 2008; Miller, East, Fitzgerald, Heston, & Veenstra, 2002). Sometimes visuals are used as part of the analysis and representation of self-study. For instance both Hamilton (2005) and Perselli (2005) use paintings like this. Biddulph (2005) and Derry (2005) use their imagery as both analysis and synthesis of their self-studies. Other examples can be found in Weber and Mitchell (2004). The self-studies reported in this chapter also use visual analysis and visual presentation as well as visual data.

The Context for the Study: Previous Studies in Nottingham

The first of the Nottingham self-studies confronted the often hidden power relations which underpin everyday relationships and practices within a teacher education institution, by examining the complementary roles of a senior academic and
two members of support staff within a research unit. The study proceeded through
iterative cycles of data collection, analysis, re-formulation of the method/question
and further data collection. At the start, digital photos were taken of typical or significant instances of everyday work. The analysis took the form of physically and
collaboratively discussing them and putting them into arrangements in the form of
posters. This analysis uncovered new questions, such as the absence of the photographer himself or herself in the photos. As a result, more photos were taken, with these
questions in mind. These were then printed and arranged, this time in collaboration
with some colleagues who took an interest in both the meanings of the pictures and
also their presentation as posters. Again the process was repeated. The study was
presented as an exhibition of posters, inviting visual and verbal contributions from
the audience. The study is reported in Griffiths et al. (2006).

The second study drew on the first. It investigated everyday social justice in the
workplace – or lack of it – by focusing on workspaces in the academy: how such
spaces affect and are affected by the self-identity, social status and actions of those
working in them. The four researchers had the following roles: full professor, post-
doctoral research fellow, research assistant and a senior member of the support staff.
The study was similar to the previous one in its iterative collecting of pictures which
were then analysed, resulting in the formulation of further questions. In contrast to
the previous study, the researchers rarely saw each other at work. One of them was
employed at a different university; the others were in quite different parts of the campus. At the start of the study, photos were taken as if a workspace was just a tangible
three-dimensional place. These photos were circulated using email, but also printed
and brought to a meeting. The analysis and discussion was far more verbal than
had been the case in the previous study. Comments were made on the pictures using
email and also during discussions. Perhaps precisely because this analysis was more
verbal, in one cycle metaphors of workspace were created (e.g. mulching space,
switch-off space) which were the focus for a subsequent cycle. Arrangements on
posters were not part of the analysis but were used for the presentation of the study.
The study is briefly reported in Simms (2007).

Both studies had used visual representations at the stages of formulation of
research questions, data collection, analysis and presentation. However, there are
significant differences between the studies, especially in relation to the analysis.
Both studies used pictures/images as well as words as part of the analysis. However, in the first study, the discussion was focused on a visual arrangement of
the data; in the second there was more verbal discussion of individual pictures.
Both studies used images of physical reality as ways of conveying ideas. However in the second, the ideas were conveyed through images which expressed a
metaphorical understanding of the situation. The presentation in both cases was
a kind of bricolage. This term is used here in the sense intended in methodolog-

ical texts as indicating the inclusion of different, incommensurable, forms of data (Denzin & Lincoln, 1998). It is also used in its original sense of collage or montage, indicating the use of a range of material to create a visual image which conveys visual meaning. As Khudu-Petersen (2008) explains, a collage is created piece by piece, in a nonlinear arrangement which is carefully constructed to make a whole.

The Edinburgh Study

All staff in this study work in one department in the University of Edinburgh's School of Education. The department is large and complex. About 45 staff members mostly focus on teaching beginning teachers within their subject specialisms, but also teach on TESOL courses and a range of in-service courses, doctoral courses, etc. The department is housed in four separate buildings. Expressive Arts is found in one. This is where Amanda, lecturing in Art and Design, has her office. Science and Technology are in another building. A third houses everyone else, including Rosemary who lectures in TESOL. The fourth contains Mathematics and the main administration. Here Zoè, lecturing in Information Communication Technology (ICT), is to be found, as are Heather and Morwenna. For a number of reasons the members of the department had not been much involved with research. In September 2006, Morwenna and Heather were appointed with the task of encouraging research.

A concern about space and place had been significant for Heather and Morwenna ever since they took up their appointments. They had become increasingly aware of the constraints on research opportunities in the department resulting from its physical and social geography: separate buildings, coffee rooms, social networks, professional networks. The two were also increasingly impressed by the energy and optimism generated when the academic staff were presented with an opportunity for professional conversations across these geographical divides. They thought this geography was worth investigating.

Such a study seemed well suited to a visual or visualizing approach like the ones used at Nottingham. Places can be photographed and described. Visual metaphors readily presented themselves. For instance, members of staff had described departmental separations as 'silos', 'rabbit holes' and 'earth's core and crust.' So a visual methodology seemed to be a useful way of generating understanding, to create some joining up into more fruitful, congenial spaces. Accordingly, we decided to explore that area.

Methods Used and How They Evolved

Colleagues were invited to join the collaborative self-study group. Criteria for participation in the group were having a range of subject disciplines represented, having colleagues from different locations on campus with different research experiences and having a group of between four and seven. We began with a group of six, although this quickly became five as one member withdrew due to significant other work commitments. The remaining five were all enthusiastic – even while showing some proper scepticism about how it might work. This scepticism, informed by our own individual conceptions of research, became one of the strengths of the group and encouraged dialogue about the study.

The initial research question was, Where do we find or create places and spaces for research and how do they affect our research? In line with the guiding principles of exploration, collaboration, openness and reflection, the question was general and open to interpretation. In the spirit of the democratic and collaborative design of the group it was left open how literally or metaphorically the phrase 'spaces for research' was to be understood. Indeed, the question was only a tentative formulation which changed and developed during the study.

The process of our research could broadly be described as being iterative and cyclical. Morwenna created a diagram as a way to represent visually the process of our study (see Fig. 1). This visual helped her/us to consider and understand our research process and be clear about what we were doing. At this point Morwenna recognized the process as cyclical, commenting,

> *I have expressedthis in the cycle diagram by putting that we reach tentative conclusions at the end of each cycle. And that we may then go on to generate new questions, but equally we might generate new themes.* (Blog, March 27, 2008)

However, as valuable as this was in helping us see what we were doing, it presented a somewhat false simplicity of the way the project was progressing. This

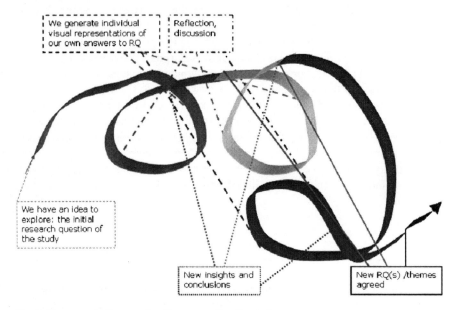

Fig. 1 Morwenna's diagram visually representing the study

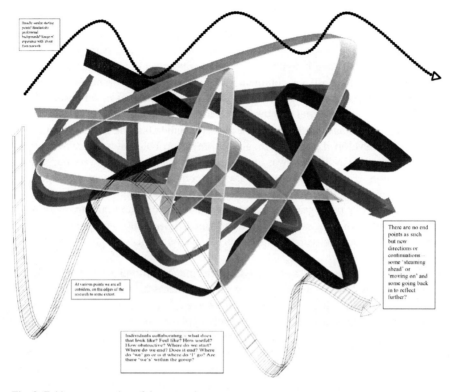

Fig. 2 Zoè's representation of the research process

was not a linear process. Zoè, in response to Morwenna's diagram, produced her own representation of how she understood the research process (see Fig. 2). This visual, in contrast to Morwenna's, presented the process as messy and complex. It captured the collaboration and the research paths of the five 'selves' of the study. Our research process was full of stops and starts, changes in direction, moments of involvement and withdrawal and sometimes an apparent absence of direction. This was not a tidy process of data gathering, reflection and discussion, generation of themes and/or further research questions. Instead the tidy research spiral was filled with loops, twists and branches – some connected and intertwined and others splintered off to the outskirts of the study, darting in and out momentarily. There was a constant sharing of pictures, ideas and thoughts (by blog, informal chats, formal meetings, email) throughout this process. These generated discussion, and themes emerged, developed and evolved. New focus was placed on the research questions.

The visual element was present at every meeting – from photographs, pictures and other images created to diagrams and pictures that formed part of the visual analysis and interpretation. For each of us time was precious and often hard to find, so other methods of communication and forums for continuing discussions and keeping the study active were sought. Email was an important part of this although predominantly for the exchange of information and administrative issues. A *Spaces and Places* blog was started. The motivation for this was twofold: first it was a place we could share pictures without clogging up our (very limited) work email allocation; second it could be a space to continue and extend our discussions, share thoughts and post our comments about our project, helping to nurture and promote the collaboration. The blog became an essential part of the research process. Although the potential was there for it to simply be a digital depository for our pictures, discussion about these and our evolving understanding and questions about the research developed in this space, albeit some contributed more often than others.

As worthwhile as the blog was, it was certainly not a substitution for our face-to-face meetings. These were invaluable, and probably too infrequent. Dialogue was central to our study. There was something so rich about coming together as a group, spreading out our photographs, pictures and other visuals and talking about them. We commented on what stood out for us and made observations on each other's pictures – often these discussions helped to challenge our own conceptions and develop our thinking.

We continued the process of discussing our images through email, blog and face-to-face meetings. It was a messy and uncertain process as we felt our way towards answering the research questions using our images. Through the face-to-face discussions we came up with common themes and explored those. Our understanding of the process was informed by our different experiences of research and scholarship: research as spirals of enquiry, evaluative research, self-study, practical philosophy and/or creative art. We often felt we were starting and stopping and changing direction, all the time reflecting on the process through (sometimes quite heated) discussions on the blog, in meetings and during casual encounters. After 4 months of discussion and visual data creation (pictures and diagrams, etc.) we each produced a carefully written reflection on what we had learnt. These were published on the blog (April 22, 2008).

The use of the visual was key at every stage. It did not take long for us to see its revelatory power as it continually generated ideas and discussion. Discussion about our collection and creation of images helped us identify themes which informed further data creation, and this often overlapped with analysis. For example, as we have already explained, we turn to the visual to help us understand our overall process (see Figs. 1 and 2). Another example of the use of the visual was the word clouds (see Fig. 3). They provided a quick textual analysis of a selection of blog posts. One was produced in February (Zoè's blog, February 22, 2008) and a second in April (Zoè's blog, April 20, 2008). These graphic images of the changing focus of our discussions helped us reflect on the process. In both cases the visual perspective added a different dimension and made visible ideas that had previously gone unnoticed.

We each commented on the value of using visual methods and the ways the visual has helped us to (re)construct our thinking and understanding about research spaces and research culture. However, we have not all been comfortable with the method. Heather enjoys images but they do not (yet) speak to her with the same directness as words. Amanda forced us to reflect on our capacity to create images. As an artist,

Fig. 3 The word cloud and blog extract

she strongly believes the snapshot does not provide the quality of image needed to communicate to others. In an email she explains,

> *Do you think it might be an idea to get one good photo each rather than several snapshots? This way there is a little more thought going into the image... Photographs are an art form too and can be poor. A photographer (say from the students at the Art school) [would be] a helper for you not a hindrance.* (Email, December 20, 2007)

Disagreeing, Heather replied,

> *I see the photographs as data that just happen to be in visual rather than textual form, rather than as products having value in themselves, in the same way that a record of an interview with someone will tell me useful things rather than in itself being a candidate for a prose competition.* (Email, December 20, 2007)

We each had our own individual and developing understanding of the nature and role of the visual in the research process. Through this research we were curious about the ways in which the visual could add to our research. Could the visual tell a story that would be different from a textual account? Could the visual in some way disrupt the verbal story we may tell? What was the relationship between the visual and the textual? Did the use of the visual allow us to think differently about our research spaces and places?

The different images that we all produced at the first meeting, and then again later on, show what different interpretations can be placed on 'visual'. Zoè brought photographs, a speeded-up video of herself at work with a colleague, collaborating on some research (see Fig. 4) and, to our amazed delight, a comic strip of herself struggling to write. Amanda produced a composition made of many photos of her art studio, all taken on one day. She had created a beautiful image of her studio,

Fig. 4 Zoè working
collaboratively on the
computer

including her feet planted in the middle of it. Morwenna and Heather brought snap-shots of significant places, though Morwenna found she had taken a lot of pictures of spaces which hindered research – such as the long walk between buildings. Rosie's pictures brought images in five abstract categories. One of these was mental space represented by a photograph of the back of her head as she worked over a computer

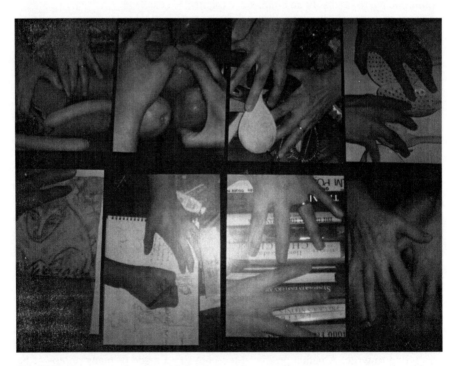

Fig. 5 Visual representation of teaching and research connections

keyboard. Others included time (a timetable), elevation (looking down on things) and obstacles to getting somewhere (a 'road closure' notice near the campus). At a future meeting Amanda brought a striking sequence of photographs that she had created (see Fig. 5). For her, these represented her own research process and through this process she recognized how her teaching and research connect.

Later on, between us, we also produced: diagrams, a word cloud (see Fig. 3) and picture 'stories.' Sometimes pictures were produced with powerful captions. One such example was when one of the group explained to us why her picture of her workspace at home was taken from the outside window looking in (rather than from within the room itself), because she wanted to retain these private spaces. She said, "I didn't feel I wanted just anyone to look into my soul" (Meeting notes February 21, 2008, see Fig. 6). Powerful images were also conveyed through words, as one group member shared her feelings about her own progress with the research and feeling "dismally left behind" but also recognizing when "the clouds have passed" (Blog, March 11, 2008).

It became clear to us that trying to represent or conceptualize something through picture or image is surprisingly different from trying to represent it in plain words. Although the image was a significant aspect of our research the importance of talk throughout the process became evident. The visual images appeared to stimulate

Fig. 6 Not just anyone can look into my soul

much discussion and themes began to emerge from the photographs. To a certain degree we were able to make the familiar strange. The visual was able to shine light on issues, ideas, spaces and places previously not considered. When the visual was used to help construct understanding or conceptualize the process, salient issues emerged, insights were gained and some silences in the research were recognized.

Making Sense of It All – A Messy Business

The above account of the way our methodology evolved has already suggested that we began analysing our data almost the minute we saw it. (In admiring, exclaiming over and commenting on each other's pictures, how could we not?) We did not necessarily realize this at the time, though, as Heather wrote in her reflections,

> *Looking back I can see that my analysis of my own data began as I realized I needed to broaden my ideas of where I did research. The process continued as an internal dialogue, assisted tremendously by group discussions.* (April 16, 2008)

So our analysis started with the discussions described earlier, even with the first images-sharing session prompting themes to emerge. At subsequent meetings we revisited and re-worked our thinking, the iterative and cyclical nature of the research process evident in data collection and analysis too. This analysis could be astonishingly creative. Once, for example, Morwenna brought along various physical objects inspired by thoughts about the research (a snakes and ladders game, a dancing ring, drawings of the body as metaphor).

Partly because of its iterative nature, analysis was somewhat messy. Nevertheless there were three points at which data came under more focused scrutiny. The first was preparation in early April for writing our personal reflections, which took as a common guide the question, What have I learned? We each looked separately and closely at the data, distilling our own most important outcomes from them. The second was preparing a paper for the 2008 conference at Herstmonceaux, England, when Zoè drew on those reflections in addition to the blog, emails and meeting notes to convey some of the central themes for the group. The third focused stage came in writing this chapter, when using Zoè's analysis as a base we concentrated on the strongest (most often recurrent and most passionately debated) of the themes.

What We Learned

Diverse Space

From the start it was clear how different we were – the hugely varied visuals shared at our first meeting make the point strongly. Later, other differences often surprised us. Some of us were dedicated collaborators, while others preferred working individually. Some loved and frequented the blog, others did not. And we discovered that we understood research differently.

Indeed, as we began to realize this, the word 'research' became increasingly problematic. The data suggest our different understandings stemmed partly from our different research histories. For example, Heather and Rosemary had experience of traditional, relatively tidy research. Rosemary had also carried out much *messier research*, as she says, *action research, self-reflection and the subjective end of qualitative research* (Email, December 5, 2008). While Heather was content leaving traditional research behind, she acknowledged that the current collaboration moved her beyond her comfort zone, as did Morwenna, although her research identity was rooted in collaborative action research. Amanda sought research links to art, writing in her reflections that *making the connections of my real research and the development of art education in the university setting, and to do this through the visual* (April 16, 2008) was particularly important; but she found it hard to step back from being a professional artist. *The group has been collecting images which I consider to be a set of sketches towards a finished drawing*, she wrote. *It is difficult for me to interpret these photographic sketches as finished items worthy of an exhibition* (April 16, 2008). The term 'exhibition' also proved problematic, with Amanda comprehending the concept from a professional artist's perspective, while the others saw this more as a research presentation happening to take visual form.

Morwenna's reflections record a growing realization of these differences, which brought her to see that *while for*[her]*spaces for research and a research culture are strongly overlapping, this is not true for everyone.* She came to question her assumptions about collaboration and how to do research, recognizing that *we need* **both** *spaces/places for a research culture and* **also** *spaces/places for research.*

Collaborative Space

Perhaps because of our diversity, at some point we all described collaboration as a *hard space* (Heather's reflections, April 16, 2008), *disconcerting, even uncomfortable sometimes* (Morwenna's reflections, April 16, 2008) that brought *raw nerves, conflict* (Morwenna's reflections, April 16, 2008) and a complexity and chaos clearly captured in Zoè's visual representation of our process (see Fig. 2). Tensions and frustrations were apparent. Some of us found the public nature of genuine collaboration, even within our small group, difficult. Blog entries and reflections show a growing awareness that collaboration had destructive potential: individuals had chosen very carefully what images to share and with whom. Zoè's reflections described initial discomfort at contributing to the blog. She regarded her posts as 'musings' – the kinds of thoughts she would not normally commit to print until crafted into a coherent story. For her, the process of making them public was powerful. This unease at the openness that collaboration requires is perhaps mirrored in Amanda's discomfort at sharing 'snapshots'.

Though Heather's reflections noted our group's democratic nature, other data suggest that members varied in their feelings of involvement. Some distanced

themselves through emails such as *Hope my comments are of some help to you
... not sure if this is what you had in mind* (Email, April 16, 2008) and *thoughts
which you may, or may not find of use* (Email, April 21, 2008).

Our attempt to further collaboration in the absence of physical time/space for
regular meetings through the 'Spaces and Places' blog is interesting. For some it
became important for the research: Zoè came to see it as *a useful yet very public
space where I/we can share our thoughts* (Reflections, April 16, 2008). She and
Morwenna contributed to it often, others with varying frequency. For several months
one of the group refused to use it, the notes from two meetings recording her view
that the work to become familiar with it would be too burdensome.

Perhaps surprisingly in light of the bumpiness, we all agreed our collaboration
was worthwhile. In their reflections, Heather and Morwenna separately employed
the word *exhilarating*, Zoè described collaboration as *a space to question, challenge,
consider and negotiate ideas* and Amanda wrote that *the sharing of these concepts
... has been worthwhile in making clear the varied and complex idea of what is
a research space*. In Rosemary's words, *Working as a group definitely resulted in
synergy: the shared outcomes being more than the sum of individual parts.*

Relevant Space

That research should connect with teaching was crucially important for those of
the group who taught. If the two overlapped and informed one another, they felt it
easier to create research-engaged space. For Rosemary, Amanda's sequence of photographs (see Fig. 6) illustrated this process: *beautiful in themselves, [they] helped
to conceptualize clearly ways in which research and teaching are inextricably linked
through a teacher's creation of materials and their metamorphosis in the pedagogic
process* (Reflections, April 16, 2008).

Powerful Space

We all acknowledged the power of visual images. Though unconvinced of her ability to 'read' them, Heather acknowledged they had taught her something about herself, *Looking at the images, taking part in our discussions and reading the emails
and blogs has made me realize I do most of my creative thinking in the comfortable spaces'* (Reflections, April 16, 2008). Rosemary's reflections pointed to *the
catalytic power of visual imagery for generating and eliciting ideas*. For Amanda
the visual was so powerful that explanations were unnecessary; one blog entry
(February 26, 2008) reads,

> *The image is much more important to me than the perceived meaning as I think that if the
> image is strong then there is a kind of encouragement to understand the artist's meaning.*

It was particularly important for understanding our own research situations that
images – like photographs of a desk full of marking (see Fig. 7), and Rosemary's

Fig. 7 Scripts to be marked

Fig. 8 The bath is an
'off-duty' space for research

image of a 'road closed' sign showing how we keep having to circumvent obstacles – helped us recognize some of the constraints and barriers we faced, and perhaps created, in trying to find research spaces. In contrast, other images showed what diverse spaces we create, like the airport photograph taken by one of us returning from a meeting, or the picture of a bath to illustrate the 'off-duty' places where research happens (see Fig. 8).

Looking to the Future

And now to the crunch question, Will any of what we have learned make a difference to what we do? As far as it is possible for anyone to see into the future, we say yes, it will. Most of us are keen to continue exploring ways of using the visual in our research, to encourage students to use them and get students to get pupils to use them. Discussing the pictures was something rich and strange that yielded insights more fruitful, even, than discussion of words would have done. We are not about to let go of words though, because we think they are needed, too.

And we seem to want more collaboration – about which we learned a great deal – though that had not been at all what we set out to investigate. Its challenges generated a rich mix of images – a rocky road, hitting wild rapids – but perhaps most powerful of all, an iceberg, whose surface presents as smoothly serene but which conceals bulky depths where no one knows what is happening (see Fig. 9). We are coming to wonder how far a collaboration without those jagged depths can truly be collaboration. We now know we can ride the rapids, using and working with the challenges, because the richness is worth it.

Is there anything in what we have learned that we think others might find useful? That it is always worth trying to do something in more than one mode. That it is worth trusting in the process of doing things that are fun (most of the time!) and just out of the comfort zone, when it is concerned with something you have a passion for. The connections will be made. The passion and the new approach come together in creative and unexpected ways. And knowledge really is better found/constructed/acted upon when it was a pleasure getting it. Laughter is good.

And oh yes: get blogging! Although for our group the blog was a mixed bag, on the whole it provided a great space for thinking and sharing. And now we can revisit our thoughts any time we like. So we will be doing more of that. Now, what was the password for our Spaces and Places blog again . . .?

Fig. 9 Collaboration drawn as researchers floating as an iceberg in the water

References

Allender, J., & Manke, M. (2002). Reflecting and refracting self-study artifacts: Jazz poetry. In C. Kosnik, A. Freese, & A. Samaras (Eds.), *Making a difference in teacher education through self-study. Proceedings of the Fourth International Conference on Self-Study of Teacher Education Practices, Herstmonceux Castle, East Sussex, England* (Vol. 1, pp. 15–19). Toronto: OISE, University of Toronto.

Biddulph, M. (2005). The monochrome frame: Mural-making as a methodology for understanding "self." In C. Mitchell, S. Weber, & K. O'Reilly-Scanlon (Eds.), *Just who do we think we are? Methodologies for self-study in education* (pp. 58–68). London: RoutledgeFalmer.

Cavarero, A. (2002). Politicizing theory, *Political Theory, 30*, 506–532.

Denzin, N. K., & Lincoln, Y. S. (1998). *The landscape of qualitative research: Theories and issues.* London: Sage.

Derry, C. (2005). Drawings as a research tool for self-study: An embodied method of exploring memories of childhood bullying. In C. Mitchell, S. Weber, & K. O'Reilly-Scanlon (Eds.), *Just who do we think we are? Methodologies for self-study in education* (pp. 58–68). London: RoutledgeFalmer.

Dewey, J. (1916). *Democracy and education: An introduction to philosophy of education*, New York: Free Press.

Diamond, C. T. P., & van Halen-Faber, C. (2005). Arts-based methodology as a poetic and visual sixth sense. In C. Mitchell, S. Weber, & K. O'Reilly-Scanlon (Eds.), *Just who do we think we are? Methodologies for self-study in education* (pp. 58–68). London: RoutledgeFalmer.

Griffiths, M. (1998). *Educational research for social justice: Getting off the fence.* Buckingham, England: Open University Press.

Griffiths, M. (2003). *Action for social justice in education: Fairly different.* Buckingham, England: Open University Press.

Griffiths, M. (2006). The feminization of teaching and the practice of teaching: Threat or opportunity? *Educational Theory, 56*, 387–405.

Griffiths, M., Bass, L., Johnston, M., & Perselli, V. (2004). Knowledge, social justice, and self-study. In J. J. Loughran, M.L. Hamilton, V. K. LaBoskey, & T. Russell (Eds.), *International handbook of self-study of teaching and teacher education practices* New (Vol. 1, pp. 651–708). Dordrecht: Kluwer.

Griffiths, M., & Macleod, G. (2008). Personal narratives and policy: Never the twain? *Journal of Philosophy of Education, 42*, 121–143.

Griffiths, M., Poursanidou, D., Simms, M., & Windle, J. (2006). Defining workspaces: Defining ourselves. In L. M. Fitzgerald, M. L. Heston, & D. L. Tidwell (Eds.), *Collaboration and community: Pushing boundaries through self-study. Proceedings of the Sixth International Conference on Self-study of Teacher Education Practices, Herstmonceux Castle, East Sussex, England* (pp. 288–289). Cedar Falls, IA: University of Northern Iowa.

Griffiths, M., & Tann, S. (1992). Using reflective practice to link personal and public theories. *Journal of Education for Teaching, 18*(1), 69–84.

Griffiths, M., Windle, J., & Simms, M. (2006). 'That's what I'm here for': Images of working lives of academic and support staff. In D. Tidwell, & L. Fitzgerald (Eds.), *Self-study and diversity* (pp. 227–248). Rotterdam: Sense.

Hamilton, M.L. (2004). Professional knowledge, teacher education and self-study. In J. J. Loughran, M.L. Hamilton, V. K. LaBoskey, & T. Russell (Eds.), *International handbook of self-study of teaching and teacher education Practices* (Vol. 1, pp. 375–419). Dordrecht: Kluwer.

Hamilton, M. L. (2005). Using pictures at an exhibition to explore my teaching practices. In C. Mitchell, S. Weber, & K. O'Reilly-Scanlon (Eds.), *Just who do we think we are? Methodologies for self-study in education* (pp.58–68). London: RoutledgeFalmer.

Khudu-Petersen, K. (2008). *Intercultural arts education: Initiating links between schools and ethnic minority communities focussing on the Kweneng West Sub-District in Botswana.* Unpublished doctoral dissertation, University of Edinburgh.

LaBoskey, V. K. (2004). The methodology of self-study and its theoretical underpinnings. In J. J. Loughran, M.L. Hamilton, V. K. LaBoskey and T. Russell (Eds.), *International handbook of self-study of teaching and teacher education practices* (Vol. 2, pp. 817–869). Dordrecht: Kluwer.

Le Doeuff, M. (1989). *The philosophical imaginary* (C. Gordon, Trans.). London: Athlone.

Lighthall, F. (2004). Fundamental features and approaches of the S-STEP enterprise. In J. J. Loughran, M.L. Hamilton, V. K. LaBoskey, & T. Russell (Eds.), *International handbook of self-study of teaching and teacher education practices* (Vol. 1, pp. 193–245). Dordrecht: Kluwer.

Loughran, J. J., Hamilton, M. L., LaBoskey, V. K., & Russell, T. (Eds.). (2004). *International handbook of self-study of teaching and teacher education practices.* Dordrecht: Kluwer.

Magee, D. (2008). I am the airplane: The use of metaphor as a nodal moment. In M. L. Heston, D. L. Tidwell, K. K. East, & L. M. Fitzgerald (Eds.), *Pathways to change in teacher education: Dialogue, diversity and self-study. Proceedings of the Seventh International Conference on Self-Study of Teacher Education Practices, Herstmonceux Castle, East Sussex, England* (pp. 241–245). Cedar Falls, IA: University of Northern Iowa.

Miller, C., East, K., Fitzgerald, L. M., Heston, M. L., & Veenstra T. B. (2002). Visions of self in the act of teaching: Using personal metaphors in a collaborative study of teaching practices *Teaching and Learning, 16*(3), 81–93.

Mitchell, C., & Weber, S. J. (1999). *Reinventing ourselves as teachers: Beyond nostalgia.* London: Falmer.

Mitchell, C., Weber, S. J., & O'Reilly-Scanlon, K. (Eds.). (2005). *Just who do we think we are? Methodologies for self-study in education.* London: RoutledgeFalmer.

Perselli, V. (2005). Re-envisioning research, re-presenting self: Putting arts media to work in the analysis and synthesis of data of "difference" and "disability." *International Journal of Qualitative Studies in Education, 18*(1), 63–83.

Simms, M. (2007, Spring). Social justice of workspaces, *Escalate, 7,* 4–5.

SSTEP website. (2008). Home Page. Retrieved from the world wide web 26 May 2008, http://sstep.soe.ku.edu/

Tidwell, D. (2006). Nodal moments as a context for meaning. In D. Tidwell & L. Fitzgerald (Eds.), *Self-study and diversity* (pp. 267–286). Rotterdam: Sense.

Tidwell, D. L., & Tincu, M. (2004). Doodle you know what I mean? Illustrated nodal moments as a context for meaning. In D. L. Tidwell, L. M. Fitzgerald, & M. L. Heston (Eds.), *Journeys of hope: Risking self-study in a diverse world. Proceedings of the Fifth International Conference on Self-Study of Teacher Education Practices, Herstmonceux Castle, East Sussex, England* (pp. 241–245). Cedar Falls, IA: University of Northern Iowa.

Van Leeuwen, T., & Jewitt, C. (2001). *Handbook of visual analysis.* London: Sage.

Weber, S. J., & Mitchell, C. (2004). Visual artistic modes of representation for self-study. In J. J. Loughran, M. L. Hamilton, V. K. LaBoskey, & T. Russell (Eds.), *International handbook of self-study of teaching and teacher education practice* (Vol. 2, pp. 979–1038). Dordrecht: Kluwer.

Facing the Public: Using Photography for Self-Study and Social Action

Claudia Mitchell, Sandra Weber and Kathleen Pithouse

Introduction: Visual Approaches to Self-Study and Social Action

"[I]t's a challenge or a calling to everybody. Nobody has to neglect that call. Everybody has to respond positively." (Tembinkosi, a teacher in rural South Africa).

How can teacher educators, inservice, and preservice teachers really see their present situations? Their problems? Their pasts and futures? In order to see, to really notice that which we may have overlooked, not seen clearly, or even avoided thinking about, we need to look carefully, to pay attention in what Maxine Greene (1977) would call a wide-awake manner, or with what Bell Hooks (1995) or Jennifer Gore (1993) might call a critical or feminist gaze, or what Bateson (1994) would call peripheral vision, or what Eisner (1998) would call an enlightened eye, or through what Cochran-Smith et al. (1999) call careful listening. Even as we study ourselves, we need to engage in dialogue that will allow us to look through other people's eyes to gain "perspectives beyond the self" (Bullough & Pinnegar, 2004, p. 313) and thus to reconsider what we see from different vantage points. As we argue both here and elsewhere (see, for example, Mitchell & Weber, 1999; Weber & Mitchell, 2004), the use of visual approaches to self-study can literally help us see things differently. The strength of visual methods lies in harnessing the power of images to bring things to light in both personal and public ways and to offer multiple theoretical and practical perspectives on issues of social import. Using images connects us to the self, yet distances us from ourselves. When done with a critical gaze, self-study facilitates professional growth in ways that not only end up changing oneself, but also serve as impetus for tackling the wider social problems that contextualize our individual lives. Far from being a route to a blinkered focus on 'me,' self-study can actually encourage a wider view of the broader situation that shapes our individual practice.

As the chapters in this volume about self-study illustrate in ways that are often implicit, studying one's own practice, knowledge, and values is inevitably linked to

C. Mitchell (✉)
McGill University, Faculty of Education, 3700 McTavish Street, Montreal, Quebec H3G 1Y2, Canada
e-mail: claudia.mitchell1@mcgill.ca

D.L. Tidwell et al. (eds.), *Research Methods for the Self-study of Practice*,   119
Self-Study of Teaching and Teacher Education Practices 9,
DOI 10.1007/978-1-4020-9514-6_8, © Springer Science+Business Media B.V. 2009

questions of change: What kinds of changes are needed in specific contexts? How can people encourage those changes, and on whose "say so"? How can we imagine and provoke change? How can we connect imagined change and practicable action? And do we even recognize change when it happens? How do we evaluate what happens? These are difficult questions—and it may be easier to theorize about social action than to engage in it—but self-study is all about asking difficult questions.

In exploring ways to address the challenge of change in relation to self-study, we have worked with a variety of visual modes, including drawings (Mitchell & Weber, 1999; Weber & Mitchell, 1995), video documentary (Mitchell, Kusner, & Charbonneau-Gowdy, 2004), school photographs (Mitchell & Weber, 1999), photovoice (Mitchell, de Lange, Moletsane, Stuart, & Buthelezi, 2005), performance (Weber, 2005), dress (Mitchell & Weber, 1999; Weber & Mitchell, 2004), and collage (Pithouse, 2007). Each approach has something valuable to offer, but they have in common a participatory element that involves going public and gathering multiple perspectives. One of the most adaptable and promising of the methods we have used involves the construction of a 'curated' photo album, something we shall describe in detail in the sections to follow. We are particularly interested here in the ways in which working with photographs contributes to the public face of self-study (see also the work of Griffiths, Poursanidou, Simms, & Windle, 2006). As a number of other researchers in the area have noted (see, among others, LaBoskey, 2004; Loughran & Northfield, 1998), 'the public face' in and of itself is a critical component of engaging in self-study.

In the work we draw on for this chapter, we relied on relatively low-budget traditional technologies that were appropriate to local contexts. But in looking toward the future, we have also begun to explore the ways in which new media and new technologies can complement (and expand) the possibilities for self-representation in the public face of self-study. These range from the use of digital cameras in creating PowerPoint albums (St. John-Ward, 2008; Weber & Mitchell, 2007), digitizing projects using metadata (Park, Mitchell, & de Lange, 2008), and MovieMaker, and the use of blogs. Not only can digital technologies contribute to expanding the repertoire of visual approaches to self-study, they also contribute to expanding the range of audiences.

Seeing for Ourselves: Curating Self-Study Photo Albums as Social (Action) Texts

By focusing on our work with teachers in South Africa, where the practices of teachers and teacher educators are critical in relation to addressing the impact of the HIV and AIDS epidemic, this chapter will illustrate how specific ways of working with photo albums in self-study involve performance that can lead to social action. We will start with some background that situates this aspect of our practice.

There is a general consensus that education, broadly defined, is a key to having a meaningful and sustainable impact in the fight to contain the spread of HIV and the effects of AIDS. Ironically, the one area of education that has received relatively little attention to date relates to teachers themselves, even though they remain on the front lines when it comes to working with youth. Education policy in South Africa identifies a complex range of HIV and AIDS-related responsibilities that all teachers and school managers are meant to assume. Some examples are: giving HIV and AIDS-related advice to learners, parents, and the wider community; challenging customary attitudes toward sex and talking about sex; giving emotional help and guidance to learners who are bereaved or orphaned; giving special academic assistance to HIV-positive learners; taking action to deal with HIV and AIDS-related discrimination in schools (see Department of Education, South Africa, 2000). However, there appears to have been little exploration of how teachers can become actively involved in developing context-specific strategies for meeting these additional responsibilities in their diverse school settings. Instead, as is so often the case in many countries, the reform emphasis has been placed on developing teacher-proof materials, youth-to-youth peer education programs, and strategies for getting health-care personnel into the schools so that they can be involved in giving out correct information. While youth-to-youth programming can indeed be an effective approach, and there is definitely a need for health-care workers to be involved with schools, the issues are far too complex and vast to leave teachers out of the equation. After all, they are the professionals who work with young people everyday and may have the closest and most direct relationship with them. Research (see, among others, Brookes, Shisana, & Richter, 2004; Nelson Mandela Foundation, 2005; Pettifor et al., 2004; Shisana, Peltzer, Zungu-Dirwayi, & Louw, 2005; Vass, 2008) confirms that teachers are indeed an important source of HIV and AIDS-related information for young South Africans. These studies also highlight the pressing need for South African teachers to receive additional support in dealing with the multiple personal and professional challenges that are brought by the HIV epidemic and often exacerbated by poverty, inequality, and violence in schools and communities. (See also the South African Human Rights Commission's (2008b) *Human Rights Development Report*). Consequently, in a number of projects operating out of the Center for Visual Methodologies for Social Change at the University of KwaZulu-Natal, we have seen how self-study can bring teachers front and center in looking for solutions to serious problems. Among the various visual methods used in these projects, one of the most interesting, the use of photo albums, is also one of the most portable and adaptable.

Creating, Curating, and Using Photo Albums for Self-Study

Our use of photo albums for self-study in education is informed by two sets of visual practices that combine study of self with social critique in order to imagine, inspire, or instigate change: photovoice and critical memory work with photo albums.

Photovoice

Caroline Wang's (1999) visual methodology, appropriately called 'photovoice,' enables project participants to be researchers. They are invited, guided, and equipped to produce their own images, making visible their voice around a particular social issue that affects them directly. A carefully considered prompt or question is provided to encourage participants to explore, through the lens of a simple point and shoot camera, issues of concern. The images themselves contain elements of social critique, which is further interrogated through eliciting responses to the photographs, often by displaying them in public venues or showing them to specific community or policy groups. Participatory in nature, photovoice is often used in the context of community work or social activism to better understand what really matters to people. It follows the premise that, as Wang explains, "What experts think is important may not match what people at the grassroots think is important" (http://www.photovoice.com/background/index.html, retrieved June 9, 2008). As we have explored elsewhere, photovoice offers a fascinating approach to research in education (de Lange, Mitchell, & Stuart, 2007; Mitchell et al., 2005).

Critical Memory Work with Photo Albums

The work of Jo Spence (1988), in her book, *Putting Myself in the Picture*, along with her collaborations with Joan Solomon (Spence & Solomon, 1995) in *What Can a Woman do with a Camera?* offers an up-close self-study component of producing images and working with photo albums. *What Can a Woman do with a Camera?* draws together a fascinating collection of essays describing visual projects based on still photography carried out by ordinary girls and women. From Sylvia Ayling's (1995) "We have nothing to lose but our invisibility" to Linda Troeller's "The TB/AIDS diary," the book takes up the questions: How can we as women tell stories that eradicate the disparity between how we are seen and what we think and feel, what we actually do? How do we present who we really are in terms of images? For us, these questions and methods could be used to nicely frame the enterprise of self-study in education. They have become the cornerstone of our work.

When we first started working with photo albums, it was in the broader context of documentary studies (Allnutt, Mitchell, & Stuart, 2007; Mitchell & Allnutt, 2008). There has been a considerable amount of scholarship on family albums, most of it outside of education, particularly in the area of the visual arts and art history. These studies range from work on one's own family album(s) (Faber, 2003; Kuhn, 1995; Spence, 1988; Spence & Holland, 1991; Weiser, 1993) to the work of Arbus (see Lee & Pultz, 2004), Chalfen (1987, 1991, 2002), Hirsch (1997), Langford (2000), and Willis (1994), to name only some of the scholars who examine other people's albums. These various album projects have highlighted the personal in looking at or working with one's own photographs, but there is also, as in the case of Langford, the idea of explicitly looking at other people's photo albums through a socio-cultural lens. The issues that these scholars have explored range from questions of cultural identity and memory through to the reconfiguring of one's own family albums (Spence, 1988). Recognizing the relevance of this scholarship, we use it to ground our methods of using photography for self-study in education.

It was only when we started to engage in this kind of photo-based work with teachers in Media Studies and Visual Studies classes at the University of KwaZulu-Natal and McGill University, respectively, that we began to see its potential for teachers' self-study. Example 1, which draws on the work of Tembinkosi, a young teacher in rural KwaZulu-Natal, South Africa, who was enrolled in a graduate course in Cinematic and Documentary Studies, demonstrates the ways in which one can work with family photographs to explore social documentary. In that course, the starting point for the study of documentary video was for the students (all of them practicing teachers) to first create their own photo documentaries, using domestic photographs that had already been taken by others. Later, in another course and drawing on our work with photovoice and the idea of teachers taking their own pictures (see, for example, Mitchell et al., 2005), we expanded the album project to one that could also include photos that teachers had taken themselves. Thus, in Example 2, which came about as part of a course on Gender and Leadership involving 50 women vice principals and principals in the province of Gauteng in South Africa, each of the participants took pictures and constructed a social documentary to address issues of gender in her school.[1]

Protocol for Creating and Curating Self-Study Albums

The approach we have used to creating albums is quite simple, on the surface at least, and is adaptable to working with archival and family photographs and to photovoice projects where teachers themselves take up cameras to represent issues that are important to them:

- Find (not take) or take (not find) some photos that appear (to you) to be linked to some sort of theme, narrative, or question that is relevant to your life (to your self-study inquiry).
- Choose (select) and organize seven or eight (no more) of these photos into a small photo album.
- Provide a title, and write a short 'curatorial' statement of 150–200 words to introduce and frame your collection.
- Write short captions to accompany each photo, and include acknowledgements and dedication (where appropriate), and 'about the artist' (optional).
- Contain each aspect of the textual material (e.g., curatorial statement, captions, images) to what can be placed within a plastic album window (or single page).
- Make an oral presentation of your album to your intended audience (for example, colleagues, administrators, community leaders, policy makers) and take note of their responses/critiques.
- If possible, display your album (make it available) where most appropriate.

---

[1] The Gender and Leadership program is part of the Matthew Goniwe School of Governance and Leadership in Johannesburg, South Africa.

Although the steps we presented above may appear simple, doing them well requires insight or a thoughtful eye. Part of the challenge is in recognizing the potential significance of individual photographs as well as the links between them and in framing and ordering them so that they speak with eloquence. Further, as we shall see in the examples below, in presenting and displaying these images taken from our lives, we are performing; we are forced by the process to go public, to articulate, and to take ownership of our images and ideas. Not only are we able to see how others react, but also we are compelled to step back and almost literally look at ourselves. Self-study indeed.

It is also important to stress that the photographs do not have to be directly related to school: our frame for self-study in education is much broader than that. Asking teachers to use photographs taken from their lives requires that they examine the personal, the everyday, and the totality of their experience, which is, after all, the context in which professionals work. Many of the participants in the photo album projects we shall describe below found this new and wider perspective on their domestic photos to be challenging, freeing, and expansive. It freed them to think differently about their own lives—in a compact yet concrete and materialist manner. As we discuss elsewhere (Mitchell & Allnutt, 2008), our protocol pointed them to their own backyard—an often overlooked source of material in professional self-study. A related point is that unlike so many other research projects in education, in constructing their albums, the participants could, and often did, include bodies, whether their own or other people's. In self-study, the body is crucial, for it is through our bodies that we act, teach, and think. In the case of the following projects in South Africa, the very existence of the body is in question, a matter of life and death.

Example 1: Reconfiguring the Family Album: "And today I am a teacher"

Tembinkosi, a teacher enrolled in a graduate course, documented the story of his sister who in her early 20s died mysteriously, leaving behind her 6-year-old son to be raised by the grandmother. Tembinkosi used the project to explore the silences not just about the cause of his sister's death, and the importance of naming the disease, but also the position of AIDS orphans—in this case, his young nephew. In Tembinkosi's performance of the album when he presented it to the class, he offered the image of his mother falling asleep with the album under her arm. It was a moving representation of what the album project meant to his family in terms of breaking silences. It was also a poignant representation of a teacher's self-study.

The process includes both the production of the album and also the presentation to other teachers in the group, with the result that there are both the material text of the album and what might be described as the performance of the album. Tembinkosi's performance of his album and others in the group was also videotaped and can be viewed in the documentary *Our Photos, Our Videos, Our Stories* (Mak, Mitchell, & Stuart, 2005).

"When I first began, it wasn't my aim really to be a part of this class, the media studies class, I mean, because there was a lot of lecture that was made on the computer, camera...So, I was a bit scared. I didn't think that I was really suitable for this course. But, as time went on there was this documentary. We were asked to collect photos—about eight photos—and I didn't really know what to do with the photos because I think that photos are just wonderful being placed in the album and put over there in the drawer or in the cupboard or anywhere. But finally, I ended up being in a position to do my own work.

Photo 1: Here I am as a baby. Mainly my history consists of certain memories because I was born to an unmarried couple. My father did not take care of us. He did not take care of my mother. So, we grew up under very very challenging and threatening conditions.

Photo 2: Here I included my photo from my first graduation... This is my Mom and this is my Gran. If you go through the story—here, in the last sentence—my mother failed to address the guests on the evening. Instead, she cried. I was crying for the whole time in the few days before the graduation because I didn't really know that I was actually reaching the end of the process of studying and no one predicted the outcome. We never thought that at the end of the day there would be such a wonderful history. And today I am a teacher.

Photo 3: For the very first time, I wanted to tell a story about my late sister. She died in 2002. When I fetched the medical report from the hospital, they stated that the cause of death was streptococcal meningitis, which later I discovered that it's associated with HIV/AIDS.

Photo 4: My sister's son, he's age 11 now, and he's very close to my heart. I'm always worried because he never spoke about his late mother and I keep on wondering what's going on in his life. What does he think about his mother? Obviously, he misses her. . . .

My Mother, she took the album and went through it until she fell asleep with the album—holding it like this. And in a way it was, in a way I was touched, and I said to myself "Oh, for the very first time I managed to deliver a message," because of its history of my family, it's a shared history but we never had a chance to discuss it, to revise, to look back and talk about the future, let alone the challenges within my household.

As a teacher, I have discovered that the number of child-headed families is rising. Sometimes I find a child is absent from school. Maybe for a week or two, or for the day or two. When you try to dig deeper about the situation you will find that the child could not come to school for the past two weeks or past two days simply because he or she has to look after his or her dying father. Or both parents are very very sick and the child cannot pull the door and leave for school. Instead, he or she must remain at home with the aim to prepare food, wash the parent, feed them. And some of the children have witnessed the death of their parent. If the family is not being lead by a child, you find that an elderly person, a grandfather or a grandmother, is now actually responsible for the education of their grandchildren. Those are common cases in my country especially in my environment or in my province—Kwazulu-Natal—so it's a challenge or a calling to everybody. Nobody has to neglect that call. Everybody has to respond positively."

But Tembinkosi's project does not stop there. Several years later, as we have explored in follow-up interviews, he described one outcome of this work, the setting up of a small center in the community that serves the needs of children in the community who have been orphaned as a result of the pandemic. Tembinkosi teaches children in the fifth and sixth grades all day where he sees directly the impact of the disease. And after school he offers what help he can. He talked of what the center is currently doing (providing a meal for children before they go home after school and offering a place to do homework, socialize, play sports) and also what else he would like to be able to offer if they could raise more funds:

"I am imagining a bigger place. We want to have a television room so that the children can just relax. And we want more space so that they are not all crammed in together. Right now we just have a small hotplate to prepare the food. But if we had a proper kitchen we could do so much more."

A seemingly simple photo album process thus empowers a teacher to look critically at his world, and to imagine how it could be or what it should be.

Example 2: Photovoice: A School Principal Looks at Gender Violence in Her School

Margaret, a secondary school principal enrolled in a Gender and Leadership course, decided to use photovoice to engage in a self-study on how she was dealing with gender violence in her school. She reviewed the cases of violence in her school over a period of several months, photographing every single place in the school where an act of violence had taken place. Interestingly, she decided to take places rather than people and indeed the shots are not unlike police shots, each with a distinct and somewhat eerie scene-of-the-crime look, reminiscent of Joel Sternfield's (1996) photos in *On This Site: Landscape in Memoriam*, or the photo work of Sultan and Mandel (2005) in *Evidence*. Like Margaret's, Sternfield's photos show the ordinary landscape that is left behind after the act of violence.

Once Margaret had taken all the photographs, she selected eight for the album project that she shared with the group of women in the course. The following are two examples of the captions she wrote for her chosen photographs:

> *Photo 1: It is easy to overpower a girl in a dark corner*
>   *Caption 1: The school building itself presents a minefield of opportunities for boys to harass girls...Every nook and cranny bears witness of forceful experimentation...It is easy to overpower a girl in a dark corner...*
>
> *Photo 2: It is not only the girls who are at risk*
>   *Caption 2: It is not only girls that are at risk. Behind this door a boy was offering blowjobs @ R2 per person for pocket money, because he apparently had to do it for free at home...*
>   *Where does it come from? Who teaches me to abuse or how do I end up a victim? It can be my own parents! Poverty also plays a major role. We need to break the chain!*

In addition to consulting the literature on gender violence in schools in South Africa, an issue that has been the subject of a number of international and local studies (see, for example, the Human Rights Watch 2001 report, *Scared at School*, and the South African Human Rights Commission (2008a) report on school-based violence), Margaret added to her album a curatorial statement about her own relationship to the images:

> *I grew up in the rural areas during a time when a school was seen as a sacred place. When I came to the city, the first school I taught at had a classroom that was pointed at as "that room where a woman was killed a few years ago." I was shocked. Suddenly a school building was not safe anymore.*

I focused on the notion that, although a school building is sexless, it is a backdrop for, or rather it sets the right stage for, sexual harassment to happen: all those dark corners and cozy spaces we find in schools make it easy for girls to become victims.

But these things that happen at our school also point fingers at the teachers and parents of those children. Why are we quietly watching on while our boys are taught to disrespect girls? And when we address these issues, why is it not effective to stop gender violence from reoccurring?

Margaret did not stop there, however. In addition, she created an exhibition that she set up in the school. In commenting on her project as whole, Margaret observed, "I wanted to see for myself and then I wanted to see how the images would help our whole school work as a team to make the school safer." As was the case for Tembinkosi, Margaret's photo-based self-study pointed to changes needed at both the individual and the collective levels.

Methodological Considerations: Features of Curated Photo Albums as Self-Study

Through our work in both photo album and photovoice projects, we have identified nine significant features of these methods that in a very practical (and often observable) way point to the educative and social value of creating and performing photo albums or mounting exhibits.

1) 'Looking, gazing, seeing, noticing: Gathering evidence and evaluating'. These are at the heart of any self-study, especially those using photography-based methods. In the examples we presented earlier, we see how the personal experience of looking, when shared (even with an imagined absent audience), can evolve to critical reflection and social action through the process of making one's photographs public in an album. The personal seeing leads to a contextual noticing that turns outwards, inviting a broader audience to gaze and see, perhaps differently. "Do you see what I see?" "What do you think of what I see?" "What else do you see?" These are the visual and conceptual questions that test the worthiness and evaluate the evidence of the kinds of projects we do.

2) 'Remembering, considering, and gathering information through dialogue' is crucial. During the process of searching for suitable photographs taken by others, or in arranging to take photos themselves, the participants often need to consult other people, to ask for their help in locating, identifying, or staging photographs, to engage in conversation that sparks ideas and leads to insight into what images might be the most useful for their self-study. Photographs act as powerful memory prompts. Participants often comment on how asking a family member or friend or colleague for photographs often provokes lengthy reminiscences and conversations that reveal surprising or forgotten elements that prove to be invaluable to the project. Important details for a fuller or more authentic interpretation of the images are gathered, often incidentally, as part of the

search/shoot. Sometimes in the process of taking or looking for images, the central theme or question changes as a more basic or important thread becomes evident.

3) 'Choice' is central to the inquiry process that underlies curated photo albums. Having to select photographs to include in a themed album or exhibit encourages participants to identify personal and social issues that they genuinely care about and want to highlight and explore through the displaying and curating of a collection of photos. Choosing the theme or issue is in itself a performance of values, self, and context. Moreover, in the act of choosing, the participants review photographs they have taken or found in order to think about their suitability and significance to their chosen theme and to imagine how the audience might view them. Although invisible to the audience, the images that are deliberately set aside, not selected, are just as important to the method. Making a choice is an act of commitment that results in a public visual statement, a performance. It is the behind-the-scenes process that underlies the public face.

4) 'Constructedness' is another key feature of photo albums. As we have explored elsewhere in our discussions of media and identity (Mitchell et al., 2008; Weber & Mitchell, 2007), the actual assembling of the text (in this case the album) can be framed as a type of playfulness—a tentative Lego construction that could incorporate a variety of shapes, be it grandiose or small, and denote different meanings, depending on how things are put together and taken apart. In looking at an album, one can imagine it differently, for example, by wondering why a certain picture was included or put in a particular frame. There is a transparency to the process. What starts out to be one thing can turn out to be another as pieces are tried in different positions. Ultimately, the construction relies on matters of the aesthetic, the intention, and the technical, the ordering of the particular photos, the arrangement of the print text, and of course the negotiation of space (particularly the containment to using only eight photos, and producing short captions and curatorial statements). In constructing a photo exhibit, the self is explored, re-constructed, and performed in ways that help uncover issues that need further attention.

5) 'Explication' is an important feature of the curatorship of photo albums. It is important to note that our approach to photo albums combines images and text (both written statement and oral presentations). The challenge in writing or talking about a photo collection is to set the context, situate one's theoretical or political stance, and guide interpretation. It is not easy to find the best words to complement, sum up, contextualize, or add to the visual statements made by the photographs. Writing captions and curatorial statements for the chosen photos and preparing to speak about the album prompt participants to become more conscious of the noteworthy aspects and possible implications of their collection. In thinking about how to address their audience in writing, they are obliged to step back and look again, pushing the self-study process even further.

6) 'Materiality' is a seldom acknowledged, tacit feature of photo album work. As Edwards and Hart (2004) observe:

> Albums in particular have performative qualities. Not only do they narrativize pho-
> tographs, such as in family or travel albums (see Hirsch, 1997; Holland & Spence,
> 1991; Langford, 2000; Norstrom, 2004), but their materiality dictates the embodied
> conditions of viewing, literally, performing the images in certain ways. How are albums
> used? Are they intended to be read formally? In a large group? Privately? Albums have
> weight, they smell, often of damp, rotting card—the scent of 'the past' (Langford, 2000,
> p. 5). Large presentation albums, viewed by two or more seated persons with the object
> spread across their knees, would link the group to one another physically, determining
> the social relations of viewing. Conversely, small albums, held in the hand, suggest a
> private relationship with the object: to view jointly with another person would again
> require very specific and close physical proximity. (p. 12)

This idea of materiality is critical, as Tembinkosi reminds us, not only in relation to the individual photographs contained in the album but also in relation to
the actual album as a material object: "My Mother, she took the album and went
through it until she fell asleep with the album—holding it like this."

7) 'Embodiment' is a basic modality of curated photo albums. The photos, the
album, the public presentation—all these are forms of embodiment. Education
and academic discourse centers on words and ideas, often entirely omitting the
body from learning, an act that is embodied whether we acknowledge the fact
or not (see Chapter 4 in Mitchell & Weber, 1999). Visual methods such as
photography force participants to bring their own bodies and those of their students back, literally, 'into the picture' (Mitchell & Weber, 1998). Seeing, taking pictures, revealing the direction of one's gaze—all these evoke the body.
Even when people use objects as stand-ins or signifiers for their bodies, they
are linking, extending, or representing their corporeal existence and identity.
Further, the requirement that participants present their albums orally obliges
them to put their bodies on the line to give voice to their interpretations and
indings.

8) 'Performance,' closely linked to embodiment, is central to the curating process.
It may seem strange to think of the photo album as a public performance, but
as Langford (2000) asserted, "The showing and telling of an album is a performance" (p. 5). Having the participants perform the album project moves them to
a different place very quickly. As Hirsch (1997) says, "To step into the visual is
not to engage in theory as systematic explanation of a set of facts, but to practice theory, to make theory just as the photographer materially makes an image"
(p. 15). Presenting the album is a crucial step in articulating problems and imagining change. Indeed, our contention is that the very act of looking at the performance produces change (see also Pithouse & Mitchell, 2007). This looking-
as-change is characterized by creative engagement on the part of the participant who is simultaneously a producer and a viewer of the photograph. Creative
engagement involves both absorption in the present moment and an opening to
imagination and possibility.

The production and presentation of such albums contribute to a type of
reflexive performance which in and of itself becomes a critical component
of self-study. Edwards (2002) reminds us that our experience of photographs
is situated in space and time, and mediated by the presentational format and

the context of looking. In a sense, then, the display of the albums becomes an embodied performance of meaning, which is understood as such by the audience.

9) 'Reflexivity' is a key to the success of photo album work. Participants comment on the ways in which the processes of selecting photos, assembling the photos for the album, composing the captions and curatorial statement, and finally presenting and engaging in dialogue contribute to reflexivity as they contemplate such questions as: "How best to represent my narrative through images and words?" "How will teachers and others respond to the album?" "Who am I, anyway, in this album?" "What can I learn from this process, what should I change?" In other words, the process of creating and curating the album positions each participant as simultaneously producer of the image/text and reader/consumer. Visual anthropologist Jay Ruby (2000) discusses how reflexivity, autobiography, and self-awareness figure in the process of working with visual texts. Like any performance, a photo exhibit is interactive, a call to dialogue, an effort to communicate, and possibly, a provocation to think or act differently. Moreover, through discussion with their audience, and through revisiting the photos in the album format, participants can become more aware of characteristics or connotations they had previously not noticed. They can gain new and multiple perspectives that enrich and broaden their own thinking about their theme, raising new questions and ideas in relation to the album. They can even envisage and share possibilities for taking action, making changes in their practice, which after all, is the very purpose of self-study.

It is important to note that although we articulate the above features in relation to curated photo albums, as we argue in detail elsewhere (Mitchell & Allnutt, 2008; Weber, 2008; Weber & Mitchell, 2004), other visual approaches to self-study, notably video production (see also Whitehead, 2004), drawing, and theatrical performance, have much in common in terms of methodology.

Self-Study and Change Revisited

Elected politicians all over the world periodically announce broad school reforms to assure constituents that social ills will be addressed. Teacher education is often singled out as the most suitable vehicle for initiating or sustaining these reforms. Indeed, at the time that we are writing this chapter, South Africa has singled out teacher education as the most critical area of Higher Education for addressing HIV and AIDS. One of the six main objectives of the Higher Education HIV and AIDS Programme (2004) in South Africa is to identify and clarify the specific role to be played by teacher education faculties in addressing HIV and AIDS. However, it is not always easy to really see the specifics of what really needs to be changed. And, as Fullan (2001) and Hargreaves, Earl, Moore, and Manning (2001), among others, explain, top-down efforts are doomed to failure if teachers and students have no real voice, if no one has deep insight into what teachers and students themselves think needs to be changed both in their local contexts and in the broader society. In addition, a single-minded focus on change can promote a deficit view of teachers by implying that they need to be somehow perfected. This approach overlooks the idea that there is a necessary imperfection in our day-to-day endeavors as human beings that feeds our ongoing processes of learning and development. It is also important to recognize the contextual constraints that might prevent teachers from making immediate or sweeping changes and to support them in developing their own practicable strategies for taking some action (no matter how small) within or in response to those constraints (Pithouse, 2007). In Tembinkosi's case, taking action in relation to breaking the silence around his sister's death became a starting point for more sustained work in the community in relation to the AIDS pandemic. In Margaret's case, she set up a dialogue with the whole school and community around violence.

In an era where teachers are increasingly interested in or even called to teach for social justice (see Zeichner, 2003), it becomes more important than ever for self-study, as a field, to take on the challenge of examining teaching practices in the context of social issues. As this chapter has argued, participatory and performative visual approaches to self-study can play a key role in teaching for social justice by illuminating pressing social challenges that have resonance beyond the self and stimulating creative, context-specific responses to those challenges. The projects of Tembinkosi and Margaret point to the possibilities for teachers and teacher educators to develop their own strategies—or as Tembinkosi expressed it, "[F]inally I ended up being in a position to do my own work."

Acknowledgments We gratefully acknowledge the key contributions of a number of colleagues in work with teachers around photovoice and curated photo albums: Jean Stuart, Susann Allnutt, Naydene de Lange, Relebohile Moletsane, and Ann Smith.

References

Allnutt, S., Mitchell, C., & Stuart, J. (2007). The visual family archive: Uses and interruptions. In N. de Lange, C. Mitchell, & J. Stuart (Eds.), *Putting people in the picture* (pp. 89–99). Amsterdam: Sense.

Ayling, S. (1995). We have nothing to lose but our invisibility. In J. Spence & J. Solomon (Eds.), *What can a woman do with a camera?* (pp. 127, 132). London: Scarlet.

Bateson, M. C. (1994). *Peripheral visions: Learning along the way.* New York: Harper Collins.

Brookes, H., Shisana, O., & Richter, L. (2004). *The national household HIV prevalence and risk survey of South African children.* Cape Town: Human Sciences Research Council Press.

Bullough, R. V., & Pinnegar, S. E. (2004). Thinking about the thinking about self-study: An analysis of eight chapters. In J. J. Loughran, M. L. Hamilton, V. K. LaBoskey, & T. Russell (Eds.), *International handbook of self-study of teaching and teacher education practices* (Vol. 1, pp. 313–342). Dordrecht: Kluwer.

Chalfen, R. (1987). *Snapshot versions of life.* Bowling Green, OH: Bowling Green State University Popular.

Chalfen, R. (1991). *Turning leaves: Exploring identity in Japanese American photograph albums.* Albuquerque: University of New Mexico Press.

Chalfen, R. (2002). Snapshots "r" us: The evidentiary problematic of home media. *Visual Studies, 17*(2), 141–149.

Cochran-Smith, M., Albert, L., Dimattia, P., Freedman, S., Jackson, R., Mooney, J., et al. (1999). Seeking social justice: A teacher education faculty's self-study. *Leadership in Education, 2*(3), 229–253.

de Lange, N., Mitchell, C., & Stuart, J. (Eds.). (2007). *Putting people in the picture: Visual methodologies for social change*. Amsterdam: Sense.

Department of Education, South Africa. (2000). *The HIV/AIDS emergency: Guidelines for educators*. Pretoria: Government Press.

Edwards, E. (2002). Material beings: Objecthood and ethnographic photographs. *Visual Studies, 17*(1), 67–75.

Edwards, E., & Hart, J. (2004). Introduction: Photographs as objects. In E. Edwards & J. Hart (Eds.), *Photographs, objects, histories: On the materiality of images* (pp. 1–15). New York: Routledge.

Eisner, E. W. (1998). *The enlightened eye: Qualitative inquiry and the enhancement of educational practice*. Upper Saddle River, NJ: Prentice Hall.

Faber, P. (Ed.). (2003). *Group portrait South Africa: Nine family histories*. Cape Town: Kwela Books.

Fullan, M. (2001). *The new meaning of educational change*. (3rd ed.). New York: Teachers College Press.

Gore, J. M. (1993). *The struggle for pedagogies*. London: Routledge.

Greene, M. (1977). Toward wide-awakeness: An argument for the arts and humanities in education. *Teachers College Record, 79*(1), 119–125.

Griffiths, M., Poursanidou, D., Simms, M., & Windle, J. (2006). Defining workspaces; defining ourselves. In L. M. Fitzgerald, M. L. Heston, & D. L. Tidwell (Eds.), *Collaboration and community: Pushing boundaries through self-study. Proceedings of the Sixth International Conference on the Self-Study of Teacher Education Practices, Herstmonceux Castle, East Sussex, England* (pp. 288–289). Cedar Falls, IA: University of Northern Iowa.

Hargreaves, A., Earl, L., Moore, S., & Manning, S. (2001). *Learning to change: Teaching beyond subjects and standards*. San Francisco: Jossey-Bass.

Higher Education HIV/AIDS Programme. (2004). *HIV and AIDS audit: Intervening in South African higher education 2003–2004*. Pretoria: The South African Universities Vice-chancellors Association Higher Education HIV/AIDS Programme (HEAIDS).

Hirsch, M. (1997). *Family frames: Photography, narrative and postmemory*. Cambridge, MA: Harvard University Press.

Holland, P., & Spence, J. (Eds.). (1991). *Family snaps: The meaning of domestic photography*. London: Virago.

Hooks, B. (1995). *Art on my mind: Visual politics*. New York: New Press.

Human Rights Watch. (2001, March). *Scared at school: Sexual violence against girls in South African schools*. Human Rights Watch. Retrieved February 9, 2005, from http://www.hrw.org/reports/2001/safrica/

Kuhn, A. (1995). *Family secrets: Acts of memory and imagination*. London: Verso.

LaBoskey, V. K. (2004). The methodology of self-study and its theoretical underpinnings. In J. J. Loughran, M. L. Hamilton, V. K. LaBoskey, & T. Russell (Eds.), *International handbook of self-study of teaching and teacher education practices* (pp. 817–869). Dordrecht: Kluwer.

Langford, M. (2000). *Suspended conversations: The afterlife of memory in photographic albums*.Montreal: McGill-Queen's Press.

Lee, A., & Pultz, J. (2004). *Diane Arbus: Family albums*. New Haven, CT: Yale University Press.

Loughran, J., & Northfield, J. (1998). A framework for the development of self-study practice. In M. L. Hamilton, S. Pinnegar, T. Russell, J. Loughran, & V. K. LaBoskey (Eds.), *Reconceptualizing teaching practice: Self-study in teacher education* (pp. 7–18). London: Falmer.

Mak, M., Mitchell, C., & Stuart, J. (2005). *Our photos, our videos, our stories* [Video documentary]. Montreal: Taffeta Productions.

Mitchell, C., & Allnutt, S. (2008). Working with photographs as objects and things: Social documentary as a new materialism. In G. Knowles & A. Cole (Eds.), *Handbook of the arts in qualitative research: Perspectives, methodologies, examples and issues* (pp. 251–263). London: Sage.

Mitchell, C., de Lange, N., Moletsane, L., Stuart, J., & Buthelezi, T. (2005). The face of HIV and AIDS in rural South Africa: A case for photo-voice. *Qualitative Research in Psychology, 2*(3), 257–270.

Mitchell, C., de Lange, N., & Thuy, X. (2008). Let's just not leave this problem: Exploring inclusive education in rural South Africa.*Prospects*, 1573–9090.

Mitchell, C., Kusner, C., & Charbonneau-Gowdy, P. (2004). Seeing for ourselves: When classroom teachers make documentary films. *Changing English, 11*(2), 279–289.

Mitchell, C., & Weber, S.J. (1998). Picture this! Class line-ups, vernacular portraits and lasting impressions of school. In J. Prosser (Ed.), *Image-based research: A sourcebook for qualitative researchers* (pp. 197–213). London: Falmer.

Mitchell, C., & Weber, S. (1999). *Reinventing ourselves as teachers: Beyond nostalgia.* London: Falmer.

Nelson Mandela Foundation. (2005). *Emerging voices: A report on education in South African rural communities* (Researched for the Nelson Mandela Foundation by the Human Sciences Research Council, with the Education Policy Consortium). Cape Town: Human Sciences Research Council Press.

Norstrom, A. (2004). Making a journey: The Tupper scrapbooks and the travel they describe. In E. Edwards & J. Hart (Eds.), *Photographs objects histories: On the materiality of images* (pp. 81–95). London: Routledge.

Park, E., Mitchell, C., & de Lange, N. (2007). Working with digital archives: Photovoice and meta-analysis in the context of HIV & AIDS. In N. de Lange, C. Mitchell, & J. Stuart (Eds.), *Putting people in the picture: Visual methodologies for social change* (pp. 163–172). Amsterdam: Sense.

Park, Eun G., Mitchell, C., & de Lange, Naydene. (2008). Social Uses of Digitization within the Context of HIV and AIDS: Metadata as Engagement. *Online Information Review, 32*(6), 716–725.

Pettifor, A. E., Rees, H. V., Steffenson, A., Hlongwa-Madikizela, L., McPhail, C., Vermakk, K., et al. (2004). *HIV and sexual behaviour among young South Africans: A national survey of 15–24 year olds.* Johannesburg: Reproductive Health Research Unit, University of the Witwatersrand.

Pithouse, K. (2007). *Learning through teaching: A narrative self-study of a novice teacher educator.* Unpublished doctoral thesis, University of KwaZulu-Natal, Durban, South Africa.

Pithouse, K., & Mitchell, C. (2007). Looking into change: Studying participant engagement in photovoice projects. In N. de Lange, C. Mitchell, & J. Stuart (Eds.), *Putting people in the picture: Visual methodologies for social change* (pp.141–151). Amsterdam: Sense.

Ruby, J. (2000). *Picturing culture: Explorations of film and anthropology.* Chicago: University of Chicago Press.

Shisana, O., Peltzer, K., Zungu-Dirwayi, N., & Louw, J. (Eds.). (2005). *The health of our educators: A focus on HIV/AIDS in South African public schools.* Cape Town: Human Sciences Research Council Press.

South African Human Rights Commission. (2008a). *Report of the public hearing on school-based violence.* Johannesburg: Author.

South African Human Rights Commission. (2008b). *Human rights development report.* Johannesburg: Author.

Spence, J. (1988). *Putting myself in the picture: A political, personal and photographic autobiography.*Seattle, WA: The Real Comet Press.

Spence, J. (1995). *Cultural sniping: The art of transgression.* London: Routledge.

Spence, J., & Holland, P. (Eds.). (1991). *Family snaps: The meanings of domestic photography.* London: Virago.

Spence. J., & Solomon, J. (Eds.). (1995). *What can a woman do with a camera?* London: Scarlet.

Sternfield, J. (1996). *On this site: Landscape in memoriam.* San Francisco: Chronicle Books.

St. John-Ward, M. I. (2008) *Enhancing second language learning: Exploring a visual approach to working with the bedroom culture of pre-adolescent girls*. Unpublished MEd thesis, University of KwaZulu-Natal, Durban, South Africa.

Sultan, L., & Mandel, M. (2005). *Evidence*. New York: D.A.P.

Vass, J. (2008). The impact of HIV/AIDS. In A. Kraak & K. Press (Eds.), *Human resources development review 2008: Education, employment and skills in South Africa* (pp. 90–110). Cape Town: Human Sciences Research Council Press.

Wang, C. (1999). Photo-voice: A participatory action research strategy applied to women's health. *Journal of Women's Health, 8*, 85–192.

Weber, S. J. (2005). The pedagogy of shoes: Clothing and the body in self-study. In C. Mitchell, S. Weber, & K. O'Reilly-Scanlon (Eds.), *Just who do we think we are? Arts-based methodologies for self-study* (pp. 13–21). London: RoutledgeFalmer.

Weber, S. (2008). Visual images in research. In J. G. Knowles & A. L. Cole (Eds.), *Handbook of the arts in qualitative research* (pp. 41–53). Thousand Oaks, CA: Sage.

Weber, S., & Mitchell, C. (1995). *"That's funny, you don't look like a teacher:" Interrogating images and identity in popular culture*. London: Falmer.

Weber, S. J., & Mitchell, C. A. (2004). Visual artistic modes of representation for self-study. In J. J. Loughran, M. L. Hamilton, V. K. LaBoskey, & T. Russell (Eds.), *International handbook of self-study of teaching and teacher education practices* (pp. 979–1037). Dordrecht: Kluwer.

Weber, S. & Mitchell, C. (2007). Imaging, keyboarding, and posting identities: Young people and new media technologies. In D. Buckingham (Ed.), *Youth, identity, and digital media* (pp. 25–48). Cambridge, MA: MIT Press.

Weiser, J. (1993). *Phototherapy techniques*. New York: Jossey-Bass.

Whitehead, J. (2004). Can I communicate the educational influence of my embodied values, in self-studies of my own education, in the education of others and in the education of social formations, in a way that contributes to a scholarship of educational enquiry? In D. L. Tidwell, L. M. Fitzgerald, & M. L. Heston (Eds.), *Risking the journey of self-study in a diverse world. Proceedings of the Fifth International Conference on the Self-Study of Teacher Education Practices, Herstmonceux Castle, East Sussex, England* (pp. 276–278). Cedar Falls, IA: University of Northern Iowa.

Willis, D. (Ed.). (1994). *Picturing us: African American identity in photography*. New York: New Press.

Zeichner, K. (2003). The adequacies and inadequacies of three current strategies to recruit, prepare, and retain the best teachers for all students. *Teachers College Record, 105*(3), 490–519.

Making Meaning of Practice through Visual Metaphor

Deborah Tidwell and Mary P. Manke

The use of metaphor in the form of a visual representation of practice grew out of our initial interest in examining our work as administrators through the use of nodal moments (Tidwell, 2006). This approach focuses on particular moments in time that are perceived as significant occurrences. We are both administrators in teacher education, with different responsibilities for our administrative work but with similar interests in the self-study of that work. Mary serves as associate dean in the College of Education at her university. Deb serves as coordinator for her division of Literacy Education and co-director of the reading clinic in the College of Education at her university. Deb's administrative duties are only a part of her work as an associate professor in the Department of Curriculum and Instruction. In our previous self-study research, we have both used forms of visual representation to examine practice, whether through photography (Allender & Manke, 2002; Manke & Allender, 2006) or through illustrative drawings (Tidwell, 2002; Tidwell & Fitzgerald, 2004; Tidwell & Tincu, 2004; Tidwell, 2006). Our decision to draw illustrative nodal moments as data for our self-study grew out of Mary's work in the use of artifacts as a method for self-study (Allender & Manke, 2002; Manke & Allender, 2006) combined with Deb's work in the use of nodal moments for examining student knowledge (Tidwell & Tincu, 2004) and for self-study of her own practice (Tidwell, 2002; Tidwell & Fitzgerald, 2004; Tidwell, 2006).

We began this self-study with very different experiences both in administrative work and in the use of illustrations to study practice. Deb had worked with nodal moments as visual data in her own self-study research about her teaching and in her instructional work with students enrolled in her courses on the assessment of literacy. She approached our study with confidence and comfort in using illustrated nodal moments as data to examine her own practice and as someone comfortable with doodling and drawing. What was new for Deb was using nodal moments in a less structured setting and in partnership with a colleague who was also using illustrated nodal moments in self-study practice. Mary came to this self-study with

D. Tidwell (✉)
University of Northern Iowa, 618 Schindler Education Center, Cedar Falls, IA 50614-0606, USA
e-mail: deborah.tidwell@uni.edu

D.L. Tidwell et al. (eds.), *Research Methods for the Self-study of Practice*,
Self-Study of Teaching and Teacher Education Practices 9,
DOI 10.1007/978-1-4020-9514-6_9, © Springer Science+Business Media B.V. 2009

confidence in the visual image as a reflective symbol/representation for examining meaning. However, as she states in her reflective journal, Mary was less comfortable with the idea of actually drawing, "When you see the drawings you will know that it is not that I am an artist" (March 16, 2006). Mary probably would not have entered into this project if it had not been for Natalie Goldberg, author of *Writing Down the Bones* (1986) and *Living Color* (1997), who took up drawing as a Zen practice even though she could not draw. Reading Goldberg's books and looking at her drawings of corners of her rooms, Mary thought, "I could probably draw like that." Underneath was a thought, "as badly as that . . . ." So Mary created a folder of drawings of the corners of the rooms she lives in, and thus she was made bold enough to give this project a try. At the start, Mary only half-believed what Deb said about the insight-creating power of drawing nodal moments in one's practice.

The Emergence of Metaphoric Representations

To begin our self-study, we decided to meet to discuss how we would use nodal moments in studying our practice. In mid-May 2005, we met face-to-face to consider what we meant by nodal moments and by self-study, and how we might begin the process. We agreed to use the nodal moment format Deb had used with her students to begin our study. In this way, each of us would highlight a key moment in our work that we found important and draw a concrete representation of that moment, ideally rich with context. We would then scan the drawing and send it electronically to each other along with a written description of the moment. Because we lived about 5 hours apart, we had planned to conduct most of this collaboration over the Internet and by phone. But this initial face-to-face meeting had been so helpful in getting our ideas out and in planning our study, we agreed to meet in person again, about every 2 months, to discuss our work. Between times we would converse electronically.

As we started our work with nodal moments, we focused on the question, "How do specific nodal moments in our administrative practice influence our work and our administrative lives?" Typically, when Deb has used nodal moments in the past, the drawings of those moments were fairly concrete representing what was happening within a particular context. Our initial plan was to be concrete in our drawings of our nodal moments as well. But from the start, our first drawings did not reflect concrete representations of nodal moments, but rather they reflected what appeared to be a broader archetype of similar critical events in our practice (M. L. Heston, personal communication, September 16, 2008). What we found ourselves drawing and using for our initial discussions were visual representations that, while focused on what each of us perceived as an important critical event in our professional work, actually resonated with similar moments across time and space. In essence, when we began drawing, we actually created an archetypal image of an event that seemed familiar to our practice. As we thought about and discussed those initial drawn moments, we realized that we were naturally moving toward metaphoric representations. We then made the decision to continue drawing our nodal moments metaphorically rather than try to force ourselves to focus on 'being concrete.' Our research question evolved to reflect this change: "How can we better understand our administrative work and our administrative lives through metaphoric representations?" We still considered our research as focusing on nodal moments in our practice, but how we defined nodal moment in this context was broader, encompassing an archetypal representation of similar nodal moments over time.

We created our drawings from reflections on our administrative practice. What we found ourselves reflecting upon were moments that intrigued us and that we found important to our administrative work. The metaphoric drawings from these key moments became the artifacts for our self-study. We used these nodal moment artifacts as the catalyst for discussions about our administrative work through which we were able to connect the actions within our practice with the known and with the unknown (Schön, 1987). We found that by using these illustrative metaphors of archetypal nodal moments, we were able to make sense of our various administrative experiences, especially those that seemed particularly challenging. Through the interpretation of these experiences the meaning then became the learning (Mezirow, 1990).

Lakoff and Núñez (2000), in their work with metaphor in mathematics and learning, suggest that the creation of metaphors supports and makes possible the process of abstract thinking. It can be argued, then, that the creation of metaphors can be an effective tool for examining the more complex and possibly abstract meanings embedded within our own practice. Additional support for our use of metaphor comes from the work of other self-study researchers who have used metaphor to represent their own practices in various ways. Some self-study researchers (e.g., Magee, 2008; Pritchard & Mountain, 2004) have used key terminology as metaphoric representation that helps describe their practice and their self-study process. Researchers (e.g., Aubusson, 2004; Linzey, 1998; Miller, East, Fitzgerald, Heston, & Veenstra, 2002) have used metaphor in their self-studies as data for discussing and explaining practice. Other self-study researchers have used metaphor in their descriptive titles of research to reflect the meaning within their research experience, such as "When Professionals Divorce: Who Keeps the Dog?" (Gassman, 2008), "Walking Through the Rose Bush Thicket" (Austin, 1998), "Through a Murky Mirror" (Freidus, 2002), and "Herding Cats and Nailing Jello: Reflections on Becoming a Dean" (Mills, 2002).

In Aubusson's (2004) self-study research, he saw the use of metaphor as a method for eliciting his own and preservice teachers' beliefs and understandings of teaching approaches. He provided a strong argument for the use of metaphor for understanding practice, describing metaphors as analogies in which an implied comparison is contained within a figure of speech. Our research builds on this use of metaphor to understand and explain practice. In addition to self-study research using metaphor, we drew upon the literature from visual literacy (Goldsmith, 1987; Graber, 1990; Levie, 1987; Stonehill, 1998; Waddell, McDaniel, & Einstein, 1988), the nature of metaphor (Lakoff & Johnson, 1980; Lakoff & Turner, 1989), reflective practice (Campoy, 2005; Henderson, 2001; Schön, 1987), and the more specific genre of self-study research (Bullough & Pinnegar, 2001; Loughran, Hamilton, LaBoskey, & Russell, 2004; McNiff, Lomax, & Whitehead, 1996; Tidwell & Fitzgerald, 2004; Whitehead, 2000).

In the following sections of this chapter, we will describe the process by which we both learned and grew as administrators, and developed and tested a research tool that we call 'metaphoric representation.' We used drawings and collaborative dialogue to understand and conceptualize our administrative work. We used metaphoric representations as a tool for understanding the meaning of a particular moment in our practice, as an effective means to elicit reflection on practice, and as a frame for our self-study research. Through our development of metaphors to represent our practice, we learned how to repeatedly consider each metaphoric representation and to extract from it contextually based understandings which came to inform our practice. We will describe the recursive reflective process that developed and the changes this process generated in our practices over time.

How We Made Meaning from Our Drawings

Drawing what Deb referred to as "moments in time that mattered in our work" was more complex than we expected. For Deb, moving from her structured teaching setting to her administrative work was initially difficult. In her previous work with nodal moments, the familiar context of teaching provided a focus for thinking about specific actions and interactions with students in her class. Studying her administrative work was new and her focus was less clear. What stymied her was the lack of an established framework from which to draw. She could choose among many contexts and actions. "For me, the greatest initial struggle was just trying to determine where to focus, what would be the context, and where I should begin" (Tidwell, Manke, Allender, Pinnegar, & Hamilton, 2006, p. 258). To get started, Deb used a doodle she had created at a faculty meeting. While this moment did not depict her immediate administrative work, it did depict the effects of a typical meeting, where her attention span breaks easily, she feels trapped, and the faculty (and her faculties) are slowly being smothered by the contents of the meeting (see Fig. 1). Without fully recognizing what she was doing, Deb introduced the use of metaphor in this very first drawing.

Here are some of Deb's comments about her first drawing, sent June 2005,

This was a picture I drew at a faculty meeting as I was "in training" to be the coordinator for my division. The official coordinator was still in charge, but I also attended meetings and was involved in the decision making process and the planning. I wanted to use this picture because the issues addressed are still issues I have with meetings and administrative work. Not sure where to go with this. What are your thoughts?

In this drawing, Deb had represented herself within several different aspects of a meeting: As someone boxed in and trapped inside the meeting, as someone straining to make the meeting move forward while time seemed to slowly drag out, and as body components (of herself and others attending the meeting) being crushed by

Fig. 1 Deb's nodal moment drawing #1

the meeting's content. She saw this requirement of her administrative duties to meet more often across her work week as a real issue in her practice. It prompted her initial thinking and discussion about how she balances what she considered her real job as an associate professor with administrative duties.

Like Deb, Mary had similar problems in finding nodal moments in the many facets of her administrative work. Her first nodal moment focused on her interactions with a particular faculty member. She wanted to represent a recurring pattern in her administrative work, one that she found frustrating and perplexing (see Fig. 2).

Fig. 2 Mary's nodal moment
drawing #1

Mary reflected on this drawing in June 2005,

This drawing represents moments when somebody goes on the attack, I'm drawing a particular somebody here. But fortunately, my drawing skills are such that he would never recognize himself.

But it's not just a gender thing. This happens with women too. The situation is what's constant. I have put work and thought into a problem, I've taken some action steps, I feel pretty confident that what I'm doing makes sense. And I certainly could, in the right environment, explain what I'm doing and why.

But instead, typically in a meeting with several people there, someone does this really aggressive thing that I represent as Gr-rrr-r! In the case of the guy I drew, it IS a loud voice as well as an aggressive manner, and making claims that this is his decision and I (or the Dean's Office, meaning me) should let him make it. But in the past it's happened with someone who didn't raise her voice, but stated her (erroneous, I really think) views with such certainty that I couldn't respond – the same as when Professor G-rrr-r went after me.

I have to admit that these experiences (and there have been more than the two I'm referring to, with the same people and a few others) have led me to formulate strong arguments and explanations that I have later been able to pull out and use effectively. But I hate that frozen feeling. . . .

Both of us had been struggling to find a foothold to begin our self-study, and these initial drawings were critical in helping us begin the conversation. We understood the power of professional dialogue in accessing the epistemological dimensions of our work, helping us to make the connections between ourselves and what is known (Guilfoyle, Hamilton, Pinnegar, & Placier, 2004), and we used our drawings as the impetus to begin these dialogic exchanges. After sharing our first two attempts, we focused on developing a usable and meaningful process for analyzing our drawings. In an email discussion of our first two nodal moments, Deb responded to Mary's drawings and comments with some suggested patterns:

> (July 2005) . . . *I looked at what you had drawn and discussed, and then I looked at what I had drawn and discussed, and it seems like there are possibly three themes or areas we could continue to discuss as women who are administrators:*
>
> *(1) The existence of aggression from individuals we "administer" in our roles as administrators.*
> *(2) This feeling of "too much" that you expressed in your second nodal moment and that I expressed in my second nodal moment as well. This could be a really interesting discussion/interaction/interdoodle(!) on this dynamic.*
> *(3) Meetings – especially the ones that you have obligations to attend and the dynamics that happen with these kinds of meetings. I don't know if this is a real issue for you, since you talked about having the choice not to attend meetings you think are not of interest to you. I don't have that choice, and sometimes the meetings are my nemesis. Might be interesting to discuss.*
>
> *What do you think about these ideas/themes/foci?*

Deb's comments provided specific and concrete topics to discuss, as if she were trying to find one specific area of administrative practice on which to center our study. Her focus on concrete specifics was very much like her original framework for nodal moments: Examining specific moments in time, and representing those moments concretely in drawing and writing. But these concrete suggestions for topics on which to focus our drawings and discussion went nowhere. We recognized that our process was not 'covering topics' but one of 'seeking meaning.' We began to understand how a drawing of the moment (concrete representation) was not as useful as a drawing about the moment (metaphoric representation). This realization changed what we meant by the term nodal moment. It was at this point in our study that we shifted our understanding of nodal moment from a concrete-specific time frame to a broader context of an archetype encompassing several moments over time. In our exchange of ideas about what our first nodal moments represented to us, we discovered the power of the archetypal nodal moment as depicting something that had meaning for our practice. We agreed that we should continue in this vein, creating metaphoric representations of what we found important in our practice. An integral part of this endeavor was the constant exchange of ideas and reactions to our drawings and their meanings. These interactions reaffirmed the value of talking and sharing about practice, thus making meaning through social construction (Berger & Luckmann, 1990; Palincsar, 1998). We also learned that questioning one another about our drawings helped us to extract more meaning from them. We asked questions like, "Why did you represent it that way?" and discovered more in our drawings than we knew was there. Since our first drawings had inspired such shifts in our understanding of nodal moments, we decided it was time to meet again, face-to-face, to continue our discussions that began electronically. At this second meeting, we looked at each other's drawings again, each explaining the actions depicted, both discussing what the drawings meant to each of us now, and exploring how these drawings related to our administrative work.

Our plans to meet regularly both electronically and in person helped to create an accountability (Miles & Huberman, 1994) that assisted us in both completing drawings and in thinking about and writing about our creations. We each drew a second nodal moment and sent them to each other. Our electronic exchanges of drawings and texts continued across 6 months, with each of us sharing a drawing about once a month. We also met two more times (August and October) face-to-face to evaluate our progress and to discuss our drawings, the meanings within the drawings, and the understandings that evolved from them.

As our drawings developed over time, we found ourselves more and more comfortable with the process of drawing metaphorically about our professional lives. Deb found it very helpful to have Mary as an audience for her drawing. When she drew, her initial purpose was to capture what was real for herself in her own practice. At the same time, knowing that the metaphoric drawing and her reflection on that drawing would be shared with Mary, Deb made a concerted effort to think through her reflection more fully so that her own understanding of the moment would come alive for Mary as well. As Mary described it, Deb wanted her to understand Deb's 'self-as-administrator.' Mary continued to find the act of drawing a real challenge and was helped to stay with the process by Deb's interest in the meanings derived from the drawings. Mary was also intrigued by her own interest in the new learning these drawings were providing for her.

In Mary's second drawing, she drew herself in front of a bulletin board with a list of tasks and goals related to her work (Fig. 3).

In July 2005, Mary wrote to Deb about her drawing:

> *This drawing was cued by Deb's June drawing – and represented a bulleting board I don't actually have, though the lists and the meetings and the feelings are very real. There are few things on my list that I don't value and want to do. My first dean always had a bunch of tasks she wanted me to do that were her agenda, not mine. But with this dean that happens rarely.*
>
> *I don't have to go to many meetings that I don't think are important – which is good because I have a hard time behaving in a truly boring meeting (boring meaning I have no interest in what is going on).*
>
> *Most of the stuff I need to read (and it turns out that reading is a BIG part of my job) is definitely interesting. But I often feel that it's just TOO MUCH. I feel sliced and diced. Where I'd like to feel like faceted glass, I feel like shattered glass – sometimes even like the little chunks of glass you find on the floor if your car window gets broken. I don't need to have just one goal, but ten or twelve would be nice. And with the hours that there are in a life the lists are just too long!*

We were both surprised by the understandings and knowledge about our work that came out of this process. Deb better understood her hesitancy about being in an administrative position. It was not that she was unable to do the work, it was that she did not find the administrative work of professional value. In fact, she saw her administrative demands as taking away from her real work as a professor. Unlike Mary, Deb administers as a service more than as a professional choice. She is not a full-time administrator and does not perceive herself as one. Mary *is* a full-time

Fig. 3 Mary's nodal moment drawing #2

administrator and approaches the work in a completely different light. This came as a realization for Deb in writing about Mary's second drawing:

> *After reading your comments associated with your nodal moment #2, a statement you made helped me to rethink my own administrative work: "There are few things on my lists that I don't value and want to do." I began to realize that I perceived my administrative work as ancillary to my real work, as controlling me, as taking over my time and my energies, and I viewed myself as having little or no control over the demands of the work. ... My administrative work is only part of my workload at the university, where I was asked by the department to become involved in some administrative duties in order to help facilitate the running of the programs in our department. ... I didn't perceive this administrative work as part of what I "liked" to do, but rather what I had to do. From this stance, any tasks became burdensome to my real work as an associate professor. But "... few things ... that I don't value and want to do..." really struck home for me. Have I really looked at what I value as my administrative work? Is there value in what I do? I sketched out the overall components of my three administrative areas. In the process of sketching these components I realized that I do actually value all of them as important to the success of the clinic or the division or of the America Reads program. This was a big change in how I viewed my interactions with this part of my job. In essence, I felt the control of the administrative work shifted from an outside pressure on me to an inner sense of management. Very different perspective.*

This inner sense of management was an epiphany for Deb in this self-study. It was a turning point as well in her understanding of what she perceived as her professional work. She realized she did not really want to be an administrator, nor to continue with administrative work as an integral part of her career. This was a big change in how she approached administrative duties. She saw them as important to the successful running of a program, and as necessary for a program to function, but she also saw them as not a part of her interests in developing her long-range professional goals.

As the metaphoric representations took shape, they deepened our conversations about our practice and what it meant to us. In Fig. 4, Mary found herself using metaphoric representation to portray conflicts and questions of which she was essentially unaware. The drawing grew out of a feeling or sense that she had so much to do and so much to keep track of that being an administrator was like walking on a tightrope, balancing herself across the demands of her work. It was not until she wrote about the drawing for Deb that she began to grasp the meaning of what she had drawn. In our discussions we found that this was true for both of us: Meaning was generated by the creation of the drawings and uncovered through our electronic and face-to-face discussions.

In August 2005, Mary created the drawing (Fig. 4) and wrote to Deb about the insights that the drawing had generated:

> *Presto, I'm a tightrope walker, carrying a long pole that should help me balance. I hope so, because there's a hole in the safety net below. My feelings here are related to the ones I drew in July. With a job so big I can't even remember all parts of it at one time, I sometimes feel unsure that I'll be able to do everything there is to do well enough to stay on the rope. So the fear of falling is always with me, someplace in my mind.*

Fig. 4 Mary's nodal moment #5

Looking at this drawing, I see that the balance pole I need to hold in my hands to keep from falling is also keeping my hands from doing their work. So I think I could do more and better if I weren't worrying about not doing. I notice that something I like about Friday and Saturday night is that if I wake up in the night with my mind racing I have the time to turn on the light, read for a while, and sleep later in the morning. With meetings starting early most work mornings, and emails to answer before I go to the first meeting – I have to discipline myself to turn over and play the mind games that let me stop fussing and go earback to sleep. Then, just sleeping becomes a form of work ....

These early reflections on this drawing were concentrated on the negative aspects of the drawing, but at a later point in the process, Mary developed a different point of view (discussed later in the chapter). This development of changed responses to each of our drawings was a hallmark of our reflective self-study process.

After Deb's first drawing of the dynamics within a meeting (Fig. 1), she began creating drawings that focused more on her work as the coordinator of her division. In her second nodal moment drawing, Deb represented herself as a juggler trying to juggle the roles of an administrator with those of a teacher and a researcher. In her third drawing of a talking bulletin board, Deb focused more narrowly on the dynamics she addressed within her administrative work. By the fourth drawing, Deb singled out a specific responsibility as the coordinator, that of developing the division's schedule of course offerings, represented as a metaphor of running the gantlet of all the distractions and interruptions that she negotiated in the process. The cumulative effect of these four drawings were the understandings she gained about her administrative work, which led to the fifth drawing seen in Fig. 5.

Fig. 5 Deb's nodal moment drawing #5

In September 2005, Deb drew herself as a weight lifter and wrote this reflection to Mary:

Learning to let it go .... It's difficult for me to know when to do something myself and when to delegate. It helps to keep reflecting on my role as the coordinator of the division. I keep asking myself, What is my role? This has become a particularly interesting question as our dean (now in his third year at the university) has a strong commitment to democracy in education. His interest in the democratic process and in establishing our laboratory school as a First Amendment School (the only one of the 21 in the country that is associated with a teacher education program) has sparked some interesting conversations in the hallways and in division meetings about the process of democracy in the running of our university. Traditionally we have had a very top-down model of administration. Not only was this a model at the institution, but it was also the way I handled most tasks given to me – get it done and move on.

This nodal moment is about changing my role from the do-bee, the weight lifter, to the "delegator." This change in my role came out of my reflections on "What is my role as the coordinator?" coupled with discussions with colleagues about the dean's interests in education and democracy and with our (Mary's and my) discussions/stories about our administrative work. What was amazing to me about this moment is that my colleagues in the division were more than willing to volunteer to take a piece of the work.

What came out of this weight lifting metaphor for Deb was a clear understanding of her management style and the realization that delegating to others served her need to reduce her work load, the faculty's willingness to participate, and the dean's expressed interest in a more participatory and democratic style for the college. Deb believes she would not have reached this understanding without the metaphoric representation that revealed her to herself.

Mary sees the analysis of archetypal nodal moments as providing her with a self-description of her work as an administrator through her re-reflection on these moments. These depictions of her work could not have been created without the mental processes that drawing metaphoric representations evoked for her. In March 2006, Mary took the recursive process of analysis a step further by revisiting the drawings she created from June 2005 to November 2005. She reflected upon them as a collection of drawn memories and gained additional insights into the meanings they represent in studying her administrator-self. In the texts that follow, Mary highlights her re-reflections on three of her original nodal moments (the metaphoric representation of Professor G-r-r-r, the metaphor of a tightrope walker, and her metaphoric representation of herself as a spider) and provides a summation of those reflections on her practice.

Mary's first reflection on her Professor G-r-r-r (Fig. 2) took place in June 2005. In March 2006 she returned the drawing and wrote:

I'm still working with Professor G-rrr-r, and I'm interested to observe the amount of change that has taken place in this relationship. Not that he has changed, but the frozen feeling has melted away over the winter. He can snarl at me all he wants, and I just keep doing what I'm doing. Can this possibly be the result of Nodal Moments therapy? Am I experiencing the outcomes of self-study in a new way? I'm thinking I didn't believe it could change me for the better... What I want to start observing is whether this change is confined to Professor G-rrr-r, or is more widespread in my administrative life.

Again, in March 2006, Mary returned to the tightrope metaphor (Fig. 4). She wrote,

> *This one has stayed with me since last September. I often think these thoughts resentfully as I exercise that 2 am discipline so I can go back to sleep. What happened to considering letting go of the balance pole and stepping confidently across the rope, ignoring the hole in the safety net? Who needs a safety net anyway? Could I fly across if I let go?*

In October 2005, Mary created a metaphor using a fat spider resting in the middle of her web. She reflected on her pleasure in the many connections she makes in her job between and for teachers, students, faculty, and other administrators. In March 2006, she wrote,

> *There seems to be less to say about a drawing that represents a positive aspect of my self-as-administrator. But I think I may be perceiving part of the power of the drawings here. If I were keeping a written journal and wanted to return to the reflection [described above], I'd have to search for it in pages of text. But the nodal moments can be flipped through easily, and bring alive the thought and the mood that produced them. . . . So I'd say that the drawings have the capacity to hold a positive memory – and keep me away from my tendency to focus on what I didn't get done. . .*

As Mary completed her March reflections, she commented,

> *Writing these March reflections as a group, instead of one at a time, naturally encourages me to make connections among them. I see that three times I focused on the stress caused by over-commitment in my job. Each time I've found some cause for optimism in my drawing, but I keep returning to the stress. In June, I wrote about another kind of stress – one that occurs less often. Twice I wrote about positive aspects of my work as an administrator. What I'm finding interesting as I sum this up is that one reason I've stayed away from journal writing – that is, the free-writing, put the pen down and keep writing until the bell rings kind of journal writing – for a while now is that I feel that it drags me down, feeds the tendency to focus on what's not going well in my life. So you might think that the same thing has happened with the nodal moments. But that's not how it feels to me as I write. The richness of the drawings, and what appears to be an inability to make a drawing that says only what I want it to say, has preserved in each one of them at least two points of view. One is the stress or the happiness – the other is a flip side to that. It might be making connections that lead to new possibilities, or it might be reflecting on how the positive moments (like the spiderly satisfaction with the web and the glow of having done something that pleases both me and others) do make their own contribution to the stress. . . .*

Mary looked back at an earlier question that came up during our discussions about using nodal moments and written reflections in this self-study, "Why drawings, then, when words would do?" It turns out that Mary is finding that Deb is right about the value of the drawing process. Mary knows from periods of journal keeping what kinds of insights she gets from writing, and she has realized that using metaphoric representations is definitely different. So, although Mary's depiction of self-as-administrator is really a word portrait, the sketches for that portrait are real sketches. And it is these sketches that she finds so powerful in making sense of the meanings within her practice.

What We have Learned from Using Metaphoric Representation

The use of nodal moments drawn as metaphoric representations of archetypal moments in our practice was a powerful tool for both of us in studying our administrative work. Each of us gained insights into who we are as administrators, how we work with others, and how the role of administrator impacts our lives. From these insights we have been able to make meaningful decisions about our professional work both for the immediate and for the long term.

For Mary, the metaphoric representation process we carried out together led to some significant changes in her practices as a full-time administrator. In the following text, Mary speaks to the impact of this self-study on her practice: As I drew myself and represented what my practice looked like, I came to insights that were significant for me – and used them to make changes. When I saw myself cowed by Professor G-r-r-r, I was able to recognize what was happening in such interactions, and make a conscious effort to feel and act more courageously. When I drew the pleasure I felt in using my position to make connections, I became more attentive to opportunities to do so, and do so more often. And when I saw that my anxiety about my over-crowded schedule was keeping me from trying new possibilities, I was able to spend less time feeling overwhelmed and more time doing what I want to do (in my job and elsewhere). This process of creating visual metaphoric representations, reflecting on them over time, and sharing my reflections with a colleague with similar interests led to real changes in my practice and improved the quality of my professional work. The outcomes were similar to the kinds of outcomes I had previously experienced in self-study of my teaching practices.

Like Mary, Deb also saw change in her practice stemming from her interactions with the visual texts she had created and through her conversations with Mary about the meanings within the metaphors. What follows are Deb's reflections upon the changes that occurred in her professional work as she engaged in metaphoric nodal moments: For me, the process of drawing was cathartic, in a sense, as I like to draw. But the real power in the drawing came from writing about the metaphoric representation. I think the writing after the drawing, before discussing the drawing with Mary, really helped me think about context and meaning. The most profound change that grew out of this process was my realization that administrative work, while important as a function of facilitating programs and supporting the needs of the larger institution, was not professionally fulfilling for me; and more importantly, administrative work did not need to be a part of my professional life long term. This realization changed my perspective toward and my engagement with the administrative demands that were asked of me as coordinator of a program, while also changing the context of the coordinator role in my professional life. Through the process of creating and discussing metaphoric representations, I was better able to examine the different contexts of my work as well as the interactions within those contexts. Through my discussions with Mary I was able to deconstruct those metaphors into meaningful insights that led to practical change. Following the year of our research into metaphoric representations about our administrative work, I made the conscious decision to step down from the role of coordinator for my program. I do not think

I would have been able to do so without the insights I gained from the process. Ironically, 2 years later I am now back in the role of coordinator, but from a very different perspective. I view this administrative work as facilitating our program and as ancillary to my professional work as teacher and researcher.

The power of this recursive process of reflection was in the uncovering of multiple layers. This reflective process helped us to more deeply understand our practice. We found that as we revisited our drawings over time, we unfolded new layers of meaning and saw how the act of making and reflecting on the drawings had changed our practice. We discovered that reflecting in thought and in conversation, or even in writing, lacked the power of a metaphoric drawing as a basis for our reflection. When we returned to our drawings, we returned to the moment in which they were made which revealed for us new understandings about the metaphors and thus about our practice.

Suggestions for Self-Study Using Metaphoric Representations

In working with metaphor we realized the process was as important as the metaphor itself. This process can be seen as twofold: The process for the actual development of a metaphoric representation, and the process for analyzing that representation to better understand practice. The following are suggestions for engaging in both of these processes.

Suggestions on How to Develop a Metaphoric Representation

We started with each of us thinking about an experience that we found significant in our practice, and we created a simple drawing from that experience focusing on how that particular experience spoke to us. We allowed the drawing to represent both the event and how we felt about the event. The idea was not to ask "What metaphor would help me understand what is happening in my practice?" But instead, the self-study began when we thought about something that was happening in our professional work and represented those dynamics visually. This put less pressure on us to be clever and metaphoric. We could then focus on being in the meaning behind the moment. We think it is a good idea to create several metaphoric representations over a period of time. In the process of drawing metaphoric representations, a particular issue would arise that had been on our mind and a drawing related to that issue emerged. We found that once some salient issue has been represented, other issues are likely to arise as well.

Mary was initially uncomfortable about drawing. A source that was helpful to her in realizing how she might begin drawing was a guide that Deb has put together for her reluctant students to help them draw simple characters with expression (see Tidwell, 2006). In addition, Mary was encouraged to draw from reading Goldberg's work (1986, 1997) where she uses illustrations in connections with writing and thinking about writing. Bottom line, the metaphors are not about drawing but are about expressing the dynamics and meaning within our practice. The more we focused on the meaning-making process the less concerned we were about how well we drew.

Suggestions on How to Analyze a Metaphoric Representation

Reflections are essential to the analysis of metaphoric representations. We found that the inclusion of written reflections about the drawings was quite helpful in making sense of the metaphors depicted. We also returned to these reflections to help us think about and discuss the meanings within the metaphoric representations. We shared our reflections and our drawings with each other through email, phone and face-to-face meetings. When we met, we recorded our discussions in summary notes. These notes were very helpful as a document of what we had said and as a source for thinking about those discussions after the meeting. The process of creating multiple layers of reflection on our metaphoric representations helped us generate deeper and deeper understandings of our practice. Because we were far apart, we relied on email and phone for much of our interactions. When we emailed each other our scanned drawings and our written reflections, we gave ourselves approximately 2 weeks to study our partner's drawing and to read through her reflections on that drawing. Having an electronic version of our drawings and reflections also helped make the data more accessible. We responded to each other with comments, questions, and queries about what we understood about each other's metaphors. These responses to our drawings helped us to see our metaphoric representations through a different perspective. We used our partner's comments and question prompts to push us further in our thinking about our practice. Using these comments and questions, we would re-reflect upon our own drawing and writing, then email our partner additional insights and comments about our metaphors. This recursive reflective process really helped us think about the meaning within our metaphoric representations.

Mary took the recursive nature of this reflective process a step further and returned later to her metaphors and the reflections we had shared. Her re-reflection of these earlier metaphoric representations occurred several months after creating and reflecting upon the drawings. She found her reflections conducted after the initial study were very helpful in eliciting additional insights, in discovering thoughts that may have been left out, and in providing a greater understanding about the meaning within the metaphoric representations.

In the future, when we do this again, we have some changes we are considering in our process for analyzing metaphorical representations. We found our summary notes of our meetings not only adequate but very helpful. However, we realize being able to capture the exact wording of our conversations through digital or tape recording would be useful in documenting our discussions. We found the face-to-face meetings important; yet because we live 5 hours apart we were not able to meet more frequently. We are considering the use of podcasting on the Internet to facilitate more opportunities for virtual face-to-face meetings.

We found that when both of us were using this metaphoric representation process as our method to self-study, we became less self-conscious about sharing our reflections and about responding to one another. In fact, we found our concern about the quality of our drawing became a moot point as the writing and discussions moved the drawings to a different plane – to a position of informative data emerging from a meaningful metaphoric context. Each of us had different issues concerning our practice, and each of us had different outcomes from this self-study experience. Yet we feel that we would not have reached the outcomes that changed our practice without our interactive process of discussing, reflecting, revisiting, and re-reflecting upon our data. As in self-study of teaching practices, we found that studying our administrative practices collaboratively opened our minds to new ideas and to new ways of thinking about our practice. We are convinced that the value of this process is multiplied through involving one or more collaborators. Neither of us believes that we could have experienced the knowledge building and practical change resulting from this process if we had worked alone.

References

Allender, J. S., & Manke, M. (2002). Reflecting and refracting self-study artifacts: Jazz poetry. In C. Kosnik, A. Samaras, & A. Freese (Eds.), *Making a difference in teacher education through self-study. Proceedings of the Fourth International Conference on Self-Study of Teacher Education Practices, Herstmonceux Castle, East Sussex, England* (Vol. 1, pp. 15–19). Toronto, Canada: OISE, University of Toronto.

Aubusson, P. (2004). Reflecting on and with metaphor in teacher education. In D. L.Tidwell, L. M. Fitzgerald, & M. L. Heston (Eds.), *Journeys of hope: Risking self-study in a diverse world. Proceedings of the Fifth International Conference on Self-Study of Teacher Education Practices, Herstmonceux Castle, East Sussex, England* (pp. 28–31). Cedar Falls: University of Northern Iowa.

Austin, T. (1998). Walking through the rose bush thicket: Self assessment by preservice teachers. In A. L. Cole & S. Finley (Eds.), *Conversations in community. Proceedings of the Second International Conference on Self-Study of Teacher Education Practices, Herstmonceux Castle, East Sussex, England* (pp. 98–100). Kingston, Ontario: Queen's University.

Berger, P. L., & Luckmann, T. (1990). *The social construction of reality: A treatise in the sociology of knowledge.*New York: Anchor Books.

Bullough, R. V., Jr., & Pinnegar, S. (2001). Guidelines for quality in autobiographical forms of self-study research. *Educational Researcher, 30*(3), 13–21.

Campoy, R. W. (2005). *Case study analysis in the classroom: Becoming a reflective teacher.* Thousand Oaks, CA: Sage.

Freidus, H. (2002). Through a murky mirror: Self study of a program in reading and literacy. In C. Kosnik, A. Freese, & A. P. Samaras (Eds.), *Making a difference in teacher education through self-study. Proceedings of the Fourth International Conference on Self-Study of Teacher Education Practices, Herstmonceux Castle, East Sussex, England* (Vol. 1, pp. 87–91). Toronto, Canada: OISE, University of Toronto.

Gassman, G. (2008). When professionals divorce: Who keeps the dog? In M. L. Heston, D. L. Tidwell, K. K. East, & L. M. Fitzgerald (Eds.), *Pathways to change in teacher education: Dialogue, diversity and self-study. Proceedings of the Seventh International Conference on Self-Study of Teacher Education Practices, Herstmonceux Castle, East Sussex, England* (pp. 139–142). Cedar Falls: University of Northern Iowa.

Goldsmith, E. (1987). The analysis of illustration in theory and practice. In H. Houghton & D. A. Willows (Eds.), *The psychology of illustration: Instructional issues* (Vol. 2, pp. 53–85). New York: Springer-Verlag.

Goldberg, N. (1986). *Writing down the bones: Freeing the writer within.* Boston: Shambhala.

Goldberg, N. (1997). *Living color: A writer paints her world.* New York: Bantam.

Graber, D. A. (1990). Seeing is remembering: How visuals contribute to learning from television news. *Journal of Communication, 40*(3), 134–155.

Guilfoyle, K., Hamilton, M. L., Pinnegar, S., & Placier, P. (2004). The epistemological dimensions and dynamics of professional dialogue in self-study. In J. J. Loughran, M. L. Hamilton, V. K. LaBoskey, & T. Russell (Eds.), *International handbook of self-study of teaching and teacher education practices*(pp. 1109–1168). Dordrecht: Kluwer.

Henderson, J. G. (2001). *Reflective teaching: Professional artistry through inquiry.* Upper Saddle River, NJ: Merrill.

Lakoff, G., & Johnson, M. (1980). *Metaphors we live by.* Chicago: University of Chicago Press.

Lakoff, G., & Núñez, R. E. (2000). *Where mathematics comes from: How the embodied mind brings mathematics into being.* New York: Basic Books.

Lakoff, G., & Turner, M. (1989). *More than cool reason: A field guide to poetic metaphor.* Chicago: University of Chicago Press.

Levie, W. H. (1987). Research on pictures: A guide to the literature. In D. A. Houghton & E. M. Willows (Eds.), *The psychology of illustration: Instructional issues* (Vol. 2, pp. 1–50). New York: Springer-Verlag.

Linzey, T. (1998). Life on the icefloe: A metaphor for studying change in the teacher's model. In A. L. Cole & S. Finley (Eds.), *Conversations in community. Proceedings of the Second International Conference on Self-Study of Teacher Education Practices, Herstmonceux Castle, East Sussex, England* (pp. 167–172). Kingston, Ontario: Queen's University.

Loughran, J. J., Hamilton, M. L., LaBoskey, V. K., & Russell, T. (Eds.). (2004). *International handbook of self-study of teacher education practices.* Dordrecht: Kluwer.

Magee, D. (2008). I am the airplane: The use of metaphor as a nodal moment. In M. L. Heston, D. L. Tidwell, K. K. East, & L. M. Fitzgerald (Eds.), *Pathways to change in teacher education: Dialogue, diversity and self-study. Proceedings of the Seventh International Conference on Self-Study of Teacher Education Practices, Herstmonceux Castle, East Sussex, England* (pp. 222–225). Cedar Falls: University of Northern Iowa.

Manke, M. P., & Allender, J. S. (2006). Revealing the diverse self in self-study: The analysis of artifacts. In D. L. Tidwell & L. M. Fitzgerald (Eds.), *Self-study and diversity* (pp. 249–265). Rotterdam: Sense.

McNiff, J., Lomax, P., & Whitehead, J. (1996). *You and your action research project.* London: Routledge.

Mezirow, J. (1990). Conclusion: Toward transformative learning and emancipatory education. In J. Mezirow & Associates (Eds.), *Fostering critical reflection in adulthood: A guide to transformative and emancipatory learning* (pp. 354–376). San Francisco, CA: Jossey-Bass.

Miles, M. B., & Huberman, A. M. (1994). *Qualitative Data Analysis: An expanded sourcebook.* Thousand Oaks CA: Sage.

Miller, C., East, K., Fitzgerald, L., Heston, M. L., & Veenstra, T. (2002). Visions of self in the act of teaching: Using personal metaphors in collaborative study of teaching practices. *Teaching and Learning: The Journal of Natural Inquiry, 16,* 81–93.

Mills, G. (2002). Herding cats and nailing jello: Reflections on becoming a dean. In C. Kosnik, A. Freese, & A. P. Samaras (Eds.), *Making a difference in teacher education through self-study. Proceedings of the Fourth International Conference on Self-Study of Teacher Education Practices, Herstmonceux Castle, East Sussex, England* (Vol. 2, pp. 72–73). Toronto, Canada: OISE, University of Toronto.

Palincsar, A. S. (1998). Social constructivist perspectives on teaching and learning. *Annual Review of Psychology, 49,* 345–375.

Pritchard, P., & Mountain, A. (2004). Woodstock to hip hop: Convergent lifelines and the teaching journey. In D. L. Tidwell, L. M. Fitzgerald, & M. L. Heston (Eds.), *Journeys of hope: Risking self-study in a diverse world. Proceedings of the Fifth International Conference on Self-Study of Teacher Education Practices, Herstmonceux Castle, East Sussex, England* (pp. 206–209). Cedar Falls: University of Northern Iowa.

Schön, D. A. (1987). *Educating the reflective practitioner: Toward a new design for teaching and learning in the professions.* San Francisco: Jossey-Bass.

Stonehill, B. (1998). *What is visual literacy?* Retrieved March 28, 2006, from http://www. pomona.edu/visual-lit/intro/html

Tidwell, D. (2002). On stage: The efficacy and theatrics of large group instruction. In C. Kosnik, A. Freese, & A. P. Samaras (Eds.), *Making a difference in teacher education through self-study. Proceedings of the Fourth International Conference on Self-Study of Teacher Education Practices, Herstmonceux Castle, East Sussex, England* (Vol. 2, pp. 111–116). Toronto, Canada: OISE, University of Toronto.

Tidwell, D. (2006). Nodal moments as a context for meaning. In D. L. Tidwell & L. M. Fitzgerald (Eds.), *Self-study and diversity* (pp. 267–285). Rotterdam: Sense.

Tidwell, D., & Fitzgerald, L. (2004). Self-study as teaching. In J. J. Loughran, M L. Hamilton, V. K. LaBoskey, & T. Russell (Eds.), *International handbook of self-study of teacher education practices* (pp. 69–102). Dordrecht: Kluwer.

Tidwell, D., Manke, M., Allender, J., Pinnegar, S., & Hamilton, M. L. (2006). Contexts for using illustrative nodal moments in self-study. In L. M. Fitzgerald, M. L. Heston, & D. L. Tidwell (Eds.), *Collaboration and community: Pushing boundaries through self-study. Proceedings of the Fifth International Conference on Self-Study of Teacher Education Practices, Herstmonceux Castle, East Sussex, England* (pp. 257–262). Cedar Falls: University of Northern Iowa.

Tidwell, D., & Tincu, M. (2004). Doodle you know what I mean? Illustrative nodal moments as a context for meaning. In D. L. Tidwell, L. M. Fitzgerald, & M. L. Heston (Eds.), *Journeys of hope: Risking self-study in a diverse world. Proceedings of the Fifth International Conference on Self-Study of Teacher Education Practices, Herstmonceux Castle, East Sussex, England* (pp. 241–245). Cedar Falls: University of Northern Iowa.

Waddell, P., McDaniel, M., & Einstein, G. (1988). Illustrations as adjuncts to prose: A text-appropriate processing approach. *Journal of Educational Psychology, 80*(4), 457–464.

Whitehead, J. (2000). How do I improve my practice? Creating and legitimating an epistemology of practice. *Reflective Practice, 1*(1), 9–14.

Creating Representations: Using Collage in Self-study

Mary Lynn Hamilton and Stefinee Pinnegar

Our Context

As scholars from very different places and experiences, we have known each other for a long time. Mary Lynn grew up on the East Coast not far from New York City. Her teacher preparation occurred in an alternative but university-based program in the urban southwestern United States where she began her teaching in secondary social studies. Stefinee grew up and was educated in the rural Southwest. She completed a traditional teacher education program in English education at a small college and then began teaching on a Navajo reservation. After finishing her master's degree in English at a large private religious institution, she taught several more years in the rural Midwest. We met at the University of Arizona where we began doctoral programs in the college of education at about the same time. Stefinee focused on educational psychology and Mary Lynn's work focused more on the foundations of education, particularly cultural anthropology. Because both of us were interested in teacher education and we shared professors, we have similar beliefs about educational preparation, as well as similar notions of collaboration and community.

We, along with our colleagues Karen Guilfoyle and Peggy Placier (the 'Arizona Group'), began as new professors at the same time, and in the torrent of academia, we provide shelter when needed or a good push if appropriate. We encourage each other to stand outside the expectations of that academic world to look with unshaded eyes at the traditions that might blind us. Across time we have developed ways to challenge ourselves, each other, and colleagues in an examination of academic life and theoretical perspectives using representations beyond traditional writing. These alternative visual/tactile artistic representations of our world provide nonverbal conduits to our written work and propelled our written work beyond

M.L. Hamilton (✉)
University of Kansas, 1122 W. Campus Road, Joseph R. Pearson Hall, University of Kansas, Lawrence, KS 66045
e-mail: hamilton@ku.edu

D.L. Tidwell et al. (eds.), *Research Methods for the Self-study of Practice*,
Self-Study of Teaching and Teacher Education Practices 9,
DOI 10.1007/978-1-4020-9514-6_10, © Springer Science+Business Media B.V. 2009

conventional expectations. Throughout this process, we have created a collaborative team and developed a strong community of support within the self-study of teacher education practices research group.

The Development of our Approach

In 1994, we (Arizona Group, 1994a) presented a piece entitled, *A chorus of voices: Studying the cycles of teaching in academia*, on behalf of the Arizona Group at the Third World Congress on Action Research at Bath University in the United Kingdom. Originally, since all four of us were planning to attend we anticipated that each of us would represent the ways in which the overarching cycles we had identified in our research project played out in particular ways in our own settings (Arizona Group, 1994b). Thus, within our presentations we planned to capture the value of the particular and local while simultaneously capturing what had seemed common across contexts. Soon after the group had written the piece for the proceedings and sent it off, it became apparent that Karen and Peggy would not be attending.

As we contemplated presenting the work of the full Arizona Group, we decided we wanted a way to make visible the contexts in which we worked in terms of our experience in the academy, our roles as teacher educators and our teaching, our students, and our institutions. We wanted a way to physically carry all of us to the World Congress and as simultaneously as possible to make visible to our audience the common and unique themes of our experience. We wanted whatever we chose to represent ourselves to make clear our individual and particular voices and yet also make visible the commonalities across contexts.

It was at this moment that our first foray into collage began. Since Peggy and Karen would not be attending, they each made short videos of themselves in their spaces which presented their understanding of their experience in academia within their context. We developed collages that communicated similar themes. Thus, our first use of collage as a research tool was one which emerged as a strategy for representation rather than explicitly as a tool for research or data analysis. We constructed individual collages that captured our institutional contexts, our relationships with faculty and students, our teacher education contexts, and our experience, and presented them simultaneously with video accounts Peggy and Karen provided. Our collages made visible our individual contexts allowing our audience to examine both particularly and generally the themes being explored.

Three things surprised us in this process: (1) how helpful the construction and presentation of the collages were for deepening our understanding of our own contexts and experience; (2) how power collages were in giving us an emotional, intellectual, and holistic sense of each other's particular experiences; and (3) how much more clarity and texture collages provided for interpreting and exploring the commonalities across our contexts. Consequently, we became interested in our selection of materials, images, and texts in terms of the magazines we chose to cut apart and our strategies for selecting particular items. We were interested in the decisions we made about what might be included in the collage (i.e., the complete set of pages, images, and words we ripped and cut from printed materials), and the decisions we made in the final selection of the materials we actually used in our collages. The winnowing processes we used and the relationship between the ways in which the materials we selected for the final collages were influenced by and representative of the larger collection of pictures, words, and colors we did not include seemed to echo our strategies for data analysis. We were interested in our sometimes similar but often distinct processes of layout, gluing, rebuilding, covering over, and returning to pictures discarded, and our careful reasoning concerning the retaining and discarding of collected materials. We were interested in placement and construction. Finally we were interested in the textured nature of the final representation and the ways the texture made visible things that previously had been hidden from our thinking. We felt that our collages provided representations of both the interpretative and analytic cycles of research and data analysis and were metaphorically similar to an archeological excavation.

In creating these representations of our individual contexts, we became particularly interested in the ways in which building the collages drew on the same strategies of analysis and interpretation that we had used in qualitative data analysis in other research efforts. In reconsidering our experiences in order to represent them in a collage, we made visible the intuitive and tacit knowledge that guided us in data analysis, data interpretation, and data representation. In other words, as we reflectively selected or glued down one image or selection of text rather than another, we were made aware of how we had come to ideas that during the interpretation process had seemed almost instinctive. Examining the juxtaposition of images or pieces of the collage as we constructed it made us aware of things we knew in our bodies but which we may not previously have raised to a conscious level in our interpretations of our experience. Both the process and the final product revealed our interpretive and experiential selves to ourselves. In the aftermath of this work, we felt that the collage experience had sharpened and refined our research skills in terms of design, analysis, and representation. We puzzled about this. As a result, in 2000, we gave a session at The Third International Conference on Self-Study of Teacher Education Practices (also known as the 'Castle Conference') in which we presented new collages as a strategy for more systematically exploring the relationship between collage and the research processes of data collection, analysis, and representation.

We began our work for the Castle Conference presentation by posing research prompts to guide our development of our new collages, returning first to those prompts which had guided our task in 1994: What is our context in terms of our teaching, research, and citizenship within our particular teacher education program? How does the context constrain and facilitate our experiences as teachers, citizens, and researchers? How do our private or personal and public lives intersect within this context? We brought both the earlier and more recent collages to the conference, and during our session, we interrogated each other about the use of collage and its relationship to our research. We questioned the relationships (commonalities and differences) between our production of the collage and research design, enactment, analysis, and representation both in terms of our earlier constructions and these more current examples.

In this experience, we were both surprised by the fact that each of us brought three-dimensional rather than two-dimensional collages. Mary Lynn had constructed triptychs with drastically different frames in which the collage themes not only moved across the surface in very different ways but also hung off the edges. The triptychs were filled with passion and calm, and clarity and confusion, making visible the themes of her experiences within the academy. Stefinee's representation, while similarly complex, was more constrained. She had constructed a series of three nested pyramid-shaped boxes, with the largest box being about 4 in wide and 4 in tall with a square base. The outermost box represented Stefinee's institutional context, the second box, placed just inside the larger box represented her programmatic context, and the smallest box (located inside the middle box) represented her personal/professional context within her university. The outside of each box represented the public aspect of that feature of her context and the inside represented the private aspects of that context. Thus, in constructing the collages she attended to the interrelationships created between the personal representation of her context within the university and her professional experience within the context of her college and program, and the representation of her personal experience in the context of her college and program with her collage of her public persona as an individual faculty member.

In interrogating the processes we used in developing the collages, we became clearer this time about the metaphoric quality of our engagement in research as an enterprise. Our collages challenged the fundamental nature of the relationship of our own knowledge of our experience in academe and the ways in which we positioned ourselves as teachers, citizens, and scholars, particularly in terms of the research we pursued, the questions we asked, and the understandings we had. Through this inquiry into collage as a research tool, we also gained greater clarity about the ways in which research analysis was not just an interior process; our understandings were challenged, pushed, refined, and transformed by the materials we used in the construction process. We were made exquisitely aware of the fundamental interplay between what we bring to the research, the data and artifacts we collect, and what we learn from analysis.

Our experience with collage led to our 2002 AERA presentations on teacher education reform (Arizona Group, 2002). For this meeting, we each chose an image to represent our understanding of teacher reform. We analyzed public and private documents in which either we, our department, our college, our institution, or research on teacher education focused on issues of teacher education reform. Then we each chose an imagistic way to capture our understanding. For example, Stefinee chose an image of the near-enough cabin built without a plan and where precision was abandoned whenever things were 'near enough.' Karen represented her experience as a wolf howling in a wilderness setting with mountains, streams, and other permanent fixtures capturing her sense of aloneness in her thinking about teacher education reform in her own context. Mary Lynn used a variety of maps each capturing teacher educator reform from a different constituency and at a different level. The use of such imagistic tools pushes our thinking into uncomfortable as well as productive places as we explore our practices and the spaces that surround them.

Literature Informing Our Thinking

We find that narrative and exposition often have a strong linearity which seems to be the nature of conveying story or articulating reasoned arguments. As readers, we often seek that structure to aid in the sense-making process. In contrast, collage provides an opportunity to produce an "internalized portrait" of the world based on our experience of it (Davis & Butler-Kisber, 1999, p. 4). Collage (and other art forms like poetry and painting) usually offer some level of nonlinearity that facilitates a simultaneous understanding of person, place, theory, practice, and interior and exterior social relations through deeper, implicit cultural models and imagery (Weber & Mitchell, 2004). Collage forces the viewer and the creator to think beyond the boundaries of tradition and can be seen as symbolic narrative (Jones, 2003).

Generally, art can be used as a way of knowing or a way to capture cultural imagery (Eisner, 1997, 2002). As an art form, collage has been around for some time, including the works of Picasso and others. Recently, researchers have discussed its use as a counterpoint to positivist approaches to and strategies for research (for example, Butler-Kisber, 2002a; Denzin & Lincoln, 2005; Richardson, 2001). It has also been identified with a postmodern epistemology (Vaughan, 2005), one that pushes on the margins and borders of ideas (Harding, 1996). For example, Harding (1996) argued that collage provides ways of valuing multiple understandings of cultures and ways of knowing and presenting that multiplicity simultaneously, thus broadening traditional western perspectives on knowledge(s). Lincoln and Denzin (2005) believe qualitative research has an epistemological basis that actually invites the use of creative forms for the pursuit of important questions, and collage would be one such form, requiring artistic insight but useable by most researchers. For Davis and Butler-Kisber (1999), collage is an important way to enhance analysis and representation in pursuing educational research. The work of Finley (2001; Finley, Cole, Knowles, & Elijah, 1994), Knowles (Knowles & Thomas, 2001, 2002), and Cole (2001) also explore, articulate, and demonstrate the rich textures that art brings to research in terms of making visual the power of multiple perspectives and alternative representations of reality. Finley (2001), in particular, expresses clearly and coherently the interdependency of artistry and scholarship as each informs the other.

Synthesizing images in collage work requires that the artist be open-minded and intuitive (Abbey, 2004; Butler-Kisber, 2002a, 2002b). According to Abbey, many emotional experiences cannot be reduced to words, which can actually distort the meaning of experiences and result in an overgeneralized or insufficient understanding. Words can lack the power to represent subtle variations of meaning, and translating feelings into images rather than words can be less threatening and help make an inner impression more visible and tangible. Thus, Abbey asserts that collage can utilize images to capture simultaneously the unexpressible and the expressible. It can make visible the emotional and intuitive often hidden in more traditional written research accounts.

Stern (2004) argues that implicit knowledge is partially an intuitive understanding of the interrelationships among the nonverbal elements and interactions that contribute so much to our nonconscious understandings of the world and our action and place in it. Thus, the use of collage or other artistic tools as research facilitates scholars' ability to make explicit nonconscious understandings that are present in our interactions with and actions in the world. While not immediately present in our consciousness, such nonconscious understandings are not repressed in the Freudian sense represented by the term the 'unconscious.'

Through collage and other arts-based research, scholars work to foster critical consideration of ideas (Freire, 1998; McDermott, 2002). McDermott (2002) suggests that aesthetic knowledge and collage can be dangerous to those who seek to avoid looking closely at lives in the world. Collage is not simply a glued set of images where an individual artist presents a view. Rather, it is the initiation of a dialogue with self and viewers, inviting the skeptical self as well as audiences to disrupt and de-center traditional understandings. In this way collage allows both the scholar and the audience to break through traditional, bounded ways of knowing, since a collage can visually represent both implicit and explicit understandings. It provides a way to make visible an interior ontology—our internal, sometimes unexpressed, and sometimes intuitive construction of the world from which we act.

More than a way of knowing (epistemology), the creation of collage addresses 'what is' (ontology). As creators select and compose their work, they expose their view of reality. Indeed, in the process of collage making our view of the world, our assumptions about it, and our understanding of it are revealed. The more carefully we as self-study researchers provide coherent, articulate, and comprehensible accounts of our experience and evidence of the things we come to understand, the more likely others are to judge our scholarship trustworthy and accept our research as valuable (Pinnegar & Hamilton, 2006). We assert that research attentive to the anchoring of ontology (what is and our commitment to improving and changing) naturally addresses epistemology (what we know), since epistemology and ontology are inextricably linked. Epistemologically driven research usually centers on the establishment of truth claims. When we engage in this process, we place distance between ourselves and our experience in order to assert knowing and strive to turn our true belief into knowledge. This epistemological focus draws us away from what really engages us in studying practice in order to improve it.

Collage and Ontology

Within self-study research we find three different conversations, among many, important to our own work—dialogue, trust, and ontology. Having previously addressed dialogue and trust (Arizona Group 1997, 2004, 2005; Hamilton & Pinnegar, 2000), collage more clearly centers our attention on ontology.

In constructing collage, we attempt to create accurate, helpful, and visually powerful representations of our understanding. The collage, with its juxtaposition of image and word, provides a visual presentation of our interior representation of our experience and makes visible our interrogation of the research question we are exploring and the understandings we have come to. For example, as we select images and position them against each other, pages of carefully reasoned arguments get transformed into a single instantly visible whole in which we have juxtaposed themes from our review of the research literature, the research question, the process of our research investigation, the assertions for action, the understandings that we reached, and the conclusions we wish to make. Furthermore, the construction of collage requires us to both privilege and de-privilege themes in our research, as we present them individually and holistically within the frame of the collage project. For example, some images get pasted on top of others, some take up more space than others, and some are represented as text in contrast to pictures. Some images are placed front and center while others are pushed to the margins, and others are carried across the whole, emerging as repeated motifs. For example, in Stefinee's first collage representing her institutional context she selected thumbnail portraits of past and present presidents of the institution and leaders of the religion that funds the institution and glued them into a representation of a flame from a pioneer campfire. She placed similar clusters of thumbnail portraits in other spaces in the collage. The portraits selected have personal meaning for Stefinee and represent the theme of entanglement of professional duty and private family life present across the collage.

The finished collage presents a holistic, multilayered, interpretative visual image of what we came to understand—it represents our conception of what is—a visual image of our ontological view of the research question. We believe that a careful articulation of ontology establishes the credibility and trustworthiness of the researcher and, as a result, is a way to establish value in self-study work. We find that when researchers (including ourselves) focus on epistemology, making claims and externally seeking validity, we usually become unproductively enmeshed in discussion and debate about positivistic ideas of validity, objectivity, and generalizability, and the necessity of using such criteria to establish the worthiness of the research. We chose instead to focus on ontology—creating careful, coherent, intriguing, and enlightening accounts of studies of self in relationship to enacting or striving to understand our practice as the site for establishing the value and credibility of our work. This focus allows self-study of practice researchers to embrace their ontological commitment to improving the quality of teacher educators', teachers', and public school students' experiences in education as well as producing quality rigorous and trustworthy research. We have come to understand that a focus on ontology is more productive since "what captures the imagination, the heart and the convictions of the readers and users of educational research is attention to ontology: what is" (Pinnegar & Hamilton, 2006, p. 4).

Processes in Creating Collage

When we construct a collage we begin by developing a prompt to guide the collage we plan to construct. We pose the prompt and then critique it; a given prompt may be too general, too focused, or simply not accurate enough. The tools we use for critique include our consideration of the prompt against the critical and complementary views we read in the literature, whether the prompt is an accurate view of our understanding, and whether it attends appropriately to and could invite alternative interpretations or multiple perspectives. We also invite others to critique our prompt. For example, we pose the prompt to others both in informal conversation and in public forums as statements about teacher education, our experiences as teacher educators, or the process of becoming a teacher or teacher educator. In this way, our attention to developing a prompt that will allow us to uncover 'what is,' is fundamentally guided by dialogue as a process for knowing. When we move to considering construction we use similar strategies to develop our ideas both before and during our creation of alternative representations with color, text, and dimension represented by collage.

Since we have used collage regularly across the past 10 years, we both have extant collections of images and words from printed sources and other materials. However, as we add to and gather new collections we find ourselves engaging in the process in ways that seem similar to how we gather interview data, student assignments, or other kinds of data in response to a research question. We seek out the typical and the exotic, the commonplace and the unique. We seek to make certain that the collection we use will appropriately represent the whole we are attempting to explore.

As we move forward in building the collage, we develop plans for the structure and form of the collage itself—three dimensional, two dimensional, nesting structures, triptychs, movable pieces, and pop-up elements—which will both constrain and provide texture and structure to our interpretations. Again, we explore our plans internally and externally—by articulating the potential form of the project with each other and with others. Then we begin constructing our collage—selecting the text and laying it out against the structure. Thus, the entire process is one in which we reach understanding about an element of our project (prompt, materials, structure, final representation) and then we critique the decision we have arrived at. All of this is a fluid and interactive process much like engaging in a conversation or dialogue with ourselves, our critical self, our colleagues, our materials, and the research literature in teacher education. Thus, we explore the construction and reconstruction of ontology, where we look to see what is, according to our representation, and we think, "That's what I've created. Now, where am I?" From our use of dialogue as a process of coming to know coupled with our ontological focus, we recognize from the beginning that our work is never really finished; a sense of uncertainty accompanies us, as nothing is ever static. However, these strategies provide strength for the assertions for action and understanding we develop. These strategies and others provide depth or thickness to our findings so that we can take action leading us forward in our understandings just as truck lights (Pinnegar & Hamilton, 2008) illuminate the darkness and allow us to move forward through the night.

Variations in Our Personal Collaging Processes

In using collage as a research tool, each of us seems to construct her own process. When we began to describe the use of collages as a research tool, we realized that individually we took similar yet distinct steps. We both begin with a prompt, and then we engage in collection, purposely or randomly ripping from magazines and other printed materials, those words, images, and pages that call to us and that capture our feelings or provide images of our lives. We each have sets of rich collections of these kinds of text materials which we both add to as we begin a new collage as well as across the collage design and construction process. Next, we engage in a process of winnowing the larger set of images and words into a smaller one. We both looked at least partially for eye candy—images that seemed exotic, attention capturing, or viscerally appealing in some way. As we chose something (a word, image, etc.), we would ask ourselves, "How does this represent our notion or give insight into it (in terms of theme, symbol, evidence, definition, etc.)?" We next, or sometimes simultaneously, consider our selection in relationship to the structure, size, and aesthetics of the work, taking into account text, color, dimensionality, and subtlety. This is an iterative process that only ends when the collage is complete. Indeed, sometimes even after we have asserted that the project is done, we may go back and glue new images onto the finished project as a result of reviewing our collage with our skeptical self (see Stern, 2004), critical friends, collaborators, or experts in the area we were pursing in the research.

There is no one way to do this. While both of us spend a long time in collection, different orientations guide that process. For Stefinee, looking for big ideas seems paramount. Her interests in selection center on the understandings she has about the prompt and the relationship of the images to the form in which they will be presented. As she selects, she sorts the pictures in terms of ideas, size and color, surrounding herself with a series of piles. Her first two-dimensional collage was 14 × 17 in, so she was not particularly concerned about the size of the images and focused more on categories like color, ideas, and landscape. In contrast, in her second collage, the set of nested, pyramid-shaped boxes were small (the largest being no more than a 4-in cube) and she found herself continually attending to size. Thus, some large images that were stronger representations of her ideas were kept available as references as she selected smaller images that could together form the larger intact images abandoned because of their size.

As Stefinee sorts, she carries in her head a shifting image of the final construction—building and rebuilding mentally how it will look. She sometimes sorts into piles alternative collages she might construct to fit the form and capture the ideas she wants to express. The images can push her to alter the internal mental representation, sometimes forcing her to abandon whole sets of images because a new image reveals an alternative way of representing an idea or an inaccuracy in her understanding. For Mary Lynn, however, the approach to the work seems far more intuitive. She looks and looks at her collection of materials, relying on her nonconscious knowing from which something (usually) emerges. Thus Mary Lynn allows the collage's content and form to emerge in a spontaneous and reiterative manner directly from the process and materials.

In preparing this chapter, we examined our collages and our written works on teaching, teacher education, and experience in academia in order to determine our progress in using collage and what the contrast between the written and visual texts revealed. As we engaged in this process we came to understand that across our academic careers our writing has captured our experiences complexly; in contrast, we found that our initial collage work depicted our experiences rather simply. For example, Mary Lynn's initial collage had simpler images which were more static and constrained. They lacked the complexity and failed to communicate the emotionality that was so apparent in her later triptychs. One could find idea kernels in the early work but depth of understanding and presentation seemed absent. However, in the triptychs, these idea kernels had become strongly developed themes; the triptychs also more subtly conveyed the nuances of interpretation and experience behind the themes. Further, the rather limited emotionality of the initial collage was greatly expanded as the images in the triptychs exploded and flowed beyond the boundaries of the triptych frame.

Few metaphors and little symbology emerged in our earliest pieces. Although heartfelt, our work could be taken at face value, providing a superficial representation that presented the layers of our experienced and revealed our thinking, but lacked nuance and sophistication. We also found it particularly ironic that the issues of privilege, social justice, and cultural tensions that were especially important in our writings appeared absent in our initial collages.

In our later work, we saw a developing sophistication and symbology. For example, in one later work Stefinee created three-dimensional shapes that figuratively and literally represented her writings and yet invited the audience into a more complex understanding of her particular experience as a teacher educator at her institution and the viewers' understanding of their experience at different institutions. In her most recent collage she used a pop-up technique that allowed her to foreground an image of her professional self in tension with the layered background which contained juxtaposed images of the many dimensions of her professional life and the boundaries and constraints of her professional context. Peeking through were images of her private and personal roles. The smiling larger black and white photocopied image of Stefinee is in startling contrast to the vivid, contradictory, contrasting images that lay in the background.

In our works, the forms of the collage themselves (nested boxes, flexible collage structure, removable elements, pop-up techniques, and triptychs) conveyed cultural and personal perspectives both implicitly and explicitly. With the pictures and images mounted on the form, a complexity of ideas as well as the relationships and tensions among them emerged. The choices of icons and symbols and the placement of the imagery on the form offered views and insights into one person's understandings of academia and invited visceral and intuitive generalization by the viewers to their own experience as teacher educators in different institutional contexts.

We have returned to examine our various collages and collage as a research tool for developing our understanding of self in relationship to practice three times thus far (Arizona Group, 1994a, 2000; Hamilton & Pinnegar 2006). Each time we see a movement toward clarity of purpose, the development of our own thinking about issues, and greater skill in using collage as a research tool. For example, in her most recent collage, Mary Lynn utilized a flexible collage base approach to her background and developed clusters of images of different aspects of her experiences within teacher education, research and teaching at her institution, and in her professional life as a teacher educator. These clusters of images could be removed or repositioned during the actual presentation of the collage to the skeptical self (Stern, 2004), critical friends, and colleagues. This allowed her to construct and reconstruct the collage, removing and adding clusters, and rearranging them on the background to heighten or diminish their interrelationships. The individual clusters represent elements of her life and provide clear yet nuanced and layered images that illustrated particular themes. The flexibility of placement provides clarity about the interactive and relational nature of self-study of practice research and of experience in teacher education. Overall, movement toward clarity with deepened complexity seems to be a part of this process for us as both researchers and teacher educators.

Our different pieces represent both our perspectives and those of the self-study of teacher education practice research community at the time the piece was constructed and yet these pieces also resonate well across time. Our artistic creations have lives of their own, representing the confusion and bewilderment of our early careers and our experience of obfuscation. As we developed as scholars, our growth in understanding about teacher education and self-study research methodology is apparent. What is equally apparent is our increasing sophistication in the use of this tool and our willingness to leave dynamic our understanding of teaching and research. In our artistic choices we attempted to make the familiar strange, and the strange familiar, inviting ourselves, as well as others, to consider alternative constructions of reality and diverse frames of reference.

As we examine our earliest work we see that the questions we had then and the themes that we uncovered continue to be central in our work now. These themes include development of practices, pressures of scholarship, and the tensions found within the academic environment (Arizona Group, 2007). Even though the issues are the same over time, we do not want our earlier works to exclusively represent what we know and understand about these issues and themes. We find that the maturity of our thought about these issues is better presented in our current work, since although the themes are the same, our more current representations have both greater clarity and more depth. Yet, we also recognize the value of these earlier more confused, less sophisticated representations, not just as cultural artifacts, but as representations of the experiences of beginners in our earlier selves. In this way, our early collages continue to provide alternative and multiple perspectives for our current research. Rather than remaining static, our ideas and our representations offer a peek at shifting realities. The series of collages constructed across our careers reveal our growth, and they also reveal a tension between our earlier more naïve and our later more mature understandings which have emerged not out of experience alone but also out of our determination to study that experience and make our understanding public. We would like viewers to understand that, like our other research, our collages make visible our historic development as scholars, thinkers, and artists. What researchers do early in their careers may deal with the same themes and symbols, but as we develop we understand them differently (see Arizona Group, 2007).

Story, narrative, exposition, and text are largely characterized by linearity. Self-study of practice research focuses on uncovering practice, which Stern (2004) reminds us is implicit knowledge and therefore may be better characterized as holistic and simultaneous; we feel implicit experience holistically with its hidden depth and nuances fluttering at the edges of our knowledge. When we attempt to capture practice linguistically, these forms impose linearity on our experience. In contrast, collage avoids linearity because it allows for the existence of both simultaneity and sequentiality. In one holistic moment you can see a life (Merleau-Ponty, 1962).

In the moment of viewing, the collage presents where we are in our perception of an object and its dimensions, even if all the dimensions are not present in the scene. Moreover, even if the collage created is only two dimensional, there is a dimensionality to it, present in the layers and perspectives created by the ways in which images are layered against and over each other. This contrasts with linear texts. The holistic, implicit knowing represented by collage becomes evident when we lay our texts and the collages that represent the same research projects against each other. In our written texts we provide detailed particular analysis and evidence of our understandings and assertions about integrity, social justice, and trustworthiness. In these texts we also identified the influences of philosophical and cultural ideas. When we turn to our collages, we see those issues conveyed differently (in images, holistically, and in relationship) and therefore sometimes more powerfully. Holding an artistic representation against a written text offers a compelling juxtaposition of word and image, making clearer the value of both. The collage provides a new, yet self-created context that encompasses the whole of our experience but is represented as a particular instance. The collage image allows us to see continuity where none may have been apparent in our experience, presents the past and present as a momentary whole, captures relationships that may have been hidden, and presents as themes those fragments that may have remained hidden in the living of our experience.

Learning from seeing involves a process of choice. As creators we look at our work, ask questions, and invite ourselves to question what we see. As viewers we ask questions and invite ourselves to explore answers, perhaps seeing, for a moment, the perspective of ourselves as the creator. Viewing a collage occurs in a zone of inconclusivity and a zone of maximal contact (Bakhtin, 1981) with self where the past, present, and future are simultaneously evident in this present moment and thus are changed. The creator/viewer drops her facade(s). The tacit symbology emerges. The many layers of self (private, public, institutional, academic, etc.) are made visible both in their presence and absence in the collage. As we view the collage, we see our ideas and thus our selves more clearly and distinctly. The audience/viewers catch a glimpse into an other's world and simultaneously become more aware of their own. Learning from seeing is an ongoing process. What we choose by juxtaposing pieces against each other, looking at the edges of things, and questioning (both in the construction and viewing) whether, how, and why those pictures, words, and images work against each other, offers insight into and disruption of our ideas.

Importantly, the question remains as to whether or not the use of alternative representations supports the research of the scholar. From our perspective, the hard work of alternative representations can push ideas forward. Collage makes visible to us gaps in thinking, misinterpretations, superficiality, and confusion; collage also makes visible the complexity, clarity, depth, and coherence of ideas and understanding.

Conclusions

Several insights about our development as scholars, collage as a research tool, and our understanding of self-study of practices research emerged in our examination of our use of collage as a research tool in contrast with our more formal and traditional written accounts. While no easy task, the exploration of our use of collage has allowed us to examine our development as people, as teachers, and as scholars; it has helped us see that the questions of the development of teachers and teacher educators, the constraining experience of life in academia, and our understanding of the study of practice continue to guide our research. We have come to see more clearly what we do know as well as the immensity of the questions we ask. We can examine how our understanding has changed and grown across time, making clear to us that we are indeed different in some ways while much the same in others.

In exploring collage as a research tool, we came to understand the process of developing prompts, gathering and collecting images, winnowing and selecting, and finally constructing collages as interpretations of our experiences. We came to see the power of holistically capturing our understanding at particular places and particular times. We learned that the process for constructing collage is similar and yet each person engages in that process differently and introduces unique features. We saw that both the form of the structure of the collage and the images within the collage push and constrain development and interpretation.

In thinking about collage as a research tool within self-study of teacher education practices methodology, we came to understand how this tool makes visible unique aspects of self-study methodology for us. In addition, this process made clearer and more visible how self-study of teacher education practice research is founded in ontology. As we critiqued our development of collage and reflected on our use of it to capture our experience, we recognized how focusing on ontology rather than epistemology can be vital in establishing the value and determining the quality of self-study of practice research.

Collage offers a worthy research method that can support self-study of teacher education practices researchers in considering possibility, in capturing their understanding, and in learning more about the methodology of this kind of research. As we explored our work in a critically reflexive fashion, we contested our ideas and disputed our purposes as individuals and in collaboration. For us this strengthened our ontological understandings and made explicit our living contradictions. Although cause for considerable internal struggle, use of alternative representations deepens our understandings and perspectives. The hard work of identifying contradictions, culling integrity imbalances, and uncovering weak theoretical links can potentially undermine the strongest scholar. Yet it must be done to best serve as a model for our colleagues and students in the ways to strengthen both our research and our practice.

References

Abbey, S. (2004). "Take your soul to school": Practical applications for holistic classrooms. *Educational Insight, 9*(1). Retrieved on May 30, 2006 from http://www.ccfi.educ.ubc.ca/publications/ingisghts/v0901/articles/abbey.html

Arizona Group: Guilfoyle, K., Hamilton, M. L., Pinnegar, S., & Placier, P. (1994a). A chorus of voices: Studying the cycles of teaching in academia. In J. Whitehead & P. Lomax (Eds.), *Proceedings of World Congress 3 on Action Research: Accounting for Ourselves* (pp. 49–53). Bath, England: University of Bath.

Arizona Group. (1994b). Conversations with distant colleagues: Initiations into the academy. In R. Martin (Ed.), *Transforming the academy: Struggles and strategies for the advancement of women in higher education* (pp. 39–50). Tehachapi, CA: GrayMill.

Arizona Group: Hamilton, M. L., Pinnegar, S., & Guilfoyle, K. (1997). Obligations to unseen children: Struggling to walk our talk in institutions of teacher education. In J. Loughran & T. Russell (Eds.), *Pedagogy for reflective practice: Teaching to teach with purpose and passion* (pp. 183–209). London: Falmer.

Arizona Group: Guilfoyle, K., Hamilton, M. L., Pinnegar, S., & Placier, P. (2000). Myths and legends of teacher education reform in the 1990's: A collaborative self-study of four programs. In J. Loughran & T. Russell (Eds.), *Exploring myths and legends of teacher education. Proceedings of the Third International Conference on Self-Study of Teacher Education Practice, Herstmonceux Castle, East Sussex, England* (pp. 20–24). Kingston, Ontario: Queen's University.

Arizona Group. (2002, April). *Narratives of four teacher educators.* Paper presented at the annual meeting of the American Educational Research Association, New Orleans, LA.

Arizona Group: Guilfoyle, K., Hamilton, M. L., Pinnegar, S., & Placier, P. (2004). The epistemological dimensions and dynamics of professional dialogue in self-study. In J. J. Loughran, M. L. Hamilton, V. K. LaBoskey, & T. L. Russell (Eds.), *International handbook of self-study of teaching and teacher education practices* (pp. 1109–1167). Dordrecht: Kluwer.

Arizona Group: Placier, P., Pinnegar, S., Hamilton, M. L., & Guilfoyle, K. (2005). Exploring the concept of dialogue in the self-study of teaching practices. In C. Kosnik, C. Beck, A. Freese, & A. Samaras (Eds.), *Making a difference in teacher education through self-study* (pp. 51–68). Dordrecht: Kluwer.

Arizona Group: Guilfoyle, K., Hamilton, M. L., Pinnegar, S., & Placier, P. (2007). Reconsidering unanswered questions: Negotiating transitions from graduate student to assistant professor to associate professor. In R. Martin (Ed.), *Transforming the academy: Struggles and strategies for women in higher education* (Vol. II, pp. 53–66). Tehachapi, CA: GrayMill.

Bakhtin, M. M. (1981). Discourse in the novel. In M. Holquist (Ed.), *The dialogic imagination: Four essays by M.M. Bakhtin* (pp. 259–422). Austin: University of Texas Press.

Butler-Kisber, L. (2002a). Artful portrayals in qualitative research. *Alberta Journal of Educational Research, 7,* 229–239.

Butler-Kisber, L. (2002b). School days, school days...: A feminist retrospective. *WILLA, 11,* 25–29.

Cole, A. (2001). The art of research: Arts-informed research. *University of Toronto Bulletin, 11/12/01 19*(7), 16. Retrieved May 31, 2006 from: http://www.news.utoronto.ca/bulletin/ PDF_issues/11-12-01.pdf

Davis, D., & Butler-Kisber, L. (1999, April). *Arts-based representation in qualitative research: Collage as a contextualizing analytic strategy.* Paper presented at the annual meeting of American Educational Research Association, Montreal, Quebec. (ERIC Document Reproduction Services No. ED431790).

Denzin, N. K., & Lincoln, Y. S. (2005). Introduction: The discipline and practice of qualitative research. In N. K. Denzin & Y. S. Lincoln (Eds.), *Handbook of qualitative research* (3rd ed., pp. 1–32). Thousand Oaks, CA: Sage.

Eisner, E. (1997). The promise and perils of alternative forms of data representation. *Educational Researcher, 26*(6), 4–11.

Eisner, E. (2002). *The arts and the creation of mind.* New Haven, CT: Yale University Press.

Finley, S. (2001). Painting life histories. *Journal of Curriculum Theorizing, 17*(2), 13–26.

Finley, S., Cole, A. L., Knowles, J. G., & Elijah, R. (1994, April). *Mindscapes: Reflections of a community of researchers.* Performance presented at annual meeting of the American Educational Research Association, New Orleans, LA.

Friere, P. (1998). *Pedagogy of freedom: Ethics, democracy, and civic courage.* Oxford: Rowan & Littlefield.

Hamilton, M. L., & Pinnegar, S. (2000). On the threshold of a new century: Trustworthiness, integrity, and self-study in teacher education. *Journal of Teacher Education, 51,* 234–240.

Hamilton, M. L., & Pinnegar, S. E. (2006). Alternative representations of collaboration and community. In L. M. Fitzgerald, M. L. Heston, & D. L. Tidwell (Eds.), *Collaboration and community: Pushing boundaries through self-study. Sixth International Conference on Self-Study of Teacher Education Practices. Herstmonceux Castle, East Sussex, England* (pp. 118–122). Cedar Fall, IA: University of Northern Iowa.

Harding, S. (1996). Standpoint epistemology (a feminist version): How social disadvantage creates epistemic advantage. In S. Turner (Ed.), *Social theory and sociology* (pp.146–60). Malden, MA: Blackwell.

Jones, K. (2003). The turn to a narrative knowing of persons: One method explored. *Nursing Times Research, 8*(1), 60–71.

Knowles, J. G., & Thomas, S. (2001). Insights and inspiration from an artist's work: Envisioning and portraying lives-in-context. In A. Cole & J. G. Knowles (Eds.), *Lives in context: The art of life history research* (pp. 208–214). Walnut Creek, CA: AltaMira.

Knowles, J. G., & Thomas, S. (2002). Artistry, inquiry, and sense of place: Secondary school students portrayed in context. In C. Bagley & M. Cancienne (Eds.), *Dancing the data* (pp. 121–132). New York: Peter Lang.

Lincoln, Y. S., & Denzin, N. K. (2005). Epilogue: The eighth and ninth moments: Qualitative research in/and the fractured future. In N. K. Denzin & Y. S. Lincoln (Eds.), *Handbook of qualitative research* (3rd ed., pp. 1115–1126). Thousand Oaks, CA: Sage.

McDermott, M. (2002). Collaging preservice teacher identity. *Teacher Education Quarterly, 29*(4), 53–68.

Merleau-Ponty, M. (1962). *Phenomenology of perception.* London: Routledge & Kegan Paul.

Pinnegar, S., & Hamilton, M. L. (2008, March). *A topography of collaboration: Methodology, identity, and community in self-study research.* Paper presented at the annual meeting of the American Educational Research Association, New York.

Pinnegar, S., & Hamilton, M. L. (2006, April). *Confronting ontology.* Paper presented at the annual meeting of the American Educational Research Association, San Francisco.

Richardson, L. (2001). Writing: A method of inquiry. In N. K. Denzin & Y. S. Lincoln (Eds.), *Handbook of qualitative research* (2nd ed., pp. 923–948). Thousand Oaks, CA: Sage.

Stern, D. N. (2004). *The present moment: In psychotherapy and everyday life*. New York: W. W. Norton.
Vaughan, K. (2005). Pieced together: Collage as an artist's methods for interdisciplinary research. *International Journal of Qualitative Methods*, 4(1), 1–21. Retrieved March 15, 2006 from http://www.ualberta.ca/~iiqm/backissues/4_1/html/vaughan.htm
Weber, S., & Mitchell, C. (2004). Visual artistic modes of representation for self-study. In J. J. Loughran, M. L. Hamilton, V. K. LaBoskey, & T. Russell (Eds.), *International handbook of self-study of teaching and teacher education practices* (pp. 979–1037). Dordrecht: Kluwer.

Part IV
Self-Study on the Impact of Practice on Students

How Do I Influence the Generation of Living Educational Theories for Personal and Social Accountability in Improving Practice? Using a Living Theory Methodology in Improving Educational Practice

Jack Whitehead

The context of this self-study is my working life in Education between 1967 and 2008. Most of that life, between 1973 and 2008, has been lived in the Department of Education of the University of Bath where I am seeking to contribute to a draft Mission of the University in developing a distinct academic approach to the education of professional practitioners. The approach outlined below is focused on the generation of a living theory methodology in exploring the question, How do I influence the generation of living educational theories for personal and social accountability in improving practice? It also includes a new epistemology for educational knowledge from creating living educational theories in inquiries of the kind, How do I improve what I am doing? The living theory research methodology used to address this question emerged during the course of my 40-year inquiry. It draws on multi-media explanations of educational influences in learning to communicate the meanings of the expression of embodied values and life-affirming energy in educational relationships. The chapter emphasizes the importance of the uniqueness of each individual's living educational theory (Whitehead, 1989a) and their methodological inventiveness (Dadds & Hart, 2001) in asking, researching and answering questions of the kind, How do I improve what I am doing?

The Context for the Study

The context for the study is relationally dynamic. What I mean by this is that it has been influenced by changes in the relationships between the economics, politics, ecology and sociocultural and sociohistorical contexts that have affected my work and the evolutionary transformations in my thinking as a school teacher between 1967 and 1973 and later in the University of Bath in the UK as a Lecturer in Education between 1973 and 2008 (Whitehead, 2008). Here is the story of the evolution of a living theory methodology. All individuals can create their own living theory

J. Whitehead (✉)
University of Bath, Department of Education, Bath BA2 7AY, UK
e-mail: edsajw@bath.ac.uk

D.L. Tidwell et al. (eds.), *Research Methods for the Self-study of Practice*,
Self-Study of Teaching and Teacher Education Practices 9,
DOI 10.1007/978-1-4020-9514-6_11, © Springer Science+Business Media B.V. 2009

which explains their educational influence. I am offering a living theory methodology that you might find useful in creating your own.

The beginnings of this major transformation of context occurred in 1971 in terms of my vocation in education. Between 1967, when I began teaching, and 1971, I felt my vocation in terms of enabling my pupils to develop their scientific understandings. My sense of professionalism was focused on my teaching. This began to change with my academic studies of educational theory between 1968 and 1972 for my Academic Diploma in the Philosophy and Psychology of Education and for the Masters Degree in the psychology of education at the Institute of Education of the University of London.

In my special study on my initial teacher education program (on "A Way To Professionalism In Education?") I had written about the importance of a professional knowledge base for education. In my later studies of educational theory between 1968 and 1972 I began to see that the dominant view of educational theory, known as the disciplines approach because it was constituted by the philosophy, psychology, sociology and history of education, was mistaken. The mistake was in thinking that disciplines of education could explain educational influences in learning. The error was not grounded in mistakes in the disciplines of education. The mistake was in the disciplines approach to educational theory. It was in thinking that the disciplines of education, individually or in any combination, could explain an individual's educational influence. My recognition of this mistake in 1972 re-focused my vocation toward the creation and academic legitimation of valid forms of educational theory that could explain the educational influences of individuals in their own learning, in the learning of others and in the learning of the social formations in which we live and work. My move to the University of Bath in 1973 was motivated by this desire to contribute to the creation and legitimation of educational theory.

The explicit acknowledgment of the mistake was stated clearly in 1983 by Paul Hirst, one of the original proponents of the disciplines approach, when he said that much understanding of educational theory will be developed

> in the context of immediate practical experience and will be co-terminous with everyday understanding. In particular, many of its operational principles, both explicit and implicit, will be of their nature generalisations from practical experience and have as their justification the results of individual activities and practices.
>
> In many characterisations of educational theory, my own included, principles justified in this way have until recently been regarded as at best pragmatic maxims having a first crude and superficial justification in practice that in any rationally developed theory would be replaced by principles with more fundamental, theoretical justification. That now seems to me to be a mistake. Rationally defensible practical principles, I suggest, must of their nature stand up to such practical tests and without that are necessarily inadequate. (Hirst, 1983, p. 18)

The scholarly context of my study, in 2008, continues to focus on the creation and legitimation of valid forms of educational theory that can explain the educational influences of individuals in their own learning, in the learning of others and in the learning of the social formations in which we live and work. This contemporary focus on the significance of epistemological transformations in what counts as educational knowledge can be seen in a recent contribution to *Research Intelligence* – a publication of the British Educational Research Association.

> In this brief paper, I want to note the changes that have occurred in how research is carried out, funded, presented and assessed in the time I have been a practitioner-researcher, and the attempts that I have observed to include more diverse perspectives and presentation styles in research. I want to suggest that these changes are indicative of an epistemological transformation in what counts as educational knowledge. (Ferguson, 2008, p. 24)

In acknowledging the influence of the economic context on the study I have held a tenured contract at the University with secure employment from 1973 to the end of the contract in 2009. I do not want to underestimate the importance of this economic security in my capacity to keep open a creative space at the University of Bath to develop my research program. Neither do I want to ignore the influence of individuals and institutional power relations of the political context that required some "persistence in the face of pressure that could have discouraged and therefore constrained a less determined individual" (Whitehead, 1993, p. 94). These are the words used in a report to the University Senate in 1991 from a Working Party established to inquire into *A Matter of Academic Freedom* related to my research. While the words are not my own, they resonate with my experience of working in the University and I believe them to be true. I shall return to this point in the analysis section when I look at the theoretical perspectives that have influenced my analysis of data.

The sociohistorical and sociocultural contexts of my workplace are western and mainly white. These are changing with multi-cultural and postcolonial influences beginning to question the power relations that sustain unjust privileges and the dominant logic and languages that sustain what counts as knowledge in the western academies. I have found the work of Edward Said (1993) most helpful in the evolution of my thinking to include these sociocultural understandings of the power relations that sustain colonial privilege. I have found the work of Eden Charles (2007) on Ubuntu, guiltless recognition and societal reidentification most helpful in understanding how to engage in transformatory educational practices. These practices move beyond the power relations that reproduce social formations and into transformational practices that are living the values of inclusionality. I am also grateful to Yaakub Murray (2008) who first introduced me to the idea of Ubuntu.

In my early work between 1967 and 1973 I used a positivist and propositional view of knowledge from the influence of my first degree in physical science. During the middle period between 1977 and 1999 I extended my epistemological understandings to include dialectics, and since 2003 I have been exploring the implications of an epistemology of inclusionality which has much in common with African, Eastern and other indigenous ways of knowing (Ferguson, 2008). This is not to imply a rejection of all my insights from propositional and dialectical theories. I continue to value insights from these theories as I deepen and extend my understandings of living educational theories and a living theory methodology with the evolution of the implications of asking, researching and answering, How do I improve what I am doing?

The Research Question(s) that Emerged from the Context

The practical question, How do I improve what I am doing? emerged before my awareness of its significance as a research question. I asked the question in my first day as a science teacher in Langdon Park School, a London Comprehensive School in 1967. I felt a passion to help my students to improve their scientific understandings. In my first lessons I could see that my pupils were not comprehending much of what I was saying and doing. However, I did not feel my concern to be grounded in a deficit model of myself. I felt a confidence that while what was going on was not as good as it could be, I would be able to contribute to improvements. My imagination worked to offer possibilities about improving what I was doing. I chose a possibility to act on, acted and evaluated the effectiveness of what I was doing in terms of my communications with my pupils. I know that the idea that individuals experience problems can be seen as working with a deficit model. I think I would feel this myself if other people talked about me as having problems! Yet, I have no problem in acknowledging for myself that there always seems to be something to improve in my practice and in the way the world is organized. I think that this awareness of the importance of improving practices is grounded in a passion to see values of freedom, justice, compassion, respect for persons, love and democracy lived as fully as possible. I find much to celebrate in looking back and appreciating what has been accomplished while recognizing that there is still much to do.

I became aware of the significance of the question, How do I improve what I am doing? as a research question in 1976 as I worked on a local curriculum development project with six teachers in different schools to improve learning for 11- to 14-year-olds in mixed ability science groups. The how in the question was a research question in the sense that it was a methods question, How do I do it? I produced an initial report on the project to explain our learning in terms of the most advanced theories of the day in relation to changes in teaching and learning style, and curriculum innovation and educational evaluation. It was accepted as a 'good' report by academic colleagues and rejected by the teachers with whom I was working. Their main reason for rejecting it was that "we can not see ourselves in it." Following the rejection I reconstructed the report from the original data I had collected with the teachers. I did this with the help of one of the teachers, Paul Hunt. The teachers accepted this second report as a valid account.

I could see that the second report had the action reflection form of expressing concerns when values were not being lived as fully as they could be; imagining ways forward; acting on a chosen way forward; evaluating the influence of the actions in terms of values and understandings; and modifying the concerns, ideas and actions in the light of the evaluations. In the initial report I had used models from the most advanced theories of the day to explain what we were doing. In the reconstructed report I used the values and responses of the participants, including the pupils, to explain what we were doing as well as insights from the theories of the day.

As my research program continued, my question, How do I improve my practice, began to focus on the methodological and epistemological issues of generating valid explanations of educational influences in learning. In 1985 I published my first explanation on how to generate the explanations I call 'living educational theories':

My purpose is to draw your attention to the development of a living form of educational theory. The theory is grounded in the lives of professional educators and their pupils and has the power to integrate within itself the traditional disciplines of education. Educational theory occupies an ambiguous position in the profession of education. Its importance is due to the fact that a profession supports its skills and techniques with a body of systematically produced theory. On the other hand, teachers tend to decry educational theory because of its lack of relationship to their practical skills and techniques.

My purpose in writing this chapter is to outline how I think a professionally credible educational theory could be generated and tested from a form of self-reflective enquiry undertaken by participants in educational contexts in order to improve the rationality and justice of:

(a) their own educational practices,
(b) their understanding of these practices,
(c) the situations in which the practices are carried out.

"It is most empowering when undertaken by participants collaboratively, though it is often undertaken by individuals sometimes in co-operation with 'outsiders' ." (Carr & Kemmis, 1983)

I am assuming that a teacher action-researcher, who is interested in contributing to knowledge of the process of improving education within schools, will be faced by an academic community which will examine the legitimacy of the claim to knowledge. I am also assuming that a teacher-researcher is concerned to establish a direct relationship between the claim to know what he or she is doing and the pupils' educational development.

The educational analysis which follows is focused upon the nature of the validity of an individual action-researcher's claim to know his or her own educational development. The analysis outlines a form of educational theory which can be generated from professional practice and which can integrate the different contributions of the disciplines of education. Let me say at the beginning how I see the relationship between my own research and teacher action-research. In my work in a University I am paid to make scholarly and acknowledged contributions to knowledge of my subject, education. I characterize my attempts to make this contribution a form of academic action-research. In my investigation of my own claims to know my own educational development I have explored the nature of a form of educational theory which is directly related to educational practice. My particular concerns have focused upon the academic legitimacy of an individual's claim to know his or her own educational development. I think that my findings will be of use to those teacher-researchers who wish to justify their own claims to knowledge to the academic community. (Whitehead, 1985, pp. 53–54)

The research questions that emerged from the context of analyzing an individual's claim to know his or her educational development were the following: How can an individual's claim to know his or her educational development be strengthened in terms of its personal and social validity? What are the standards of judgment and the units of appraisal that can be used in evaluating the validity of such claims to educational knowledge? I outline the methodological implications of answering such questions in the next section and distinguish methodology from method.

The most influential paper I have written on living theory was published in 1989 on "Creating Living Educational Theories from Questions of the Kind, 'How do I Improve My Practice?' " (Whitehead, 1989a). This coincided with the publication of my 1988 Presidential Address to the British Educational Research Association on research-based professionalism (Whitehead, 1989b). The significance of the Appendix to this address is that it shows my research supervisions in terms of master's degrees. The first living theory doctorates, and ones I had supervised, were those of Mary Gurney (1988) and Jean McNiff (1989).

> Gurney, M. (1988) *An action enquiry into ways of developing and improving personal and social education.* Unpublished dissertation, University of Bath, England.
>
> McNiff, J. (1989) *An explanation for an individual's educational development through the dialectic of action research.* Unpublished dissertation, University of Bath, England.

By 1999 my question, How do I improve my practice?, was focusing on the use of narrative forms of representation and beginning to integrate visual data from video clips of practice into explanations of educational influence. My questions about explanations of educational influence were also beginning to focus on bringing evidence of my educational influence from the accounts of my students of their learning in our educational relationships. This is perhaps best seen in the publications:

> Whitehead, J. (1999a). Educative relations in a new era. *Pedagogy, Culture & Society, 7*(1), pp. 73–90.

and in my doctorate

> Whitehead, J. (1999b). *How do I improve my practice? Creating a new discipline of educational enquiry.* Unpublished dissertation, University of Bath, England.

The evolution of the meaning of my question, How do I improve my practice?, between 2000 and 2008 can be understood through 16 of my successfully completed supervisions in which I worked to enable doctoral researchers to create and legitimate their living educational theories. The supervisions between 2000 and 2004 stressed the importance of including evidence to justify claims to know the influence of one's own practice in one's own learning and in the learning of others. I think the educational influence of ideas from my research program and my supervision can be seen in the inclusion of "I" or "my" in the titles. The following are research degrees where the majority of the titles include a reference to the self:

> Eames, K. (1995). *How do I, as a teacher and educational action-researcher, describe and explain the nature of my professional knowledge?* Unpublished dissertation, University of Bath, England. Retrieved February 19, 2004 from http://www.actionresearch.net/kevin.shtml
>
> Evans, M. (1995). *An action research enquiry into reflection in action as part of my role as a deputy headteacher.* Unpublished dissertation, Kingston University, England. Retrieved February 19, 2004 from http://www.actionresearch.net/moyra.shtml. Jointly supervised with Pamela Lomax.
>
> Laidlaw, M. (1996). *How can I create my own living educational theory as I offer you an account of my educational development?* Unpublished dissertation, University of Bath, England. Retrieved February 19, 2004 from http://www.actionresearch.net/moira2.shmtl

Holley, E. (1997). *How do I as a teacher-researcher contribute to the development of a living educational theory through an exploration of my values in my professional practice?* Unpublished dissertation, University of Bath, England. Retrieved February 19, 2004 from http://www.actionresearch.net/erica.shtml

D'Arcy, P. (1998). *The Whole Story. . . . .* Unpublished dissertation, University of Bath, England. Retrieved February 19, 2004 from http://www.actionresearch.net/pat.shtml

Loftus, J.(1999). *An action enquiry into the marketing of an established first school in its transition to full primary status.* Unpublished dissertation, Kingston University, England. Retrieved February 19, 2004 from http://www.actionresearch.net/loftus.shmtl. Jointly supervised with Pamela Lomax.

Whitehead, J. (1999b). *How do I improve my practice? Creating a discipline of education through educational enquiry.* Unpublished dissertation, University of Bath, England. Retrieved February 19, 2004 from http://www.actionresearch.net/jack.shtml

Cunningham, B. (1999). *How do I come to know my spirituality as I create my own living educational theory?* Unpublished dissertation, University of Bath, England. Retrieved February 19, 2004 from http://www.actionresearch.net/ben.shtml

In answering my question, How do I influence the generation of living educational theories for personal and social accountability in improving practice?, I would say that my stress on the inclusion of "I" or "my" in the title of doctoral theses has served to highlight the uniqueness of each individual's living theory and his or her use and development of a living theory methodology. Each individual has researched his or her own processes and contexts for improving practice and evolved his or her stories with forms of personal and social accountability. They have also offered their stories freely, as gifts to others through their flow through web-space: Finnegan (2000), Austin (2001), Mead (2001), Bosher (2001), Delong (2002), Scholes-Rhodes (2002), Roberts (2003), Punia (2004).

In 2004 the University of Bath changed its regulations to permit the submission of e-media and my students were among the first to submit under this new regulation. From 2004 most of these included visual narratives with video data of their practice. In addition to the inclusion of visual narratives to communicate the meanings and influences of the expression of embodied values in explanations of educational influence, another evolution in the meaning of my question occurred as I understood Alan Raynor's (2004, 2005) idea of inclusionality. I am thinking here of inclusionality as a relationally dynamic awareness of space and boundaries as connective, reflective and co-creative. I brought this understanding of inclusionality explicitly into my question, How do I improve my practice?, and into the supervisions below while retaining an emphasis on the importance of including "I" and/or "my" as necessary to the research:

Church, M. (2004). *Creating an uncompromised place to belong: Why do I find myself in networks?* Retrieved May 3, 2008 from http://www.actionresearch.net/church.shtml

Hartog, M. (2004). *A self study of a higher education tutor: How can I improve my practice?* Unpublished dissertation, University of Bath, England. Retrieved May 3, 2008 from http://www.actionresearch.net/hartog.shtml

Farren, M. (2005). *How can I create a pedagogy of the unique through a web of betweenness?* Unpublished dissertation, University of Bath, England. Retrieved May 3, 2008 from http://www.actionresearch.net/farren.shtml

Naidoo, M. (2005). *I am because we are. (My never-ending story.) The emergence of a living theory of inclusional and responsive practice.* Unpublished dissertation, University of Bath, England. Retrieved May 3, 2008 from http://www.actionresearch.net/naidoo.shtml

Lohr, E. (2006). *Love at work: What is my lived experience of love and how might I become an instrument of love's purpose?* Unpublished dissertation, University of Bath, England. Retrieved May 3, 2008 from http://www.actionresearch.net/lohr.shtml

Adler-Collins, J. (2007). *Developing an inclusional pedagogy of the unique: How do I clarify, live and explain my educational influences in my learning as I pedagogise my healing nurse curriculum in a Japanese University?* Unpublished dissertation, University of Bath, England. Retrieved May 3, 2008 from http://www.actionresearch.net/jekan.shtml

Charles, E. (2007). *How can I bring Ubuntu as a living standard of judgment into the academy? Moving beyond decolonisation through societal reidentification and guiltless recognition.* Unpublished dissertation, University of Bath, England. Retrieved May 3, 2008 from http://www.actionresearch.net/edenphd.shtml

Spiro, J. (2008). *How I have arrived at a notion of knowledge transformation, through understanding the story of myself as creative writer, creative educator, creative manager, and educational researcher?* Unpublished dissertation, University of Bath, England. Retrieved May 3, 2008 from http://www.actionresearch.net/janespirophd.shtml

The researchers I work with in supervision have all acknowledged my influence over the course of a minimum of 5 years of sustained enquiry to their successful completion of their doctorates. One of the most delightful acknowledgments is at the end of Jane Spiro's thesis with a story about "The Thought Doctor and The Fellow Traveller" (Spiro, 2008, pp. 325–330). Jane's creation of this story and its inclusion in her dissertation reflects back to me the important principle in my methodology of recognizing the creativity and uniqueness of the other.

I too have acknowledged the educational influences of the students whose research programs I have had the privilege and pleasure of supervising. For the award of a doctorate there must be evidence, recognized by the examiners, of originality. This can be expressed as originality of mind or an original contribution to knowledge. I have learned something highly significant for the growth of my own educational knowledge from each doctoral researcher. For example, Moira Laidlaw (1996) pointed out the living nature of the value-laden standards of judgment I was clarifying through action reflection cycles. Up to this point I thought that I was clarifying the standards in the course of their emergence in practice and that the standards were then stable and fixed. I had not appreciated the significance of seeing them as living standards of judgment. Eleanor Lohr (2006) with her focus on *Love at Work* moved my insights to highlight love as a living standard of judgment. In emphasizing the importance of "loving what I am doing" in explaining my educational influences I have been helped by Cho's (2005) insights on the importance of expressing love in educational relationships for knowledge creation. One of the greatest difficulties I encounter in my supervision is in bringing the recognition of others of their talents into their explanations of their educational influence. In my experience many individuals have difficulty in publicly acknowledging their own talents. Yet, without such recognition it is difficult to produce a valid explanation of one's influence. Others can help in developing this public recognition. Moira Laidlaw has been most helpful in providing an understanding of the talents I express in my educational relationships in a narrative of celebration of my 40 years in education (Laidlaw, 2008). Moira distinguishes my listening, enthusiasm, understanding of the student's insights and pushing them further, expression of responsibility as a form of empowerment, timing, values and connectivity. I identify with the narrative form of Moira's account and recognize that I need to bring the talents she recognizes, as being expressed by me, into my own explanations of my influence.

The educational influences from my research supervisions are too long to acknowledge in detail here. Other publications acknowledge this influence (for example, Whitehead, 2005). I would, however, like to highlight some of the most recent influences. Eden Charles (2007) has helped to develop my understanding of Ubuntu as a living and relationally dynamic standard of judgment. Je Kan Adler-Collins (2007) has focused my attention on the creation of a safe learning space, and Jane Spiro (2008) has helped to develop a focus on knowledge transformation with an emphasis on creativity.

Working with the doctoral researchers at the end of their doctoral writings I take great care in making sure that the abstracts of the theses really do say what the researcher feels is their original contribution to knowledge. We focus on the title to make sure that it reflects their primary concerns. I do hope that you will take some time to access these original contributions to knowledge and to appreciate the value of the analyses in explaining their influences. I also hope that you find the analyses of value in evolving your own explanations of your own influence.

Researching the implications of asking and answering the question, How do I improve what I am doing?, has involved the evolution of the following living theory methodology.

The Evolution of the Methodology Over the Course of the Research

A distinction can be made between the uniqueness of each individual's living theory and a living theory methodology that can be used to distinguish a theory as a living theory. It is sometimes useful for researchers to be able to identify paradigmatic ideas that can be used to identify the research as belonging to a particular community of inquiry. In using the idea of a living theory methodology I want to stress that this includes the unique contribution of an individual's methodological inventiveness in the creation of a living theory, rather than referring to some overarching set of principles to which each individual's methodology has to conform, in an impositional sense of the word. There are however distinguishing qualities of a living theory methodology that include "I" as a living contradiction, the use of action reflection cycles, the use of procedures of personal and social validation and the inclusion of a life-affirming energy with values as explanatory principles of educational influence.

Living theory methodology has evolved from my initial focus on an appropriate method for researching the implications of asking the question, How do I improve what I am doing? The distinction I make between method and methodology is that I refer to a method as a single procedure used in the research such as an interview, or a questionnaire, the use of an action reflection cycle and the use of a validation group to strengthen the validity of an account. What I mean by a methodology refers to the theoretical analysis of the methods appropriate to my inquiry, How do I improve what I am doing?

Over the course of my working life in education I have evolved three different sets of principles for my theoretical analysis of the methods I use. These principles are grounded in the three different epistemologies below – propositional, dialectical and inclusional – and each carries their own ontological implications.

Using a Propositional Perspective in a Living Theory Methodology

From a propositional perspective, a living theory methodology can be understood as involving methodological inventiveness, action reflection cycles, narrative inquiry and personal and social validation.

Methodological Inventiveness

A living theory methodology is as unique as an individual's living theory. It emerges in the course of an inquiry of the form, How do I improve what I am doing? There is no predetermined way of answering this question, and the form that the inquiry takes is influenced by the individual's methodological inventiveness, Dadds and Hart (2001) have understood the importance of methodological inventiveness:

> Perhaps the most important new insight for both of us has been awareness that, for some practitioner researchers, creating their own unique way through their research may be as important as their self-chosen research focus. We had understood for many years that substantive choice was fundamental to the motivation and effectiveness of practitioner research (Dadds, 1995); that what practitioners chose to research was important to their sense of engagement and purpose. But we had understood far less well that how practitioners chose to research, and their sense of control over this, could be equally important to their motivation, their sense of identity within the research and their research outcomes. (p. 166)
>
> If our aim is to create conditions that facilitate methodological inventiveness, we need to ensure as far as possible that our pedagogical approaches match the message that we seek to communicate. More important than adhering to any specific methodological approach, be it

that of traditional social science or traditional action research, may be the willingness and courage of practitioners – and those who support them – to create enquiry approaches that enable new, valid understandings to develop; understandings that empower practitioners to improve their work for the beneficiaries in their care. Practitioner research methodologies are with us to serve professional practices. So what genuinely matters are the purposes of practice which the research seeks to serve, and the integrity with which the practitioner researcher makes methodological choices about ways of achieving those purposes. No methodology is, or should be, cast in stone, if we accept that professional intention should be informing research processes, not pre-set ideas about methods of techniques... (p. 169)

One of the methods often used in the development of a living theory methodology is that of action reflection cycles.

Action Reflection Cycles

In my experience those who explore the implications of asking, researching and answering their question of the kind, How do I improve what I am doing?, recognize that they engage in the following process with their own living "I."

I recognize that I am working to improve what I am doing because of the values I use to give meaning and purpose to my life. I think we may be similar in that when we believe that our values are not being lived as fully as they could be, we feel concerned and our imaginations begin to offer possibilities for improving practice. When the conditions permit, I chose one possibility to act on. I act and evaluate the effectiveness of my actions and understandings in relation to the values I use to judge improvements in my practice. If I am still not living my values as fully as I believe to be possible I modify my concerns, actions and evaluations. This systematic process has been recognized by all those I have worked with as something that they too have engaged with implicitly in the process of working to improve what they are doing (McNiff & Whitehead, 2005).

In my own research and my research supervision I stress the importance of producing validated explanations of educational influences in learning. The production of such explanations as contributions to knowledge seems to me to be a characteristic of research. I associate research with knowledge creation. Methods of validation are important in research so that a publicly validated knowledge base can be established. For me this involves both personal and social validation as two of the distinguishing qualities of a living theory methodology.

Personal Validation

I work with Michael Polanyi's (1958) decision that distinguishes personal knowledge. This is a decision to understand the world from my own point of view as an individual claiming originality and exercising judgment responsibly with universal intent. I know that the local identity of my "I" is influenced by the non-local flows of space and energy through the cosmos. Yet I do work with a sense of responsibility for the educational influences I have in my own learning. I do recognize myself as a unique human being with this responsibility and I do exercise a sense of personal responsibility in validating for myself my claims for what I believe to be true. In doing this I take account of responses from a process of social validation.

Social Validation

Since 1976 I have used a process of democratic evaluation, described by Macdonald (1976), together with the four criteria of social validity proposed by Habermas (1976a), to strengthen the personal and social validity of living theories. By this I mean that I submit my explanations of educational influence to a validation group of peers with a request that they help me to strengthen the comprehensibility, truthfulness, rightness and authenticity of the explanation. Within comprehensibility I include the logic of the explanation "as a mode of thought that is appropriate for comprehending the real as rational" (Marcuse, 1964, p. 105). Within truthfulness I include the evidence for justifying the assertions I make in my claims to knowledge. Within rightness I include an awareness of the normative assumptions I am making in the values that inform my claims to knowledge. Within authenticity I include the evidence of interaction over time that I am truly committed to living the values I explicitly espouse.

A living theory methodology from a propositional perspective does not seem to be capable of clarifying the meanings of the embodied values that form the explanatory principles in my accounts from the grounds of my experience as existing as a living contradiction (Whitehead, 1989a). For this I need a dialectical perspective.

Using a Dialectical Perspective in a Living Theory Methodology

A dialectical perspective holds contradiction to be the nucleus of dialectics. This resonates with the "I" in my question, How do I improve what I am doing?, as I exist as a living contradiction in the question. By this I mean that I hold together values and their denial in my practice. It is this experience of myself as a living contradiction that seems to spark my imagination into generating possibilities for improving practice and leads into the development of action reflection cycles. What these cycles enable me and others to do is to clarify the meanings of our embodied values as these emerge in practice. Following Feyerabend (1975) in his work *Against Method*, I agree that understanding freedom involves experiencing the meaning of freedom in the course of its emergence in practice. Hence, my emphasis is on understanding the meanings of values from their embodied expression in practice. For the sake of clarity I want to make a distinction between two different meanings of practice. From a cultural–historical perspective a practice can be seen as arising in response to general demands of societal need. A practice can be conceptualized as a historically developed and conditioned tradition of action for addressing societally formed needs (Chaiklin, 2007). This is not how I am using the word practice. I am using practice to mean what I or others are doing in asking, researching and answering questions of the kind, How do I improve what I am doing?

I think this distinction is important for researchers who want to avoid a gap between theorizing about their practice and their conscious lived experience. Researchers who encounter the use of practice from a sociocultural and activity theory perspective or a cultural–historical perspective might be wise to ask if there is a gap between this abstract conceptualization of practice and the conscious lived experience of the individuals who are theorizing their own practice. I am thinking here of researchers who are concerned to research improvements in practice through exploring the implications of their practical question, How do I improve what I am doing?

While a living theory methodology from a dialectical perspective can embrace contradictions and use action reflection cycles to clarify the meanings of values in the course of their emergence in practice, the nucleus of contradictions does not permit the expression of the life-affirming energy and values of inclusionality. These are not grounded in contradiction but experienced in affirmation. These affirmations of energy with values in a living theory methodology need an inclusional perspective to include them in explanations of educational influence.

Using an Inclusional Perspective in a Living Theory Methodology

My living this methodology from an inclusional perspective with life-affirming energy and values is available in the streaming video from the keynote presentation to the 2008 International Conference on Teacher Research (see Fig. 1).

Fig. 1 Streaming video at 2008 conference mms://wms.bath.ac.uk/live/education/JackWhitehead_030408/jackkeynoteictr280308large.wmv

My notes that I produced for the presentation are also available (at http://www.jackwhitehead.com/aerictr08/jwictr08key.htm) and appreciate, through the video, the qualities of affirmation and inclusion I communicate in my presentation which are different to those in the multi-media notes I posted before the presentation. I am explaining how to combine voices in living educational theories that are freely given in teacher research. The point about a living theory methodology from an inclusional perspective is that it includes a relationally dynamic and receptive response to the flows of energy and values in the living space. I think that one of my original contributions to educational knowledge is my use of multi-media narratives to communicate the explanatory power of flows of life-affirming energy in explanations of educational influence. We cannot do anything without energy, yet representations of the energy are not emphasized in explanations of educational influences in learning. The video to my keynote shows me expressing the life-affirming energy that distinguishes my love for what I am doing in education. There are other values such as freedom, justice and compassion that flow with this energy and form explanatory principles in the explanations of educational influence.

As I communicate with the audience I distinguish my way of being as a form of systemic presencing as I am seeking to be receptively responsive to those with whom I am sharing my work. Being receptively responsive implies some form of improvisation in making a creative response to the perceived needs of the other. Keith Kinsella, a colleague from Exeter University, introduced me to the idea of systemic presence. I use this in the idea of systemic presencing to describe a capability for expressing a relationally dynamic awareness of the interconnecting and branching networks of relationship in an educational space.

The flow of energy with values that I believe that I am expressing and communicating in this keynote can be distinguished by a loving flow of energy in that I am loving what I am doing. Having distinguished the contributions that propositional, dialectical and inclusional perspectives can make to a living theory methodology, I do not want to lose sight of the importance of including analyses from a range of theoretical perspectives within the methodology.

The Analyses Used to Glean Information from the Research Data

The increasing desire of individuals to research their own practice in order to understand their influence in their own learning, in the learning of others and in the learning of their organization had led to increasing requests for help about appropriate methods and methodologies for exploring the implications of seriously asking, researching and answering question of the kind, How do I improve what I am doing? In addition to the interest in methods and methodology, individuals have expressed interest in the theoretical perspectives that can be used in the creation and evaluation of their living educational theories. As each individual's explanation of his or her educational influences in learning is unique, this has implications for the analyses of the research data.

Central to the analyses of the research data in living theories are the energy and values we use as explanatory principles to explain our educational influences in our own learning and in the learning of others. For example, Naidoo (2005) uses a passion for compassion; Charles (2007) uses the relational energy and value of Ubuntu. Each individual has his or her own unique constellation of energy, values and understandings that give meaning and purpose to his or her life as explanatory principles.

Using a video of an Alzheimer's patient and her caregiver, Naidoo (2005) was able to explain the meanings of her passion for compassion as she clarified these meanings in the course of their emergence in the practice of her inquiry. To do this, she viewed a videotape of the husband's prepared reading of what he did to care for his wife, who had Alzheimer's. As her husband read his writings, his wife, sitting directly behind him, was slumped in her chair, apparently not attending to the activity. As he began reading what he did with his wife as the carer, she sat up, became animated and with a smile on her face looking directly at Naidoo, she indicated with her hands and arms a gesture that he was being bigheaded. But this was done with affection and humor. It was this expression that evoked in Naidoo her passion for compassion and which she could then bring into her analysis as a value that she uses as an explanatory principle in her work.

Chapter 6 of Charles' thesis (2007) began with a video clip of him talking about experiences of working with women in Sierra Leone whose husbands had been killed in the civil war, who had been raped by those who had killed their husbands and later had a child as a result of the rape. Charles had been working in the community following the civil war and had listened to the many stories of the women as he worked in the community. In his video he recounted his experiences with these women. Charles was powerfully affected by the love of the women for their children. It influenced his own understanding of the humanity that he associates with Ubuntu. Charles brings this value of Ubuntu informed by the meanings of the humanity of these women as an explanatory principle in the analysis of his thesis.

Because our lives are influenced by historical and cultural contexts, the analyses of the data should also integrate insights from the most advanced social theories of the day. For example, the analyses offered by Naidoo (2005), Charles (2007) and Adler-Collins (2007) include insights from these theories combined with their energy and values to form the explanatory principles of educational influences in learning. For example, Adler-Collins integrates insights from the history and culture of Japan to make sense of some of the opportunities and constraints in his implementation of a curriculum for the healing nurse.

This need for a unique explanation of our educational influences means that traditional theories cannot by their nature produce valid explanations for this influence. In a traditional theory an explanation is produced as a set of propositional relationships. These relationships are abstract and general. One of the characteristics of a traditional theory is that it is a general theory from which an explanation can be derived that applies to a particular case. Living theories are different. They are the explanations that individuals produce for their educational influences in learning. They are grounded in the relational dynamics of everyday life and explain the receptively responsive educational influences of individuals in their own lives. They are unique.

One of the reasons I became committed to supporting the development of living educational theories is that they offer individuals the opportunity to produce accounts of our influences in a way that focuses attention on the worthwhileness of our lives in terms of the values and understandings we use to give meaning to our existence. You will see that I focus attention on the idea of influence rather than causation. This is because of my fascination with our lives of intention. I see living educational theories being grounded in the conscious lived experience of individuals who are intentional and imaginative with creative capabilities. Because of these qualities I cannot say that I have educated anyone other than myself. This is fundamental to the analysis of research data. I can say that I have influenced the education of others. I do hope that this distinction is clear. Whatever I do in my educational relationships, including this writing, is mediated through a creative response of the other in making sense of what I do in terms of his or her own learning. For me to understand my educational influence in the learning of the other I must see that what I have done has been mediated in the other's learning with values to which I subscribe. I cannot distinguish something as educational without approving it. For me education is a value-laden practical activity and I rule out that all learning is educational. There is much learning of this non-educational kind in the world today as individuals learn how to do harm to each other and not to work cooperatively in each other's interests, hence my stress on educational influences in learning.

Influence

My focus on influence has been strengthened with Said's point about the value of focusing on influence in the work of Valéry:

> As a poet indebted to and friendly with Mallarme, Valéry was compelled to assess originality and derivation in a way that said something about a relationship between two poets that could not be reduced to a simple formula. As the actual circumstances were rich, so too had to be the attitude. Here is an example from the *Letter About Mallarme.*
>
> "No word comes easier or oftener to the critic's pen than the word influence, and no vaguer notion can be found among all the vague notions that compose the phantom armory of aesthetics. Yet there is nothing in the critical field that should be of greater philosophical interest or prove more rewarding to analysis than the progressive modification of one mind by the work of another." (Said, 1997, p. 15)

In analyzing data in terms of influence I do not go as far as the word-scepticism of Valéry (Hamberger, 1972). However, I shall be suggesting that adequate representations of our expressions of our embodied values that give meaning and purpose to our lives must go beyond our use of propositional language, beyond a grounding in the living contradictions of dialectics and into an inclusional flow of life-affirming energy with values that includes Valéry's insight about the significance of influence:

> Outside his poetry Valéry, like Hofmannsthal, was a word-sceptic; and the word-scepticism arose from the same awareness of the uniqueness of that which art seeks to express, and the inescapable commonness of words. If words could express it, Le Salitaire says about his own icy habitat,
>
> "It wouldn't be much. Everything that can be said is nothing. You know what humans do with what can be expressed. All too well. They turn it into base currency, an instrument

of imprecision, a lure, a trap for mastery and exploitation. Reality is absolutely incommu-
nicable. It resembles nothing, signifies nothing; nothing can represent or explain it; it has
neither duration nor place in any conceivable order or universe..."(5)

Like Hofmannsthal and other post-Symbolists, Valéry turned to mixed media – the fusion
of words with music, décor, gesture and dance in Amphion and Semiramis, of words with
music only in the Narcissus Cantata – out of an aversion to the base currency of words.
These media did not describe or relate; they enacted: and Valéry's aversion expanded to
the epic and descriptive modes: "What can be recounted cannot count for much!" (6)
(Hamberger, 1972, p. 69)

The second point about the analyses of data is that the analysis is offered within
a form of narrative inquiry (Clandinin, 2007). McNiff (2007) has shown how to do
such an analysis in her writings on "My Story Is My Living Educational Theory."

Narrative

The increasing use of narrative in educational research has enabled distinctions to
be drawn that I find most helpful in the analysis of my research data. Clandinin
and Rosiek (2007) have offered the following distinction between analyses that
privilege macrosocial conditions of life and those that privilege individual lived
experience:

Although it may seem extremely abstract, understanding the ontological as opposed to epistemological starting point of Marxist-influenced social theory is necessary for understanding the style and content of this scholarship as well as its relationship with narrative enquiry.
A mode of enquiry founded in epistemological commitments – such as positivism – takes
accurate description of the world as its primary objective. Epistemic principles, in this case,
determine the way the accuracy of research conclusions will be assessed. A mode of enquiry
founded in ontological commitments – such as Marxism or critical theory – takes transformation of those ontological conditions as its primary objective. For the Marxist influenced
scholar, research and analysis is an intervention that seeks to change the material conditions
that underlie oppressive social conditions.

As remarked on earlier, narrative enquiry shares with Marxism an explicit grounding in
ontological commitments as well as the goal of generating scholarship that transforms the
ontological conditions of living. The difference between the two traditions of enquiry is
located in the specifics of those commitments and their conceptions of intervention. Scholarship grounded in Marxism privileges the macrosocial material conditions of life as the primary influence on human life and thinking. The relational texture of everyday life, including
the personal, religious, historical and cultural narratives that provide meaning to that life,
are treated as derivative of the macrosocial conditions of life. Furthermore, these narratives
are frequently considered obstacles to be overcome on the way to a more realistic understanding of the causes of human experience.

The narrative enquirer, by way of contrast, privileges individual lived experience as a
source of insights useful not only to the person himself or herself but also to the wider field
of social science scholarship generally. As described in the comparison to post-positivism,
this approach to analyzing human experience is grounded in a pragmatic relational ontology. It takes the immediacy of lived experiences, specially its narrative qualities, as a fundamental reality to be examined and acted on. According to this view, all representations of
experience – including representations of the macrosocial influences on that experience –
ultimately arise from first-person lived experience and need to find their warrant in their
influence on that experience. (pp. 49–50)

In my own analyses of research data (Whitehead, 2005) I have used a narrative form that integrates insights from the sociocultural and sociohistorical theories of the day. I see both as necessary to explaining my educational influences in learning and in the generation of living educational theories.

Other Theoretical Perspectives

Because of limitations of space I cannot present here the details of the wide range of analyses I use with my research data. I have done this elsewhere (Whitehead, 2004, 2005; Whitehead & McNiff, 2006). Individuals' constellations of theoretical perspectives that they draw on in generating their living educational theories are unique. Mine includes insights from the life's work of Erich Fromm. I continue to value his insights into the differences between the marketing and productive personalities (1947), the fear of freedom (1942), the importance of the art of loving (1957), the revolution of hope (1956) and to have and to be (1976). From Foucault (1980) I learned to see the intimate relationships between power and knowledge and to see the importance of the power relations and procedures for determining what counts as knowledge in a particular context. This resonated with Habermas' (1976b) understandings in *Legitimation Crisis* and continues to focus my practice on transforming the standards of judgment used in the Academy to legitimate what counts as educational knowledge. In looking at video data of educational relationships my analyses and recognition of flows of life-affirming energy with the value of the being of the other continue to be influenced by the ideas of Paul Tillich and Martin Buber. I am thinking particularly of idea of "the state of being affirmed by the power of being itself" (Tillich, 1962, p. 168) and of Buber's poetic expression of the I–You relation in education in "the special humility of the educator" (1947, p. 122).

As I analyze research data in terms of educational influences in learning I draw insights from Edward Said's (1993) work on culture and imperialism. I look for the evidence that shows an awareness of the dangers of imposing one's views on another. I look for the exercise of creativity that mediates between what the educator does and what the learner learns. From Bernstein's (2000) analyses I continue to draw on his insight into the dangers of creating a mythological discourse:

> I would like to propose that the trick whereby the school disconnects the hierarchy of success internal to the school from social class hierarchies external to the school is by creating a mythological discourse and that this mythological discourse incorporates some of the political ideology and arrangement of the society.
>
> First of all, it is clear that conflict, or potential conflict, between social groups may be reduced or contained by creating a discourse which emphasises what all groups share, their communality, their apparent interdependence.
>
> By creating a fundamental identity, a discourse is created which generates what I shall call horizontal solidarities among their staff and students, irrespective of the political ideology and social arrangement of the society. The discourse which produces horizontal solidarities or attempts to produce such solidarities from this point of view I call a mythological discourse. This mythological discourse consists of two pairs of elements which, although having different functions, combine to reinforce each other. One pair celebrates and attempts

to produce a united, integrated, apparently common national consciousness; the other pair work together to disconnect hierarchies within the school from a causal relation with social hierarchies outside the school. (p. xxiii)

Concluding Insights

In answering the question, How do I influence the generation of living educational theories for personal and social accountability in improving practice, I have focused on explicating the living theory methodology that has emerged in my educational practices.

I am hopeful that you will find useful the ideas and representations of flows of life-affirming energy with values for your explanatory principles in *your* explanations of educational influence. I am thinking here of explanations in which you account to yourself and others for the worthwhileness of the life you are living.

I am also hopeful that you will feel the importance and urgency of sharing your living educational theories with others so that we may be offered an opportunity to learn from the gift of your own living theory. In my experience, individuals like to understand the how as well as the why questions, hence my emphasis on sharing each others' living theories so that we may learn useful insights from each other. I am thinking of insights on how we can research and answer questions of the kind, How do I improve what I am doing? in contributing to making the world a better place to be. I am hoping that the exercise of my imagination in creating a living theory methodology is resonating with your own.

References

Adler-Collins, J. (2007). *Developing an inclusional pedagogy of the unique: How do I clarify, live and explain my educational influences in my learning as I pedagogise my healing nurse curriculum in a Japanese University?* Unpublished dissertation, University of Bath, England. Retrieved May 3, 2008 from http://www.actionresearch.net/jekan.shtml

Austin, T. (2001). *Treasures in the snow: What do I know and how do I know it through my educational inquiry into my practice of community?* Unpublished dissertation, University of Bath, England. Retrieved February 19, 2004 from http://www.actionresearch.net/austin.shtml

Bernstein, B. (2000). *Pedagogy, symbolic control and identity: Theory, research, critique.* New York: Rowman & Littlefield.

Bosher, M. (2001). *How can I as an educator and professional development manager working with teachers, support and enhance the learning and achievement of pupils in a whole school improvement process?* Unpublished dissertation, University of Bath, England. Retrieved May 3, 2008 from http://www.actionresearch.net/bosher.shtml

Buber, M. (1947). *Between man and man.* London: Kegan Paul, Trench, Trübner.

Carr, W., & Kemmis, S. (1983). *Becoming critical: Knowing through action research.* London: Falmer.

Chaiklin, S. (2007). Modular or integrated? An activity perspective for designing and evaluating computer-based systems. *International Journal of Human-Computer Interaction, 22,* 173–190.

Charles, E. (2007). *How can I bring Ubuntu as a living standard of judgment into the academy? Moving beyond decolonisation through societal reidentification and guiltless* *recognition.*Unpublished dissertation, University of Bath, England. Retrieved May 3, 2008 from http://www.actionresearch.net/edenphd.shtml

Cho, D. (2005). Lessons of love: Psychoanalysis and teacher-student love. *Educational Theory*, *55*(1), 79–95.

Church, M. (2004). *Creating an uncompromised place to belong: Why do I find myself in networks?* Retrieved May 3, 2008 from http://www.actionresearch.net/church.shtml

Clandinin, J. (Ed.). (2007). *Handbook of narrative inquiry: Mapping methodology.* London: Sage.

Clandinin, J., & Rosiek, J. (2007). Mapping a landscape of narrative inquiry: Borderland spaces and tensions. In J. Clandinin (Ed.), *Handbook of narrative inquiry: Mapping methodology* (pp. 35–75). London: Sage.

Cunningham, B. (1999). *How do I come to know my spirituality as I create my own living educational theory?* Unpublished dissertation, University of Bath, England. Retrieved February 19, 2004 from http://www.actionresearch.net/ben.shtml

Dadds, M., & Hart, S. (2001). *Doing practitioner research differently.* London: RoutledgeFalmer.

D'Arcy, P. (1998). *The whole story. . . . .* Unpublished dissertation, University of Bath, England. Retrieved February 19, 2004 from http://www.actionresearch.net/pat.shtml

Delong, J. (2002). *How can I improve my practice as a superintendent of schools and create my own living educational theory?* Unpublished dissertation, University of Bath, England. Retrieved May 3, 2008 from http://www.actionresearch.net/delong.shtml

Eames, K. (1995). *How do I, as a teacher and educational action-researcher, describe and explain the nature of my professional knowledge?* Unpublished dissertation, University of Bath, England. Retrieved February 19, 2004 from http://www.actionresearch.net/kevin.shtml

Evans, M. (1995). *An action research enquiry into reflection in action as part of my role as a deputy headteacher.* Unpublished dissertation, Kingston University, England. Retrieved February 19, 2004 from http://www.actionresearch.net/moyra.shtml. Jointly supervised with Pamela Lomax.

Farren, M. (2005). *How can I create a pedagogy of the unique through a web of between-ness?* Unpublished dissertation, University of Bath, England. Retrieved May 3, 2008 from http://www.actionresearch.net/farren.shtml

Ferguson, P. B. (2008). Increasing inclusion in educational research: Reflections from New Zealand. *Research Intelligence*, *102*, 24–25.

Feyerabend, P. (1975). *Against method.* London: Verso.

Finnegan, J. (2000). *How do I create my own educational theory in my educative relations as an action researcher and as a teacher?* Unpublished dissertation, University of Bath, England. Retrieved February 19, 2004 from http://www.actionresearch.net/fin.shtml

Foucault, M. (1980). *Power/knowledge: Selected interviews and other writings 1972–1977* (C. Gordon, Trans./Ed.). London: Harvester.

Fromm, E. (1942). *The fear of freedom,* London: Routledge & Kegan Paul.

Fromm, E. (1947/1969). *Man for himself. An inquiry into the psychology of ethics.* Greenwich, CT: Fawcett Premier.

Fromm, E. (1956). *The sane society.* London: Routledge & Kegan Paul.

Fromm, E. (1957/1995). *The art of loving.* London: Thorsons.

Fromm, E. (1976/1979). *To have or to be.* London: Abacus.

Gurney, M. (1988) *An action enquiry into ways of developing and improving personal and social education.* Unpublished dissertation, University of Bath, England.

Habermas, J. (1976a). *Communication and the evolution of society.* London: Heinemann.

Habermas, J. (1976b). *Legitimation crisis.* London: Heinemann Educational Books.

Hamberger, M. (1972). *The truth of poetry: Tensions in modern poetry from Baudelaire to the 1960s.* Hammondsworth, England: Penguin.

Hartog, M. (2004). *A self study of a higher education tutor: How can I improve my practice?* Unpublished dissertation, University of Bath, England. Retrieved May 3, 2008 from http://www.actionresearch.net/hartog.shtml

Hirst, P. (Ed.). (1983). *Educational theory and its foundation disciplines.* London: RKP.

Holley, E. (1997). *How do I as a teacher-researcher contribute to the development of a living educational theory through an exploration of my values in my professional practice?*

Unpublished dissertation, University of Bath, England. Retrieved February 19, 2004 from http://www.actionresearch.net/erica.shtml

Laidlaw, M. (1996). *How can I create my own living educational theory as I offer you an account of my educational development*? Unpublished dissertation, University of Bath, England. Retrieved May 8, 2008 from http://www.actionresearch.net/moira2.shmtl

Laidlaw, M. (2008). *Jack Whitehead, 40 years in education. Was it worth it*? Retrieved May 8, 2008 from http://www.jackwhitehead.com/jack/ml40yeartributetojw.pdf

Loftus, J. (1999). *An action enquiry into the marketing of an established first school in its transition to full primary status*. Unpublished dissertation, Kingston University, England. Retrieved February 19, 2004 from http://www.actionresearch.net/loftus.shmtl. Jointly supervised with Pamela Lomax.

Lohr, E. (2006). *Love at work: What is my lived experience of love and how might I become an instrument of love's purpose*? Unpublished dissertation, University of Bath, England. Retrieved May 3, 2008 from http://www.actionresearch.net/lohr.shtml

Macdonald, B. (1976). Evaluation and the control of education. In D. Tawney (Ed.), *Curriculum evaluation today: Trends and implications* (pp. 125–136). London: Macmillan.

Marcuse, H. (1964). *One dimensional man*. London: Routledge & Kegan Paul.

McNiff, J. (1989) *An explanation for an individual's educational development through the dialectic of action research*. Unpublished dissertation, University of Bath, England.

McNiff, J. (2007). My story is my living educational theory. In J. Clandinin (Ed.), *Handbook of narrative inquiry: Mapping a methodology* (pp. 308–329). London: Sage.

McNiff, J., & Whitehead, J. (2005). *Action research for teachers: A practical guide*. London: David Fulton.

Mead, G. (2001). *Unlatching the gate: Realising the scholarship of my living inquiry.*Unpublished dissertation, University of Bath, England. Retrieved February 19, 2004 from http://www.actionresearch.net/mead.shtml

Murray, Y. (2008). *Welcome to my critical, colorfull and cosmopolitan living educational theory web page: Practice, research, inclusion and becoming*. Retrieved September 25, 2008 from http://www.rac.ac.uk/?_id=1568

Naidoo, M. (2005). *I am because we are. (My never-ending story.) The emergence of a living theory of inclusional and responsive practice*. Unpublished dissertation, University of Bath, England. Retrieved May 3, 2008 from http://www.actionresearch.net/naidoo.shtml

Polanyi, M. (1958). *Personal knowledge: Towards a post-critical philosophy*. London: Routledge & Kegan Paul.

Punia, R. (2004). *My CV is my curriculum: The making of an international educator with spiritual values*. Unpublished dissertation, University of Bath, England. Retrieved May 3, 2008 from http://www.actionresearch.net/punia.shtml

Raynor, A. (2004). *Inclusionality: The science, art and spirituality of place, space and evolution*. Retrieved May 4, 2008 from http://people.bath.ac.uk/bssadmr/inclussionality/placespaceevolution.html

Raynor, A. (2005). *The inclusion nature of neighbourhood – A universal dynamic solution*. Retrieved May 4, 2008 from http://people.bath.ac.uk/bssadmr/inclussionality/placespaceevolution.html

Roberts, P. (2003). *Emerging selves in practice: How do I and others create my practice and how does my practice shape me and influence others*? Unpublished dissertation, University of Bath, England. Retrieved May 3, 2008 from http://www.bath.ac.uk/~edsajw/roberts.shtml

Said, E. (1993). *Culture and imperialism*. London: Vintage.

Said, E. W. (1997). *Beginnings: Intention and method*. London: Granta.

Scholes-Rhodes, J. (2002). *From the inside out: Learning to presence my aesthetic and spiritual being through the emergent form of a creative art of inquiry*. Unpublished dissertation, University of Bath. Retrieved May 3, 2008 from http://www.actionresearch.net/rhodes.shtml

Spiro, J. (2008). *How I have arrived at a notion of knowledge transformation, through understanding the story of myself as creative writer, creative educator, creative manager, and educational researcher?* Unpublished dissertation, University of Bath, England. Retrieved May 3, 2008 from http://www.actionresearch.net/janespirophd.shtml

Tillich, P. (1962). *The courage to be.* London: Fontana.

Whitehead, J. (1985) An analysis of an individual's educational development: The basis for personally orientated action research. In M. Shipman (Ed.), *Educational research: Principles, policies and practice* (pp. 97–108). London: Falmer. http://www.actionresearch.net/writings/livtheory.html

Whitehead, J. (1989a). Creating a living educational theory from questions of the kind, "How do I improve my practice?" *Cambridge Journal of Education, 19*(1), 41–52.

Whitehead, J. (1989b). How do we improve research-based professionalism in education? A question which includes action research, educational theory and the politics of educational knowledge: 1988 Presidential Address to the British Educational Research Association. *British Educational Research Journal, 15*(1), 3–17.

Whitehead, J. (1993). *The growth of educational knowledge.* Bournemouth, England: Hyde.

Whitehead, J. (1999a) Educative relations in a new era. *Pedagogy, Culture & Society, 7*(1), 73–90.

Whitehead, J. (1999b). *How do I improve my practice? Creating a new discipline of educational enquiry.* Unpublished dissertation, University of Bath, England. Retrieved March 17, 2008 from http://www.actionresearch.net/jack.shtml

Whitehead, J. (2004). What counts as evidence in the self-studies of teacher education practices? In J. J. Loughran, M. L. Hamilton, V. K. LaBoskey, & T. Russell (Eds.), *International handbook of self-study of teaching and teacher education practices* (pp. 871–904). Dordrecht: Kluwer.

Whitehead, J. (2005). Living inclusional values in educational standards of practice and judgement. *Ontario Action Researcher, 8.2.1.*

Whitehead, J. (2008, March 28). *Combining voices in living educational theories that are freely given in teacher research.* Keynote presentation for the International Conference of Teacher Research on Combining Voices in Teacher Research, New York. Notes retrieved May 5, 2008 from http://www.jackwhitehead.com/aerictr08/jwictr08key.htm. Streaming video retrieved May 5, 2008 from mms://wms.bath.ac.uk/live/education/JackWhitehead_030408/jackkeynoteictr280308large.wmv

Whitehead, J., & McNiff, J. (2006). *Action research living theory.* London: Sage.

Assumption Interrogation: An Insight into a Self-Study Researcher's Pedagogical Frame

Robyn Brandenburg

Introduction

Embedded assumptions about teaching, and learning through teaching, are not easy to identify and are even more difficult to alter. This chapter seeks to contextualize Dewey's (1933) attitude of "responsibility" (p. 12) through identifying and interrogating taken-for-granted assumptions about learning and teaching. Using self-study of teaching as my methodology and assumption hunting (Brookfield, 1995) as a lens, I came to understand how powerful this combination was in revealing more about the complexities of teaching. Through questioning and 'suspending' (van Manen, 1990) taken-for-granted assumptions, more has been revealed about the structures which enabled the creation of new knowledge and the subsequent challenges to my conceptualization of learning and teaching as a teacher educator. A consequence of my systematic evaluation has been the modification, and in some cases, major alteration of practice.

I am a mathematics educator and teach preservice teachers in a Bachelor of Education Course, which is a 4-year degree and prepares teachers to teach in primary (elementary) or primary and secondary schools. Preservice teachers select a strand or pathway (Prep-6 or Prep-Year 10) and on completion of the degree can teach in their preferred area. Following our Bachelor of Education Course review, I developed a new approach for mathematics learning which was underpinned by reflection and reflective practice. This new approach included oral and written reflective practices and tools to foster reflection in and on learning: Roundtable Reflection (Brandenburg, 2004, 2008), ALACT (Korthagen, Kessels, Koster, Lagerwerf, & Wubbels, 2001), Freewrites (LaBoskey, 1994), and Critical Incident Questionnaires (Brookfield, 1995). My underpinning research question which prompted this research in our Bachelor of Education Course was, In what ways does reflection and reflective practice enhance preservice teacher pedagogy? It is interesting to note that at the outset, the research focus was on the ways in which reflection and reflective

R. Brandenburg (✉)
University of Ballarat, 12 Crocker Street, Ballarat, Victori 3353, Australia
e-mail: r.brandenburg@ballarat.edu.au

D.L. Tidwell et al. (eds.), *Research Methods for the Self-study of Practice*,
Self-Study of Teaching and Teacher Education Practices 9,
DOI 10.1007/978-1-4020-9514-6_12, © Springer Science+Business Media B.V. 2009

practice influenced the development of preservice teacher pedagogy. As my study progressed, however, the ongoing scrutiny of my assumptions and practices led to a deeper understanding not only of the ways in which teaching and learning were indeed intertwined, but as Kosnik (2001) had suggested, the process also confirmed for me that although often our initial desire is to "see ourselves as agents for our student teachers: motivating them, informing them, guiding them, preparing them" (p. 65), it ultimately enriches us.

In this chapter I describe one thread of my self-study research and as such, isolate and interrogate one of my key assumptions about learning and teaching. I then identify and describe the oral and written reflective practices and tools, reveal how self-study methodology enabled deeper readings of data and prompted the creation of new techniques to gather further data, and finally, discuss some possible implications for teacher educators.

Why Self-Study Methodology?

I adopted self-study as the methodology for my research (Berry, 2004b; Bullough & Pinnegar, 2004; Hamilton, 2004; Kosnik, 2001; LaBoskey, 2004; Loughran, 2002, 2004; Russell, 2004). Although different methods are employed by those conducting self-study (e.g. statistical methods, ethnography, participant observation, grounded theory) the distinctive feature of self-study is its "different philosophical and political stance" (Pinnegar, 1998, p. 31). As such, self-study is "not a collection of particular methods but instead a methodology for studying professional practice settings" (p. 33). Choosing to conduct a self-study was a deliberate attempt to understand more about practice (my own and that of my preservice teachers) and to better understand outcomes of practice in the context of a changing and complex world. In one sense, it was a response to LaBoskey's (2004) call for self-study researchers to identify and respond to 'why' questions related to understanding and researching practice:

> The purpose [of self-study] is to improve that practice, in this case teacher education, in order to maximize the benefits for the clients, in this instance preservice and in-service teachers and their current and future students. Thus, the aim for teacher educators involved in self-study is to better understand, facilitate, and articulate the teaching-learning process ... it is enormously complex, highly dependent on context and its multiple variations, and personally and socially mediated. (p. 857–858)

Increasing understanding of teacher education conducted within the context of teacher education by teacher educators has been, and continues to be, a distinguishing feature of self-study. Although other methods (such as action research, ethnographic research) are also approaches used to research the work of teacher educators, it is the 'insider perspective,' the ongoing and ever-evolving study of practice-within-context that is identified as paramount to self-study (LaBoskey, 2004). By definition the conduct of self-study research is open to individual interpretation.

My self-study research presented in this chapter explores the perception that in working from an assumption challenging base for pedagogical inquiry, learners experience levels of frustration, "discomfort, uncertainty, [and] restless inquiry" (Kincheloe, 2003, p. 44). This point has also been well made in the work of Lyons and Freidus (2004) who report on both teacher educator and preservice teacher experiences with the implementation of reflective portfolios in self-study. Initial levels of enthusiasm of those experiencing the changes as a result of self-study research are replaced by frustration as so often, learners need to learn to tolerate states of disequilibrium. However, as Bullough and Pinnegar (2004) have proposed, a disintegrative state will exist until the new knowledge has become integrated and new routines are developed.

The Learning Context

This research was undertaken over a period of 3 years with cohorts of preservice teachers who were completing the two compulsory Learning and Teaching Mathematics Units (TJ591; TJ792) of the Bachelor of Education at the University of Ballarat, a regional university in Australia. The Bachelor of Education is a 4-year undergraduate degree which aims to develop critically reflective practitioners for teaching in multiple contexts (Preparatory to Year 10, in urban, regional and rural settings). The preservice teacher cohorts constituted both males and females – averaging 20–25% males; 75–80% females – the majority of whom were white, middle class. The percentage of mature age preservice teachers (i.e. those who are non-direct school leavers and have generally had workforce experience) represented approximately 20% of the total number of preservice teachers in each cohort. The average cohort size was 85 preservice teachers and all preservice teachers referred to in this chapter have been allocated a pseudonym.

Theoretical Position

The theoretical frame for my self-study and for this analysis of my learning as a teacher educator combines the concepts of dispositions for reflective practice, namely attitudes (Dewey, 1933) and hunting and interrogating assumptions (Brookfield, 1995). Dewey describes three attitudes which underpin a reflective orientation to practice – "open-mindedness," "whole-heartedness" and "responsibility" (pp. 30–31) – and responsibility implies that one must "consider the consequences of a projected step" (p. 32) and adopt consequences which result from pursuing a practice. Studying practice inevitably leads to new understandings and challenges practices and perceptions. One aim of this chapter is to demonstrate how my research outcomes raised questions about responsibility, especially when the outcomes were not as one anticipated.

Assumption identification is difficult, as much of who we are and how we operate as teacher educators is embedded; so much so, that assumptions about teaching and learning in teacher education become both naturalized and tacit. Brookfield's (1995) assumption framework guided my understanding about assumption hunting, identification and categorization and in using his three categories (paradigmatic, prescriptive and causal assumptions) I was able to identify the nature of my assumptions. Prescriptive assumptions reflect what we think "ought to be happening in a particular situation" (Brookfield, 1995, p. 3) and the prescriptive assumption I examine as the focus of this chapter relates to my belief that the integration of multiple written reflective tools – ALACT (Korthagen et al., 2001); Freewrite (LaBoskey, 1994) and Critical Incident Questionnaires (Brookfield, 1995) – and oral practices such as Roundtable Reflection (Brandenburg, 2004, 2008) would stimulate learners to reflect critically on learning. My prescriptive assumption was grounded in the paradigmatic assumption that the promotion of critical thinking in teacher education is integral to educational, social, moral and academic advancement (Brookfield, 1995; Gore & Zeichner, 1991; Korthagen et al., 2001; Loughran, 2004). A major modification to practice in Learning and Teaching Mathematics units was the creation and conduct of weekly Roundtable Reflection sessions. This structure and practice reflected my intention to promote preservice teacher voice and encourage meaningful reflection on practice in a trusting and supportive environment.

Roundtable Reflection: Learning Through Reflective Inquiry

Integral to reflective practice is the notion of inquiry (Clarke & Erickson, 2004; Cochran-Smith & Lytle, 2004; LaBoskey, 2004; Loughran & Russell, 2002; Schön, 1983, 1987). As a means of promoting inquiry, I introduced Roundtable Reflection with each cohort of preservice teachers participating in the mathematics units. The roundtable structure was developed as a response to preservice teachers' requests for regular opportunities to verbally reflect on their professional teaching experiences in a structured and less ad hoc manner. Following a semester of data collection, which included written evaluations, forum discussions and focus group interviews (May 2002), I had identified that teaching in my mathematics classes was largely directed by me and therefore, privileged teacher educator voice. Second, preservice teachers had articulated a general lack of connection with, and understanding of the relevance of, reflective processes. Third, predetermining weekly content meant that preservice teachers' needs were not genuinely being considered – I was making assumptions about preservice teachers' prior knowledge and needs as learners of teaching mathematics. Roundtables were ultimately established to address what we (preservice teachers and teacher educator) had defined as limitations to learning and they offered an alternative practice to a traditional tutorial format together with a means to integrate inquiry into weekly learning experiences (Brandenburg, 2004, 2008).

In our context, traditional tutorials were based on the following structure: discussion related to a pre-set reading linked to the already nominated weekly topic; teacher educator led instruction related to a specified mathematical concept (for example, subtraction) and a practical activity using concrete materials to reinforce conceptual understanding. Conceptually, roundtables emphasized discussion of experiences and were based on developing the attitudes of responsibility, wholeheartedness and open-mindedness. The Roundtable Reflection on practice was therefore underpinned by the following assertions.

1. Roundtable Reflection (RR) provided opportunities for preservice teachers/ teacher educator to make sense of experience/s in a supportive environment;
2. preservice teachers generated discussion by raising issues related to their experience;
3. the role of the teacher educator was to introduce the session, clarify the framework and consciously refrain from dominating discussion;
4. all preservice teachers were provided with an opportunity to raise an issue, and hence, encourage development of their voice;
5. learning outcomes were not predetermined;
6. learning/s were made explicit;
7. opinions were respected; and,
8. references were made to the ALACT model of reflective practice (Inner/Outer cycle).

Structurally, for each roundtable session, traditional rows of tutorial seating were reorganized to form a shape representing a roundtable. The intention of this arrangement was threefold: first, to physically decentre the teacher educator, and thus challenge the traditional practice of the physical centrality of the teacher in learning; second, to establish an environment where participants have increased visual contact with others thus increase the likelihood of engagement; and third, to divest authority for learning to all members of the group and hence model reflective practice as a process in which all participants might contribute to the discourse.

Conducting Roundtable Sessions

Expectations associated with RR included an understanding that the sessions were to be regarded by participants (preservice teacher/teacher educator) as both listening and speaking spaces and that preservice teachers could choose to verbally participate in the discussion, but were not compelled to contribute. Although preservice teachers were required to attend the session as an assessment task, their verbal contributions were not formally assessed. The aim for each session, as explained to the preservice teachers, was to establish and maintain a learning environment where members felt supported and yet challenged in their thinking, and where they could therefore express concerns and expose issues regarding learning about teaching.

In doing so, assumptions about learning and teaching could then be identified and challenged. The challenge for both the preservice teachers and for me in this situation was to constantly fine-tune and monitor the balance between feelings of safety (taking professional risks and experiencing vulnerability) and developing and maintaining a professional respect and confidentiality amongst the group. This situation relates to research conducted by Berry (2004a, 2007), who refers to the experience of learner vulnerability manifested as a tension within learning environments where learners challenge both self and others.

I introduced each RR session often with a summary of the key points from the previous roundtable session. I then discussed the expectations associated with the function of RR and invited preservice teachers to identify an issue which they might like to examine further within a group learning environment. It was the content of these discussions which led to a deeper understanding of the ways in which we (preservice teachers and me) were identifying and examining a range of issues associated with learning and teaching mathematics.

A Triad of Written Reflection Tools

Together with Roundtable Reflections as an integral means to orally reflect on experience, preservice teachers were introduced to ALACT as a reflective framework (Korthagen, et al., 2001); Freewrites (LaBoskey, 1994) and Critical Incident Questionnaires (Brookfield, 1995). Extensive descriptions of these tools have been reported elsewhere (Brandenburg, 2008) but briefly, ALACT provided a guide for preservice teachers to reflect on their mathematics teaching in schools. Freewrites enabled preservice teachers to capture and specifically examine snapshots of learning. And, Critical Incident Questionnaires encouraged reflection which was based on guiding questions.

I selected and adapted Korthagen's ALACT model as it provided a cyclical (rather than hierarchical) framework for reflection. My justification for the choice of ALACT was founded on information provided by previous cohorts of preservice teachers, some of whom requested the need for a reflective framework, rather than an ad hoc approach to written reflection on experience. My adaptation of the ALACT cycle comprises five phases: Action (A) – a critical event, moment or interaction that stimulated the reflective cycle; Looking back on the action (L) – examining the action in light of the context; Awareness of essential aspects (A) – identifying specific elements that can inform the context; Creating alternatives (C) – developing/discussing alternative responses; and, Trial (T) – trying it out. The ALACT framework provided a formal structure for written lesson/critical incident/interaction reflections. This framework also provided a helpful structure for Roundtable Reflection which focused on oral discourse.

In addition to the introduction of the ALACT framework for reflecting on experience, Freewrites (LaBoskey, 1994) were chosen as they provided preservice teachers with opportunities to reflect in a structured but open-ended manner about their experiences of learning about teaching. In a Freewrite, preservice teachers were allocated approximately 10–15 minutes to write a 'snapshot' response of their experiences from the Learning and Teaching Mathematics units. During roundtable sessions, preservice teachers and I wrote for approximately 15 minutes (individually) about a recent vivid experience of teaching and/or learning. These snapshots of learning were then discussed and analysed for key points which had emerged from experience and shared in the following week. The purpose for completing the Freewrites was to establish a means by which we as a cohort could understand more about what was acknowledged by preservice teachers and myself as being both problematic and beneficial in our professional experiences in schools and during university classes. From this I summarize their Freewrites into one document and provide them with this summary at our next meeting. For my data analysis, I then examined their Freewrite responses for emergent themes, coded, categorized and analysed to inform my teaching and our learning.

Critical Incident Questionnaires (CIQ) (Brookfield, 1995) provided a further structured approach to gathering snapshots of learning related to preservice teachers' experiences, and in this case, the questions were specific, referring to particular aspects of learning. Each preservice teacher responded to the following questions: (1) At what moment in the class(es) this week did you feel most engaged with what was happening? (2) At what moment in the class(es) this week did you feel most distanced from what was happening? (3) What action that anyone (student, teacher) took in class this week did you find most affirming and helpful? (4) What action that anyone (student, teacher) took in class this week did you find most puzzling or confusing? and, (5) What about the class(es) this week surprised you the most? The CIQ questionnaire was intended to elicit elements associated with preservice teachers' emotional engagement with learning, mathematics content and the effect of the learning environment.

By introducing multiple written approaches to reflecting in and on practice, (ALACT, Freewrites, CIQ) it was anticipated that the process of reflecting on one's practice would not only become an integral practice in preservice teachers' learning about teaching, but also, provide a range of alternative approaches for reflecting on practice and, hence, cater for multiple learning styles.

Description and Analysis of a Data Thread

To examine the impact of reflection in and on practice I implemented self-study as a methodology. As a means of exploring the impact of the methodology I have selected what I have termed a data thread, or a pathway through specific data. It is a selected thread and therefore represents just one thread of data. To do this, I have the luxury of hindsight, for what seemed random and disconnected at times, now is not only obvious but has provided a springboard for further and more intensive research. I also aim to provide evidence of Hamilton and Pinnegar's (2000) claim that "Using self-study, we can confidently and immediately change our practices without waiting for new research from others . . . . In fact, in self-study, we speak with passion about a continual critique of our teaching" (p. 238). In fact, responding to critical interactions, feedback and roundtable data enabled me to reframe, create and modify my approach to teaching so that learning in my mathematics units became more effective. In doing so, I do not offer a blueprint for practice as each learning context is unique. Rather, I offer a reflection on the self-study research process which proved to be an effective process for eliciting more about the complexities of teaching and contributed to developing teacher educator pedagogy.

The Reflective Practice Thread: Roundtables, Multiple Perspectives Task, Freewrites and Critical Incident Questionnaires

My initial step was to identify my assumption related to reflective practice, and to do this I used Brookfield's (1995) categories (paradigmatic, prescriptive and causal). My prescriptive assumption (which is one that reflects what we think things ought to be like) was that the integration of multiple reflective practices will challenge learners to reflect critically on their learning. As I now know, these key assumptions were underpinned by multiple sub-assumptions. For example, I assumed learners were as passionate about reflection as I was; I assumed that multiple practices were necessary to develop reflective practice skills; I assumed that learners would have the skills to reflect critically on learning; and I assumed that the reflective process was primarily created to enhance preservice teacher learning.

One criticism, however, that commonly arises with any discussion regarding reflection (and the development of critical reflection in particular) is the lack of evidence to support claims that internalization, transformation and transportability across learning contexts can be developed (Brookfield, 1995; Hatton & Smith, 1995; Korthagen et al., 2001; Wideen, Mayer-Smith, & Moon, 1998). Other criticisms which relate to the use of reflective practice in preservice teacher education programs arise from that which has been described as a technical reflective approach, whereby particular models, frameworks and tools (which provide a guiding structure to reflective practice) become inherently prescriptive and restrictive and hence contribute to another form of the technical reductionist model of learning about teaching (Kelchtermans, 2005; Kincheloe, 2003). Inherent in my assumption about the integration of reflective practice was my belief that I could contribute to the collective knowledge about developing the critically reflective practitioner. Roundtable Reflection became a crucial practice as a means of achieving this aim.

Roundtables were conducted with each cohort of preservice teachers, and data were generated from each session and analysed. This was either by way of audio taping and transcription or by way of field notes written by me and then analysed post-session. The audio tapes were transcribed in a four-stage process (described in detail elsewhere, Brandenburg, 2008) but this process involved an initial stage where my notes were written in brackets and this highlighted an issue or added meaning or contextual information to the conversation that became apparent in listening to the audio tapes. This helped to add meaning to the written text. These notes in brackets also referred to any emphasis in terms of the dialogue; the mood, facial expressions; tone, in terms of agitation, defensiveness; agreement which was noted by preservice teachers nodding; and my interpretation of the level of emotion displayed in representing that dialogue. The second stage involved a form of tabulation whereby the transcript was then allocated a reference and a line number.

Stage Three involved coding whereby the transcript was coded and categorized. Analysis of the transcribed data then provided key categories and Stage Four involved the categorical analysis where the transcripts were read to identify "relationships between data items" (Lankshear & Knobel, 2004, p. 271) and these then were refined to a number of key categories.

Roundtable Reflection with each cohort had proved to be the cornerstone of the mathematics units. For example preserve teachers replied to the Critical Incident Questionnaire item, "At what moment in the class(es) this week did you feel most engaged with what was happening?" where 51% of the total responses referred to the roundtable sessions. Further, in response to the question, "What is your preferred reflective mode?" (Questionnaire, TJ792), almost one third of the comments referred to discussion with others during roundtables. Sam (pseudonyms were used for all preservice teachers' names) summarized preservice teacher responses to roundtables and stated

> *It's good [Roundtable Reflection] because we can really play to it, because they're our own problems they're not ... a case scenario; we can find out different ways to sort out our problems in relation to schools and work; and, we don't do it anywhere else like how to deal with that sort of thing ... this is all we do about dealing with problems.* (Sam, Roundtable Eleven, August, 2003)

Roundtables were generally embraced by each cohort and proved to be exciting learning spaces. Clearly, Roundtable Reflection worked well for preservice teachers; how was it working for me as teacher educator? It was through participating in and examining the data from Roundtable 11 (where a critical interaction occurred) that my assumption about reflection was challenged and which left me somewhat perplexed. In my discussion with preservice teachers, I asked a question

Robyn: "Okay now I'll ask you a question about my role. Now I know this is fairly new to you people; you're saying you don't have anything like this in other units, so how do you see my role; how do you see me?"

Sam: "Annoying. Only because you are too sensitive to it on the flip side – well I reckon" (Group gasp, laughter)

Robyn: "No tell me because I need to know"

Sam: "Well!"

Jen: "Would I do that?!"

Sam: "No ... I think she's sensitive to our situation and to the way that we learn ... but it's another to harp on it all the time to the point where I'm now getting out of my own natural field of development to keep thinking, "Am I fine with this? Yeh, I'm fine with this." Like I think sometimes you [should] just relax and let it happen." (Roundtable 11, Transcript 033–038)

I wrote about this interaction in my journal that evening

> *Perspective is important. Maybe I am too passionate, zealous and this can be interpreted as both imposition and over-sensitivity ... Researching practice in this systematic way and scrutinising practice and implications of practice on learners requires intense self-investment. It means initially identifying and then confronting (especially the unexpected)*

with a willingness to reflect on alternatives - to view from other perspectives. So in asking about my role as teacher educator, for example, I was opening the conversation to psts [preservice teachers] in anticipation that they would respond truthfully.

Sam – 'annoying' ... In explaining his reasoning it became clear that his impression had developed from a sense of frustration – of him having to constantly ask "Am I fine with this? Yeh, I am". I saw this from multiple perspectives. Firstly, that Sam felt comfortable in expressing an opinion. This may indicate the characteristics of the environment created as underpinning the roundtable format. Secondly Sam was involved in what could be understood as meta-reflection: an explicit aim of this approach. By constantly asking himself "Am I fine with this? Yeh, I am" then the engagement in this process is (or could be) interpreted as reflection, hence connection. The fact that this was frustrating him is an issue for me. Stating the fact that there is an over-sensitivity to reflection on my behalf was an insight - hadn't interpreted enthusiasm as over-sensitivity. And this over-sensitivity could then become a learning barrier. There is professional expertise in identifying a balance. (Journal entry, Wednesday August 27, 2003)

Needing to know more about the perspectives of participants in the class, I developed what I term the multiple perspectives task. The development of this task provided a specific example of what Hamilton and Pinnegar (2000) suggest is one key benefit of using self-study as a methodology in that it enables us to "confidently ... change our practices without waiting for new research from others" (p. 238). Although the introduction of this task was not immediate (indeed it was conducted some months post-roundtable session), it provided deeper insights into the ways in which reflective practice was being experienced by learners. Up to four preservice teachers were invited to complete this follow-up task. Participation was voluntary and the preservice teachers were not compelled to complete the task. The task was non-assessable. Two of the four preservice teachers accepted. The preservice teachers were selected randomly and the number of respondents was capped at between two and four as this allowed me to examine a sample of perspectives in detail. (Preservice teachers in each instance had received their final grade for the unit during the previous semester. Therefore, the respondents were not advantaged or disadvantaged in terms of their final unit grades.) To complete the task each preservice teacher was provided with lines of the Roundtable 11 transcript and asked to reflect on what they were thinking and feeling at the time. An example of the organization of the data is in Table 1.

The analysis of the data from this multiple perspectives task prompted me to reflect more deeply on the impact of the reflective practices being introduced with preservice teachers. I questioned my practices: Was I imposing my expectations and passion regarding reflection? Was I acknowledging preservice teachers' frustrations with the amount of reflective practice? Did I need to curtail or modify my expectations and provide choice? I was beginning to appreciate the power of systematically reflecting on multiple data sources as a means of more deeply understanding not only my practice but the preservice teacher experience of reflective practice. Parallel to the examination of roundtable and multiple perspective data, more about reflection and the impact of reflective practices were being revealed in the preservice teacher's written responses from the Freewrites and Critical Incident Questionnaires.

Table 1 Example of data analysis from roundtable discussion

	Transcript	Robyn	Mary	Sophie
R11.033 Robyn	Okay now I'll ask you a question about my role. Now I know this is fairly new to you people you're saying you don't have anything like this in other units, how do you see my role; how do you see me?	Taking a risk with the open invitation to express opinion; anticipating a comparison with past experience; clarification of my role (the anticipated and the actual – are there contradictions in my modelling, delivery, practices?) Felt I had established a trusting, supportive learning environment	My thoughts at this stage were the following: Does she really want to know the answer to this? Shall I say what I think or just what I think she wants to hear	No response to this section of transcript
R11.034 Sam	Annoying. Only because you are too sensitive to it on the flip side – well I reckon (Gasp, laughter from the group)	The word 'annoying' – what did he mean by annoying? Was I annoying him or was the process annoying him and why? Shock laughter from the group. I am surprised. This was an instantaneous response	Well at least he is truthful but it takes courage to really say what you think no matter how much the tutor or lecturer tells you so. I am amazed that he talks so	My thoughts – bloody hell Sam, that's a bit confronting. I wonder how she will handle it

Organization of data from Roundtable 11 that includes responses from three participants in the round table discussion.

Freewrites and Critical Incident Questionnaires

Data from Freewrites and Critical Incident Questionnaires revealed an even deeper insight into the ways in which reflection and reflective practices were impacting and contributing to preservice teacher and teacher educator pedagogy. The data referred to in this discussion were collected from three cohorts: Cohort One, Third Year Bachelor of Education preservice teachers ($n = 36$), was required to produce up to four emailed reflections following partner teaching in schools during Semester One, 2003, with 106 emailed reflections received. Critical Incident Questionnaires were also collected from Cohort One. Cohort Two comprised First Year Bachelor of Education preservice teachers ($n = 47$) who were required to write one written reflection on a critical incident using the ALACT framework, during Semester 2, 2003 with 47 written reflections received. Freewrites were also collected and analysed from Cohort Two. Cohort Three (TJ792, Semester One, 2004) provided 15 written questionnaire responses and ALACT reflections.

While my main intention was to encourage preservice teachers to experience a variety of reflective techniques and therefore develop some expertise in reflecting on practice, surprisingly the analysis of the data exposed new knowledge for me. A key issue that arose through systematically analysing the written data was the impact of partner teaching, which was a process whereby preservice teachers in partnership would plan, teach and reflect on lessons taught in local schools. The intensity of the feedback and the consistent themes in the written feedback revealed new learning for us all. From the preservice teachers' perspectives, although the practice was generally well regarded and led to opportunities to enhance learning, some found the practice created tensions. For some, partner teaching was described as a confusing situation for both the preservice teacher and the student. Not only did preservice teachers need to negotiate their roles in the teaching environment, but they also needed to be consistent with expectations in order to minimize student confusion. Pete articulated this dilemma in the following response: *Having two teachers in the one class influenced students' behaviour ... Chris and I accidentally told students different instructions and the students became confused. Therefore, having a buddy made the lesson difficult at times* (Pete, Cohort One). Another preservice teacher mentioned that the difficulties in teaching with a partner related to differences in methods and objectives: *I find co-teaching difficult. I think I will do better when I can manage all a particular lesson by myself. I go in to a lesson with clear outcomes and lesson structure and I find it difficult to manage with a co-teacher who has different teaching methods and probably different objectives in mind*(Cate, Cohort One).

An assumption I had made when introducing partner teaching was that partners would provide support for each other in planning, teaching, evaluating and reflecting on teaching, and in this sense, there would be a provision for peer critique and opportunities for critical reflection. Although some preservice teachers stated that they gained valuable insights into their own and others' learning from being able to share thoughts, others were less positive about this partnership and felt that they experienced confusion, frustration and lack of personal and professional control. The impact of partner teaching was also revealed in the Freewrite responses.

Partner Teaching was one of the three sub-categories which emerged from the Freewrite data analysis for Week 9, Semester Two, 2003. From the selected sample ($n = 30$), 16/30 or more than 50% of the references related to the category of aspects associated with partner teaching. Preservice teachers' responses reflected the requirement that partner teaching demanded a new set of personal skills. This raised further questions for me. What types of partnerships might be the most effective in terms of meeting everyone's needs? Although some partnerships were satisfactory according to preservice teacher feedback, clearly some partnerships were challenging. What elements of a teaching partnership contribute to extending preservice teacher's pedagogy and what elements restrict this growth? If preservice teachers work in partnership with a friend, what restrictions might this place on the levels and types of criticism that one feels are appropriate to offer a peer? If preservice teachers work with another who is less known to them, is the partnership then complicated by not knowing the other, and therefore more time must be invested in developing a trusting relationship?

It was through identifying issues and working through these tensions with individual partnerships and with the cohort of preservice teachers during university (de)briefing sessions that allowed these concerns to be raised and addressed by us. In so doing, the challenges of new learning within a teaching partnership could be made explicit; for example, discussions related to the tensions of dealing with a friendship in a teaching partnership or tensions related to accommodating the other in the teaching environment. These became the basis for subsequent Roundtable Reflection sessions.

To summarize the learning from the data thread, it became obvious that multiple levels of learning were beginning to unfold. Preservice teachers were expressing their learning using the written and oral techniques as conduits; my assumptions were being challenged as a result of this process. Using self-study as a research methodology, I not only gained new and deeper knowledge about preservice teachers' learning experiences, but had data to reveal more about my practice and understanding of pedagogy. Analysing data in a systematic and ongoing way allowed me to make modifications and adaptations to practices which I then anticipated would align more closely with our (teacher educator's and preservice teachers') needs and desires as learners.

Learning Through Self-Study

As van Manen (1990) has suggested, "the *method* [emphasis in the original] is charged with methodological considerations and implications of a particular philosophical or epistemological perspective" (p. 28) and examining the role of self-study as a methodology has revealed more about my orientation as a teacher educator/ researcher. Clearly, key new learning emerged as a result of systematically examining my practice and reviewing the data, together with some challenges to my assumptions about reflective practices and the development of critically reflective practitioners.

Reflection is a generic skill, encouraged in teacher education to enable preservice teachers to examine their experiences in deep and meaningful ways. Initially, when I began my study, I did not question the validity of this claim or the practice of using multiple tools to enhance reflection. For me, it was common sense practice. As Gore (1993) suggested, it "would be virtually inconceivable to find a teacher educator who would advocate *un*reflective teaching" (p. 149). Common sense, yes. Prescriptive for me, yes. In retrospect, some of my key assumptions combined the elements of being both common sense and prescriptive (reflecting what I believed a good educational practice might look like). By encouraging the use of multiple reflective tools, I foresaw that skills would be developed to help unpack learning. It also became evident that my prescriptive assumption about the use of reflective tools was underpinned by many sub-assumptions.

Self-study represented an approach to my research which provided an inbuilt mechanism for identifying and dealing with issues related to practice as they arose in situ. I could then respond and adapt practice. My research design was framed yet it also needed to be flexible, and in this way, I consider self-study to be generative. Generative within this context was defined as knowledge derived from experience which contributed to my knowing as a teacher educator. Coming to know was a process of incremental development (Clarke & Erickson, 2004); it was intrinsic to my way of being and understanding (Dalmau, Hamilton, & Bodone, 2002); it was non-static; it evolved over time and was deeply influenced by exploring experience and critical moments/incidents/interactions within experiences which led me to extract learning and new knowledge. Together with wanting to encourage preservice teachers to reflect effectively, I continually came to question, How am I learning as a teacher educator?

Conclusion

My initial intention as a mathematics teacher educator researching practice was to promote not only effective but critical reflection with each cohort of preservice teachers. By introducing and integrating oral (Roundtable Reflection) and written tools in the Learning and Teaching Mathematics Units and using self-study as a methodology for studying practice, more was revealed about the complexities of learning about and through teaching. My assumptions were constantly challenged. As Kelchtermans (2005) has suggested, there is always more and less happening than we expect in teaching.

Although the research was conducted in specific units in a Bachelor of Education degree in a regional university, the results of this self-study suggest that there are possible applications for teaching and learning in broader contexts. By choosing self-study as a methodology, more was revealed about a teacher/researcher's philosophical and epistemological orientation. Exposing this orientation was important as it situated the research in a context and exposed more about the researcher's pedagogical frame. I began with a research design but a crucial need for me as a self-study researcher was the ability to respond to data in timely and creative ways; hence, the development of the multiple perspectives tasks, the modification to Roundtable Reflection sessions and the ongoing research into preservice teacher's teaching partnerships. In this way, self-study was a generative process and as data were systematically analysed, deeper understandings about pedagogy evolved. It was from this ongoing scrutiny of practice that taken-for-granted assumptions were challenged. Challenging assumptions lead to new knowledge. Acting on new knowledge required certain dispositions: open-mindedness, whole-heartedness and responsibility (Dewey, 1933). Responsibility as a teacher educator conducting self-study of practice meant being prepared to open up learning and teaching assumptions for scrutiny; examine and re-examine data; modify practices, if required, and live with degrees of messiness and uncertainty. Ultimately, the focus of self-study research moved from their learning to our learning about teaching. Through reflection, which involved the acknowledgement of parallel journeys, we exposed multiple possibilities for refining our pedagogy.

References

Berry, A. (2004a). Confidence and uncertainty in teaching about teaching. *Australian Journal of Education, 48*(2), 149–165.

Berry, A. (2004b). Self-study in teaching about teaching. In J. J. Loughran, M. L. Hamilton, V. K. LaBoskey, & T. Russell (Eds.), *International handbook of self-study of teaching and teacher education practices* (Vol. 2, pp. 1295–1332). Dordrecht: Kluwer.

Berry, A. (2007). *Tensions in teaching about teaching: Understanding practice as a teacher educator.* Dordrecht: Springer.

Brandenburg, R. (2004). Roundtable reflections: (Re) defining the role of the teacher educator and the preservice teacher as co-learners. *Australian Journal of Education, 48*(2), 166–181.

Brandenburg, R. (2008). *Powerful pedagogy: Self-study of a teacher educator's practice.* Dordrecht: Springer.

Brookfield, S. D. (1995). *Becoming a critically reflective teacher.* San Francisco: Jossey-Bass.

Bullough, R. V., Jr., & Pinnegar, S. (2004). Thinking about the thinking about self-study: An analysis of eight chapters. In J. J. Loughran, M. L. Hamilton, V. K. LaBoskey, & T. Russell (Eds.), *International handbook of self-study of teaching and teacher-education practices* (Vol. 1, pp. 313–342). Dordrecht: Kluwer.

Clarke, A., & Erickson, G. (2004). Self-study: The fifth commonplace. *Australian Journal of Education, 48*(2), 199–211.

Cochran-Smith, M., & Lytle, S. L. (2004). Practitioner inquiry, knowledge, and university culture. In J. J. Loughran, M. L. Hamilton, V. K. LaBoskey, & T. Russell (Eds.), *International handbook of self-study of teaching and teacher education practices* (Vol. 1, pp. 601–649). Dordrecht: Kluwer.

Dalmau, M. C., Hamilton, M. L., & Bodone, F. (2002). Communicating self-study within the scholarship of teacher education: Herstmonceux working group. In C. Kosnik, A. Samaras, & A. Freese (Eds.), *Making a difference in teacher education through self-study. Proceedings of the Fourth International Conference on Self-Study of Teacher Education Practices, Herstmonceux Castle, East Sussex, England* (Vol. 1, pp. 59–62). Toronto, Canada: OISE, University of Toronto.

Dewey, J. (1933). *How we think: A restatement of the relation of reflective thinking to the educative process.* Chicago: Henry Regnery. (Original work published in 1909).

Gore, J. M. (1993). *The struggle for pedagogies.* New York: Routledge.

Gore, J. M., & Zeichner, K. M. (1991). Action research and reflective teaching in preservice teacher education: A case study from the United States. *Teaching and Teacher Education*, 7(2), 119–136.

Hamilton, M. L. (2004). Professional knowledge, and self-study teacher education. In J. J. Loughran, M. L. Hamilton, V. K. LaBoskey, & T. Russell (Eds.), *International handbook of self-study of teaching and teacher education practices* (Vol. 1, pp. 375–419). Dordrecht: Kluwer.

Hamilton, M. L., & Pinnegar, S. (2000). On the threshold of a new century: Trustworthiness, integrity, and self-study in teacher education. *Journal of Teacher Education*, 51(3), 234–240.

Hatton, N., & Smith, D. (1995). *Reflection in teacher education: Towards definition and implementation*. Retrieved September, 2003, from http://www2.edfac.usyd.edu.au/LocalResource/Study1/hattonart.html

Kelchtermans, G. (2005, July). *Professional commitment beyond contract: Teachers' self-understanding, vulnerability and reflection*. Paper presented at the International Study Association on Teachers and Teaching, Sydney, Australia.

Kincheloe, J. L. (2003). *Teachers as researchers: Qualitative inquiry as a path to empowerment*. London: RoutledgeFalmer.

Korthagen, F. A. J., Kessels, J., Koster, B., Lagerwerf, B., & Wubbels, T. (2001). *Linking practice and theory: The pedagogy of realistic teacher education*. Mahwah, NJ: Erlbaum.

Kosnik, C. (2001). The effects of an inquiry-oriented teacher education program on a faculty member: Some critical incidents and my journey. *Reflective Practice*, 2(1), 65–80.

LaBoskey, V. K. (1994). *Development of reflective practice: A study of preservice teachers*. New York: Teachers College Press.

LaBoskey, V. K. (2004). The methodology of self-study and its theoretical underpinnings. In J. J. Loughran, M. L. Hamilton, V. K. LaBoskey, & T. Russell (Eds.), *International handbook of self-study of teaching and teacher education practices* (Vol. 2, pp. 817–869). Dordrecht: Kluwer.

Lankshear, C., & Knobel, M. (2004). *A handbook for teacher research: From design to implementation*. New York: Open University Press.

Loughran, J. J. (2002). Effective reflective practice: In search of meaning in learning about teaching. *Journal of Teacher Education*, 53(1), 33–43.

Loughran, J. J. (2004). Learning through self-study: The influence of purpose, participants and context. In J. J. Loughran, M. L. Hamilton, V. K. LaBoskey, & T. Russell (Eds.), *International handbook of self-study of teaching and teacher education practices* (Vol. 1, pp. 151–192). Dordrecht: Kluwer.

Loughran, J. J., & Russell, T. (Eds.). (2002). *Improving teacher education practices through self-study*. London: RoutledgeFalmer.

Lyons, N., & Freidus, H. (2004). The reflective portfolio in self-study: Inquiring into and representing a knowledge of practice. In J. J. Loughran, M. L. Hamilton, V. K. LaBoskey, & T. Russell (Eds.), *International handbook of self-study of teaching and teacher education practices* (Vol. 2, pp. 1073–1107). Dordrecht: Kluwer.

Pinnegar, S. (1998). Introduction to Part II: Methodological perspectives. In M. L. Hamilton, S. Pinnegar, T. Russell, J. Loughran, & V. K. LaBoskey (Eds.), *Reconceptualizing teaching practice: Self-study in teacher education* (pp. 30–33). London: Falmer.

Russell, T. (2004). Tracking the development of self-study in teacher education research and practice. In J. J. Loughran, M. L. Hamilton, V. K. LaBoskey, & T. Russell (Eds.), *International handbook of self-study of teaching and teacher education practices* (Vol. 2, pp. 1191–1210). Dordrecht: Kluwer.

Schön, D. (1983). *The reflective practitioner: How professionals think in action*. New York: Basic Books.

Schön, D. (1987). *Educating the reflective practitioner: Toward a new design for teaching and learning in the professions*. San Francisco: Jossey-Bass.

van Manen, M. (1990). *Researching lived experience: Human science for an action sensitive pedagogy.* Ontario: Althouse Press.

Wideen, M., Mayer-Smith, J., & Moon, B. (1998). A critical analysis of the research on learning to teach: Making the case for an ecological perspective on inquiry. *Review of Educational Research, 68*(2), 130–178.

Teacher Education for Literacy Teaching: Research at the Personal, Institutional, and Collective Levels

Clare Kosnik and Clive Beck

One of the complaints about teacher education is that research done on programs tends to be local and ends at the completion of the program. As Clift and Brady (2005) found in the American Educational Research Association (AERA) panel on research and teacher education, between 1995 and 2001 only 24 studies were conducted on preservice literacy courses. And only one "studies practice beyond student teaching: most studies were conducted over one semester, typically the student teaching semester." Clift and Brady argued that "[t]he short-term nature of this research limits our ability to understand how teacher education methods courses and fieldwork lead to long-term professional growth" (2005, p. 317). The sole longitudinal study – that by Grossman et al. (2000) – concluded that it is necessary to connect the practices of beginning teachers with their teacher education program if we are to truly understand the practices of beginning teachers.

In this chapter, we report on the longitudinal study, *Teacher Education for Literacy Teaching*, which followed teachers from their preservice program through the first 4 years of teaching. It was a complicated study working at three levels: individual (e.g., studying our own practices as teacher educators), institutional (e.g., studying graduates from all three of our teacher education programs), and collective (e.g., drawing on and contributing to the literature on teacher education). This chapter focuses on the research process we used with some of the findings sprinkled throughout. Our research evolved over the years capitalizing on the researchable moment. Throughout the chapter, we describe our efforts, showing how some processes had to be abandoned while other opportunities presented themselves allowing us to follow various avenues that we had not originally planned to pursue.

C. Kosnik (✉)
Ontario Institute for Studies in Education, University of Toronto, 252 Bloor Street West, Toronto, ON M5S 1V6, Canada
e-mail: ckosnik@oise.utoronto.ca

D.L. Tidwell et al. (eds.), *Research Methods for the Self-study of Practice*, 213
Self-Study of Teaching and Teacher Education Practices 9,
DOI 10.1007/978-1-4020-9514-6_13, © Springer Science+Business Media B.V. 2009

Literature Review

In response to the criticism noted above, many schools of education have been and continue to be pressured by state and federal legislators (U.S. Department of Education, 2002) and education critics to prove that their teacher education programs make a difference to both teaching practices and pupil achievement. Numerous large-scale studies, currently underway, are studying the link between teacher education and teacher practices: Ohio (Lasely, Siedentop, & Yinger, 2006), Teachers for a New Era (in 10 states), New York City (Boyd, Grossman, Lankford, Loeb, & Michelli, 2006), and Louisiana (Noell & Burns, 2006). The National Commission on Excellence in Elementary Teacher Preparation for Reading Instruction, which was "created to address some of the important gaps in this research literature on teacher preparation" (Hoffman et al., 2001, p. 5), is studying 900 reading teacher educators and approximately 92 teachers. They are looking at graduates from exemplary reading programs to examine their "classroom literacy environments from a social practice perspective" (p. 7). Of particular interest to us is their emphasis on the processes of teacher education: "Though there is evidence of the positive effects of preservice programs on teacher attitudes and student learning ... how this process occurs is less well known" (p. 270).

Maloch et al. (2003) agreed with Anders, Hoffman, and Duffy (2000) who commented that the question of how teachers should be taught to teach reading "has received little attention from the reading research community.... Relatively few researchers have asked questions about the processes that teachers go through as they learn and continue to learn to teach reading" (2000, p. 719). The International Reading Association (2003) report, *Prepared to Make a Difference: An Executive Summary of the National Commission on Excellence in Elementary Teacher Preparation for Reading Instruction*, is one of the first studies to shed light on the structure of teacher education programs that are recognized as exemplary for literacy preparation.

Snow, Griffin, and Burns (2005), in their text *Knowledge to Support the Teaching of Reading*, began to outline the knowledge base new teachers require:

> We acknowledge that the directly relevant research basis concerning pedagogical knowledge for teaching of reading is still inadequate (compare Roller, 2001). We await the development of the kinds of powerful experimental long-term studies that definitely link specific aspects of teacher education and teacher learning to teachers' use of specific practices and then to improvements in student learning. (p. 65)

Grossman et al. (2005) systematically examined the teaching of English/ language arts and mathematics and concluded that preparing teachers to teach literacy is a complex task because students need to recognize that the domain involves "procedural, conceptual, and strategic knowledge" (p. 217). They consider the issue of the prospective teachers' own attitudes toward literacy, noting that those "who choose to become English teachers are often avid readers and writers themselves;" they say that part of the challenge is to help student teachers "move beyond their own experiences as readers and writers and understand how a diverse group of students learn to read and write" (p. 217). They also address the content knowledge that students need to have before entering the teacher credential program.

Although Ball (2000) focused mainly on mathematics teaching, her insights are relevant to learning to be a literacy teacher. She argued that student teachers and inservice teachers need to understand subject matter because it is "essential to listening flexibly to others and hearing what they are saying and where they might be headed" (p. 242). She has long wondered what kinds of knowledge teachers need and how it can be acquired. She identified the fundamental issue as follows: "The overarching problem ... is that the prevalent conceptualization and organization of teachers' learning tends to fragment practice and leave to individual teachers the challenge of integrating subject matter knowledge and pedagogy in the contexts of their work" (p. 242). Like Ball, Phelps and Schilling (2004) believe that teachers need to have specific knowledge, they "need to know content in ways that differ from what is typically taught and learned in university courses" (p. 32). Regarding the teaching of reading they suggested that we distinguish between what teachers of reading need to know in general and the content knowledge involved in teaching reading. This still leaves us with the fundamental question: How can beginning teachers acquire this array of knowledge and consolidate their learning in a pedagogy or approach that is feasible for the extremely challenging first years of teaching?

At this point we do not want to revisit the debate commonly known as the 'reading wars,' but the sharp disputes about how children learn to read and write directly influence our approach to teaching beginning teachers. As Grossman et al. (2005) noted, "how teachers define the subject will influence how they organize both curriculum and instruction" (p. 210). Barnes, Barnes, and Clarke (1984) argued there are competing views of what constitutes literacy and the particular view held by the teacher educator shapes the literacy courses.

Grossman et al. (2000) observed that while preservice education provides a "vision of writing instruction toward which beginning teachers can work," in many cases this vision is barely apparent during the difficult first year of teaching. Their research suggests that the vision tends to "stay with" the new teachers and "resurface in important ways" in later years, but they stress the need for mentoring and support if this resurfacing is to occur to a significant degree. Similarly, Ducharme and Ducharme (1999) claimed that preservice education has the capacity to keep alive "a sense of idealism and critical social vision" in the teaching profession, but acknowledge that many new teachers have "found themselves unready for some of the tasks and expectations that arise during teaching" (pp. 43, 46).

We were particularly interested in "[bettering our] understanding of teacher education practices, programs, and contexts" (Samaras & Freese, 2006, p.14); therefore, the study design included a self-study component. LaBoskey's (2004) five principles for self-study research were relevant to our work:

- Self-initiated and focused
- Improvement aimed
- Interactive

- Multiple, primarily qualitative, methods
- Exemplar-based validation. (pp. 842–852)

Without studying our own setting, we would have lost the opportunity to improve our own practice.

Context of the Study

The teacher education programs at the Ontario Institute for Studies in Education, University of Toronto (OISE/UT) are all post-baccalaureate with the elementary teacher education credential program having three streams: a 1-year program leading to Bachelor of Education (600 students), a small 2-year program leading to a Master of Teaching (40 students per year), and another small 2-year program leading to a Master of Arts (40 students per year). The 1-year program and the Master of Teaching each has one literacy course (36 hours), while the Master of Arts has two courses (39 hours each). The 600 students in the Bachelor of Education program are divided into cohorts of approximately 60–65 student teachers with a small faculty team who organize the program and practice teaching placements. At the time of this study, there were 11 literacy instructors, of whom three were tenured and the other eight were on contract. Since there was not a common syllabus for the literacy course(s), instructors had the freedom to develop their course(s) as they chose. Regarding the students, since admission to the credential programs tends to be very competitive, all the students had at least a mid-B average and had some type of experience working with children (e.g., camp counselor, volunteer teaching, teaching overseas). The average age was 28 years and 26% were self-identified as racial minority.

Clare teaches literacy courses in the preservice program and although her course evaluations by her students have consistently been very high, she has long felt that her courses were not adequate. To help her develop her courses further, she wanted to know how other literacy instructors conducted their courses. Were they more effective in preparing beginning teachers? At an institutional level, we also wanted to study the differences between the 1- and 2-year programs, in particular whether the graduates from the 2-year programs were better prepared. In general, we were interested in studying the challenges beginning teachers face. Both Clare and Clive recognized a gap in the literature on preparing beginning teachers to be effective literacy instructors and hoped to add to the emerging field of research on literacy education in teacher education. The large-scale grant for 5 years allowed us to do a longitudinal study of our graduates. We conceptualized the research as a study of the influence of the preservice literacy courses on the beginning teachers' practices. Our research questions were as follows:

- What impact does a teacher education program have on student teachers' theory and practice of literacy teaching?

- Is there a body of knowledge that student teachers need to learn to be effective literacy teachers?
- How can universities and school systems provide more adequate support and mentoring for new literacy teachers?
- How can teacher preparation programs dovetail with the many large-scale school board initiatives in the literacy area?

Although we had conducted large-scale research previously (Kosnik, Beck, Diamond, Kooy, & Rowsell, 2002) we had not embarked on such an ambitious study. We formed a research team that included doctoral students, recent graduates from the doctoral program, classroom teachers, and preservice instructors. The sheer logistics of the data gathering presented many challenges; for example, how could we create a fairly stable research team when there was a regular turnover of graduate students?

Research Process

> The rationale for doing a grounded theory study is that we have no satisfactory theory on the topic, and that we do not understand enough about it to begin the theorizing. (Punch, 2005, p. 159)

We decided to follow a grounded theory approach to research, which Punch describes as "a research strategy whose purpose is to generate theory from data" (p. 154). This we combined with the use of self-study processes (e.g., studying our own courses and overall program). At no point did we find a tension between the two approaches; rather, we felt that each informed the other. One of the principles of grounded theory is to begin data analysis early in the research process, and this is what we did. We felt this would inform our methods, allow us to pursue emerging themes in subsequent interviews, and gradually help us develop a theory of teacher education.

In the following sections, we not only describe some of the data gathering, analysis processes, and findings, but also include information about the challenges we faced and the unexpected opportunities that arose.

Research During the Preservice Program

Surveying and Interviewing the Student Teachers

Our first step in this longitudinal research was to survey all elementary student teachers. The four-page survey, a combination of multiple choice and open-ended questions, asked, among other things, about previous experiences; views on the literacy courses and their practice teaching experiences; and their level of preparedness to teach literacy. Designing the survey had a self-study element because identifying areas to investigate reflected our priorities and interests. The quantitative section of the surveys was machine-read and the responses to the open-ended questions were collated. We also interviewed a total of 20 student teachers, from the three programs, whom we intended to follow into their first years of teaching. The interviews were all transcribed. As soon as we began sifting through the data, we realized that the student teachers were very idealistic in their goals, unrealistic about their own abilities, exceptionally critical of the program, and in many cases unable to articulate their learning regarding literacy. We felt the data would have limited use because it was filled with jargon and platitudes. After many hours spent reading and analyzing the data, we made the difficult decision to abandon this part of the research.

Interviewing the Instructors

The interviews of 10 of the 11 literacy instructors were much more successful. In the interviews we inquired about their approach to their literacy courses, theoreticians who resonated with them, the assignments they devised, and suggestions for improving the program. Some of the questions had been developed for previous self-study research that we had conducted on our own courses. These interviews were conducted by Clare and were transcribed. We used *Hyper Research* (a computer program for the analysis of qualitative data, http://ssc.sagepub.com/cgi/content/citation/9/3/452) to analyze the transcripts of the instructors. We began by reading the transcripts several times to identify themes or "codes" related to the central issues of the study (e.g., induction support, course development) while other themes emerged from the data (e.g., feeling like second-class citizens). *Hyper Research* allowed us to easily match themes with interviewees, recording the references to each topic; it also established the frequencies for each code, allowing us to develop a structure for our writing. *Hyper Research* also enabled us to double and triple code passages, revealing the overlap between particular themes. We began with over 40 codes and eventually reduced these to 29 themes. As we wrote papers we kept going back to the materials for clarification, continuing to add, delete, and modify themes. For example, we split the code "research" into "conducting research" and "drawing on research."

Some of our findings include: instructors tried to "cover the waterfront" of literacy education by addressing at least 12 topics in their courses, aiming for breadth rather than depth; there were widely diverging views on the place of theory in preservice courses; all emphasized using children's literature; and, although there were no consistent assignments across the cohorts, all encouraged students to adopt a reflective stance. Overall, we felt the instructors were very strong, caring, and knowledgeable.

As we analyzed the data, we could not help but constantly compare the instructors' practices to our own. This led to us doing a self-study (Kosnik & Beck, 2008a) which we had not originally planned to conduct; however, the process of analyzing the interviews was so fascinating and informative, we felt that we could not ignore this opportunity. We used the themes that we had developed when analyzing the interviews of the instructors as a framework to analyze our own practices. As we examined our practices in this way, we not only gained insight into our own work but also understood more fully the work of the other teacher educators in our programs. For example, we could see how we tended to try to cover many topics in our courses just as the instructors did because of the pressure from the students. Recognizing this in our own work gave us greater understanding of the work of instructors.

Studying the Beginning Teachers

Our plan to follow the students we had interviewed during the preservice program into teaching quickly unraveled because, unexpectedly, only 4 of the 20 were hired for regular teaching positions; some secured teaching jobs in special education or a content-area to be taught on rotary (e.g., physical and health education) where they would not teach literacy per se; some could only get supply teaching positions (known as substitute teachers in the United States), and others moved out of the local area. As a result, we had to recruit a new cadre of teachers who had full-time positions in or near the Greater Toronto Area. We recognize that some of our new recruits most likely had a higher degree of confidence (and possibly ability) than other new teachers and this may have skewed the data. We eventually had a study sample of 22 beginning teachers, all graduates from one of the three OISE/UT programs.

Developing Interview Questions

In order to study the influence of the preservice program on the teachers, we felt we needed to interview and observe each teacher at least twice per year. Although we had clearly stated research goals, we struggled to develop interview questions to match them. Since we were not sure what we were looking for or how to ask a question about the links between their preservice program and their practice without being too leading, our interview questions were often broad (e.g., how do you go about planning your literacy program?) while at other times very specific (e.g., how would you define guided reading?). Furthermore, recognizing that beginning teachers are overworked and often disappointed with the gap between their ideals and their practices, we were extremely sensitive about the questions we asked. Since there were few longitudinal studies on this topic, we could not refer to the research instruments used by others. Once again, we found that the questions we asked reflected our priorities to some extent (e.g., to what extent do you feel your class is a community?). The interview questions addressed areas such as program planning, induction support, influence of the preservice program, and overall reflections on their literacy program.

Problems with the Interview Questions

Much to our dismay, as we started conducting the interviews we discovered that the beginning teachers had limited recall of the specifics of their teacher education program, many commenting, "It's all a blur" or "I don't remember the specifics," and a few dismissing it outright, claiming "It was a waste of time, I didn't learn anything." Our plan to examine the influence of the preservice program on beginning teachers seemed to be disintegrating because our participants could not recall much about the program with any degree of accuracy.

By the end of the first interview in the second year two other problems emerged. In each interview we tended to repeat many of the same questions in an attempt to study how the teachers' views changed over time, but our interviewees found this repetitive and tedious and were becoming bored, feeling they had nothing else to offer. We also realized the school contexts were vastly different, with some teachers receiving a high level of support and others being almost abandoned. Although an induction program for new teachers was mandated by the government, in many instances the new teachers had not received much support. The level of induction support affected the teachers to such a high degree that our goal to study the influence of the preservice program on the practices of beginning teachers seemed in some ways naïve. It was proving to be exceedingly difficult to disentangle variables such as induction support from the influence of the preservice program.

At this low point in the research, we drew on one of the pillars of self-study research – critical friends. We gathered together our research team who up to this point had done mainly the interviewing and classroom observations and asked for their input. How should we proceed? Much to our relief, they had highly useful suggestions. We abandoned to a large extent our practice of asking the same questions, developed new questions that focused more on the teachers' practices than on their reflections on the preservice program, and revised the observation form to be more analytic than descriptive. For example, we inquired "To what extent would you say that your literacy program matches the program of the teachers in your division/grade? Why is it different?" "Over the past three years, would you say that your program has become more similar to or more different from the programs offered by your colleagues?"

This practice of involving the interview team more fully has continued. For example, when we were discussing questions for the fourth-year teachers, Judy, one of the members who has a strong interest in narrative inquiry, suggested we ask the teachers to tell us the story, based on their 4 years of teaching, that they would tell someone interested in teaching.

Much to our surprise, in the second interview in the second year of teaching and even more so in the third year, the teachers became more positive about their preservice programs and seemed to have clearer recall of the specifics of the programs than they had previously. Their suggestions for improving the programs were more concrete and realistic. They also began to recognize that a preservice program could not fully prepare them. Rather than simply dismissing the program, they could identify specific aspects of it that had helped them. Our research seemed to be back on track.

Conducting Observations in Classrooms

Being interviewed we suspected was somewhat unnerving for the beginning teachers, but being observed in their classrooms actually teaching raised the stakes even higher. However, we felt the need to triangulate the interviews through observations. Just as the interview questions evolved so too did the classroom observation process. Initially, we were hampered because there are so few models to use as a basis. What should we be looking for? And what constitutes evidence of influence of the pre-service program on practice? By the end of the teachers' third year of teaching, we had a much improved form. For example, the researchers were asked to provide terms they felt described the teacher's approach to literacy. This level of description helped us make links between the preservice program and teachers' practices. For example, Julian used the terms "scholarly," "group learning," "skills acquisition," "equity," and "engagement" to describe one of the teachers he was observing. These terms were accompanied with examples and explanations which provided further information. With this level of detail we were able to appreciate that the beginning teacher's approach was consistent with the approach and practices of the literacy instructor who had taught her in the preservice program. In the teachers' fourth year, Clare wanted to use the *Classroom Assessment Scoring System* (CLASS) with the seven levels of performance indicators (http://classobservation.com/); however, some members of the team objected, feeling we should not be assessing the teachers in this way. We compromised and modified the CLASS form.

Analyzing the Data on the New Teachers

Our interviews and observations of the beginning teachers produced a significant amount of data. We had initially thought that our team of researchers could do some of the preliminary analysis but this was not feasible. The sheer volume of data we were generating was almost overwhelming, which can happen with grounded theory research. Clive volunteered to take the lead on doing the first level of analysis of the transcripts. Grounded theory analysis tends to follow a three-step process:

1. Initially identify conceptual categories. This is done through open coding.
2. Secondly, find relationships between these categories. This second set of codes which are called theoretical/axial are to interconnect the main substantive codes.
3. And finally, account for and conceptualize these relationships at a higher level of abstraction. (Punch, 2005, p. 204)

Consistent with grounded theory we began coding the data as it was collected which allowed the theory to emerge from the data. The flexibility of grounded theory allowed us to pursue areas of interest and use the literature almost as another source of data (Punch, 2005, p. 159). One of the tenets of grounded theory is identifying relationships, and in self-study research identifying and understanding relationships are pivotal.

The interviews of the beginning teachers were coded by hand. We used a similar process to the one we used for the instructors: reading the transcripts several times, identifying themes, combining categories, and adding, deleting, and modifying themes as we wrote papers. Initially, we had 34 codes; for example, did not understand some of the theory; preservice not practical enough; ELL: lack of preparation, approach used; and school-wide initiatives, constraints, pressures. Although working with 34 codes was difficult, our extensive data collection required these many codes. After applying these codes, we then examined them to group them into themes at a higher level of abstraction. Since one of our goals was to be improvement oriented we did not want to just outline the problems the beginning teachers had or their reflections on teaching literacy, we wanted to make recommendations for improving the preservice program; this led us to the beginning of a theory for teacher education. Our emerging theory is briefly described below.

Initial Findings: Seven Priorities for Teacher Education

Overall, we were impressed with the caliber of the new teachers' practice. They worked hard, cared about their students, and had somewhat balanced literacy programs. We were able to identify some of the influences of the program on their practice: for example, using multicultural literature, recognizing the need to engage students, and developing the class into a community.

By the beginning of the teachers' third year of teaching, our data analysis led us to identify seven priorities for teacher education that we see as foundational for our theory:

- program planning
- pupil assessment
- classroom organization, management, and community
- inclusive education
- subject knowledge
- professional identity
- vision for teaching.

Identifying these priorities for teacher education was a turning point for the research process because we were no longer trying to figure out what we should be looking for; we now had a structure or framework and knew the areas to pursue in our next round of data gathering (while being open to changes). This was in line with grounded theory, according to which "subsequent data collection should be guided by theoretical developments that emerge in the analysis" (Punch, 2005, p. 159). The interviews of the third-year teachers included questions about each of the priorities and the observation forms were also based in large part on the priorities. We continue to debate the actual terms (e.g., subject knowledge versus pedagogical content knowledge) and we suspect that the names and numbers of the priorities will continue to be modified. (See appendix at end of this chapter for an example of how we conceptualized and presented the program planning priority.) Although we know that through discussion with others we may modify the priorities, we feel that the concept of having priorities is an important step forward in developing a framework for teacher education.

Since our work was at the institutional level and we wanted to contribute to the literature on teacher education, we were conscious of the need to find a way to present our findings in an accessible manner. We felt that simply presenting priorities for teacher education would be too vague, and discussing a sample of 22 could become unwieldy. This led us to develop case studies of seven teachers in their third year of teaching, one for each of the priorities. Gathering the additional data for the case studies was done by Clare with the researcher who had been following the individual teacher over the 3 years. This collaborative approach, consistent with self-study principles, had many benefits: the members of the research team worked with Clare, one of the most experienced researchers on the team, which led to them improving their interviewing skills; Clare spent extended periods of time with team members which allowed them to share their views on all aspects of the research with her which she found very informative; and the data gathering was improved because two researchers were involved. The case studies have helped to make the research more accessible and our position clearer.

We have begun to disseminate our findings: our text, *Priorities in Teacher Education: The 7 Key Elements of Preservice Preparation*, will be published in 2009; we have written various articles for journals (e.g., Beck, Kosnik, & Rowsell, 2007; Kosnik & Beck, 2008a, 2008b; Rowsell, Kosnik, & Beck, 2008); and have done many presentations at conferences such as AERA, ATEE, and AACTE. With every article and book chapter we write and every presentation we give, we understand the research more fully. Discussions with other teacher educators continue to inform us, deepening our understanding of the issues and helping us recognize the applicability of our findings to other institutions. We feel that through our writing we are contributing to teacher education at the collective level because the seven priorities we have identified could be used to frame other preservice programs.

Questions that Emerged

The study to date has profoundly changed both Clare and Clive. Certainly, some of the findings were a total surprise to us (e.g., beginning teachers are at a loss regarding assessing pupils) while others were to be expected (e.g., beginning teachers are often overwhelmed and at times in despair). We continue to be intrigued by the research and anticipate our work continuing to evolve and improve. Yet, many questions have emerged.

Questions Regarding the Findings

Disseminating Our Findings in Our Institution

One of the surprising issues we have faced is the relative lack of interest in our findings within our institution. Without a doubt we have been able to identify strengths of our programs which should be an affirmation for many; however, we have identified gaps in the program. We are certain that gaps exist in all teacher education programs. OISE/UT is not unique in some of its shortcomings (e.g., finding suitable practice teaching placements). Given the importance of teacher education for the entire schooling process, we are dismayed that many continue with practices that we have found to be ineffective (e.g., trying to cover too many topics in one course). We have worked with some of the instructors in our cohort teams and Clare has worked with some of the literacy instructors. These grassroots efforts have been appreciated by our colleagues and we will continue to work at this level. However, without a vehicle to disseminate our findings to many preservice faculty, we see our efforts having limited impact within our home institution.

In some ways we are suggesting that the teacher education program in its entirety needs to be revamped, but we are realistic in knowing that this may not occur. There are many modifications that could easily be incorporated into the current program without major upheaval. For example, the beginning teachers found program planning to be overwhelming. In some of our writings about this project, we have suggested that student teachers should work closely with their cooperating teachers during practice teaching to see how the experienced teachers plan a unit. This would give the students a window into the methods used by highly effective teachers. This shift from students always planning independently to a co-planning process could be a modification to the expectations for practice teaching. This collaborative approach would certainly help students learn some of the strategies for program planning, highlight the need to prioritize curriculum expectations, and draw students' attention to key curriculum resources.

Dealing with Sensitive Findings

One gap we were able to identify in all of the programs was in preparation to work with the range of abilities in the class. Repeatedly, the teachers told us that they were not prepared to meet the needs of the students, particularly the special education students and the English Language Learners. Since there is not a course in the preservice programs on special education and learning to plan for ELL is supposed to be integrated into all courses, we were not surprised that the teachers felt unprepared for these challenges. The decision not to have a special education course and to infuse teaching of ELL and special education into the program was extremely controversial. Our findings suggest that the decision to use an infusion approach needs to be reviewed.

As we began to write papers for journals and conference presentations, we were faced with a serious dilemma. We had some extremely sensitive findings regarding particular instructors, the differences between the tenured and non-tenured instructors' practices, and the strengths/weaknesses of the 1- and 2-year programs. Since this research was at an institutional level, we knew that we had to tread carefully. We talked to a few trusted colleagues, asking their views on what should be revealed, and discussed with the research team their views about the level of disclosure. Both of us, Clive and Clare, had to be in complete agreement on how to proceed, and reaching this point was not easy because initially we had somewhat different views. After much soul searching and consultation, we decided it would be too risky to reveal certain findings. We still wonder to what degree we should be forthright and explicit.

Questions Regarding the Research Methodology

Although we have described above some of the shortcomings of our research methods and the modifications we made, we were generally pleased with our choice of methods – self-study and grounded theory.

Influence of Self-Study

The self-study component was central to our work in many ways. For example, we used our own program and studied our own teaching. Did this taint the research? We felt that it did not because we had insider knowledge, but others may conclude that our history with the program may have biased us. We have strong views on teacher education, having extensively studied our own work and the field for many years. For example, we abhor make-work assignments such as creating a curriculum unit for a phantom class, because we know from research this is not particularly helpful. How did this affect our analysis of the teacher educators' practices? Having invested so many years in teacher education, was it unfair to expect teacher educators who are only on a 3-year contract at OISE/UT to have a high level of expertise? Similarly, we have strong views on literacy instruction. For example, we feel that focusing on student learning rather than mere activity or engagement is of paramount importance. How did our views influence our analysis of the new teachers' practices, especially those who relied on a textbook with vacuous stories and trivial worksheets? We may never be able to answer these questions but it is important to be mindful of our biases.

Working with Our Cohort of Teachers

Almost all of our sample of 22 teachers have continued to be part of the study. Even when some went on maternity leave or took study leave, they still wanted to be interviewed. This we saw as very positive on many levels. We did though have a few teachers who over 4 years had not grown significantly; if anything, they seemed to have regressed, becoming less able and less caring about their students. They really did not have much to say about either the preservice program or their practice. We wondered when we should stop following a teacher. Should we persevere and hope the teacher gains greater insight and recovers enthusiasm for teaching?

Applying Our Learning to Our Work as Teacher Educators

As LaBoskey (2004) has argued, self-study has to be improvement oriented. Our initial plan was to conduct the research, write scholarly papers and books, and then revisit our work as teacher educators in light of the findings. This linear process evaporated instantly. Reading, analyzing, and writing about literacy education affected our work as teacher educators immediately. For example, many of the beginning teachers said they had been confused by all of the jargon and terminology in their literacy courses, so Clare found an excellent glossary of literacy terms and distributed it to her current student teachers.

Beyond simply tinkering with aspects of her courses, Clare took the dramatic step of reconceptualizing her literacy courses based on the priorities we had identified, completely restructuring every aspect of her courses. She felt that it would have been unethical to continue some of her practices, notably, trying to cover the waterfront of literacy topics when she knew from the research that this approach overwhelms students and leaves them unprepared and confused. In the new courses, she addressed five to seven main concepts rather than trying to do 12 topics; selected readings that blend theory and practice; implemented a Ticket Out the Door system so she could determine when students do not understand a concept; and incorporated more small-group work. Each of these processes is directly related to the research findings on beginning teachers. Consistent with self-study, she and her graduate assistant, Yiola, developed a research project to study these reconceptualized courses (Kosnik, Beck, & Cleovoulou, 2008). This is another example of the interplay of the research at all three levels – personal, institutional, and collective. Clare reconceptualized her new courses; the revisions were a result of the research on new teachers; she can describe the changes she has made to her courses which may be of value to other literacy teacher educators; and she intends to follow students who completed these revised courses into their work as teachers to see their level of preparedness, which will contribute to the collective knowledge on teacher education.

Clive for his part began to change his social foundations course in a number of ways to reflect what we were learning from the research. As a relative latecomer to preservice teacher education (until 12 years ago he taught only at the graduate level), he often felt uncomfortable in his role. This was especially so because his previous research and teaching was largely in philosophy of education. How could he convince his students – and himself – that his somewhat theoretical course was useful to new teachers, desperate for practical solutions? Fortunately, our research on new teachers helped in several ways. First, many of the study participants said they found the "philosophy of teaching" he and his colleagues presented valuable, although it was often too abstract and had crucial gaps. Second, based on the research he was able to fill some of the gaps, notably in program planning, assessment, classroom organization, and professional identity. Third, he was able to use quotes and examples from our study of the new teachers to improve the theory–practice balance. And finally, the student teachers appreciated hearing the voices of new teachers in his course. As the new elements were added, the students showed greater interest in his course and he too could see more clearly why it was important.

Concluding Comments

As described throughout this paper, we reflected on and anguished over almost every step of this study. Our highly reflective stance helped us gain insight in countless ways; for example, we recognized that our researchers needed to feel part of the team so we engaged in community-building activities. We were not detached researchers; rather, we are deeply invested in teacher education for literacy teaching (and teaching in general). By combining traditional research methods with self-study, there was a convergence of ideas and practices that was extremely powerful. Our research design allowed us to deepen our learning at a personal level and contribute at institutional and collective levels. The research process was complex and multi-layered but we believe it is one that has great potential. It is not for the faint of heart! Our advice to researchers who want to conduct longitudinal research at the three levels we have discussed is as follows:

- Be prepared to be deeply affected by the research
- Be open to adding some research processes and deleting others
- Work with a team
- Create a community for the research team
- Ask for advice
- Keep reading the literature
- Connect with colleagues in other universities
- Start writing about your findings – and implementing them – as soon as possible, and certainly before the data gathering is complete
- Follow beginning teachers beyond their first year of teaching, preferably for at least 3 years
- And, do not despair; the research will be difficult but very rewarding.

We did not address all our research objectives. In some cases achieving them was beyond our resources and in others simply not feasible. We did however learn a great deal about our preservice programs, the influence of them on beginning teachers, the challenges new teachers face, and the impact of the school context on teachers; and we gained tremendous insight into our own practice as teacher educators. And all these are leading to the development of a theory of teacher education based on the seven priorities we have identified. Maria in her second year of teaching said she would give the following advice to a beginning teacher; we think it also has applicability for those doing longitudinal research on teacher education:

> Be persistent, stick to it, don't give up. You'll have your days when you want to run away screaming, wondering what you got yourself into...and there are times when you wonder if you're good enough and doubt yourself. But know that you are, that's why they hired you.... And it's only your first year, don't expect to be able to do it all and be perfect. And allow yourself to make mistakes and learn from them.

Acknowledgments We wish to thank the Social Sciences and Humanities Research Council of Canada for their generous support of this research.

Appendix

In writing our text, *Priorities in Teacher Education: The 7 Key Elements of Preservice Preparation*, we developed a "template" for each priority. For program planning, our first priority, we used the following structure:

1. What and Why of Program Planning
2. Problems in Program Planning
3. Principles and Strategies of Program Planning

   a. Recognize the Limitations of Formal "Long-Range Planning"
   b. Identify Your Main Goals
   c. Establish Classroom Structures that Promote Learning
   d. Use Elements of Existing Textbooks and Programs
   e. Be Flexible In Following Your Plan and Using Resources
   f. Individualize Your Program
   g. Integrate Your Program
   h. Have Special Emphases in the First Few Weeks

4. Implications for Preservice Education
5. Conclusion

In our analysis and writing for all the priorities, we followed this format:

- What and Why of . . . .
- Problems in . . .
- Principles and Strategies of . . . .
- Implications for Preservice
- Conclusion.

References

Anders, P., Hoffman, J., & Duffy, G. (2000). Teaching teachers to teach reading: Paradigm shifts, persistent problems, and challenges. In M. Kamil, P. Mosenthal, P. Pearson, & R. Barr (Eds.), *Handbook of reading research* (Vol. 3). Mahwah, NJ: Erlbaum.
Ball, D. (2000). Bridging practices: Intertwining content and pedagogy in teaching and learning to teach. *Journal of Teacher Education, 51*(3), 241–247.
Barnes, D., Barnes, D. R., & Clarke, S. (1984). *Versions of English*. Portsmouth, NH: Heinemann.
Beck, C., Kosnik, C., & Rowsell, J. (2007). Preparation for the first year of teaching: Beginning teachers' views about their needs. *The New Educator, 3*(1), 51–73.
Boyd, D., Grossman, P., Lankford, J., Loeb, S., & Michelli, N. (2006). Complex by design: Investigating pathways into teaching in New York City schools. *Journal of Teacher Education, 57*(2), 230–250.
Clift, R., & Brady, P. (2005). Research on methods courses and field experiences. In M. Cochran-Smith & K. Zeichner (Eds.), *Studying teacher education: The report of the AERA panel on research and teacher education* (pp. 309–424). Mahwah, NJ: Erlbaum.

Ducharme, E., & Ducharme, M. (1999). Teacher educators and teachers: The need for excellence and spunk. In R. Roth (Ed.), *The role of the university in the preparation of teachers* (pp. 41–58). London: Falmer.

Grossman, P., Valencia, S., Evans, K., Thompson, C., Martin, S., & Place, N. (2000). Transitions into teaching: Learning to teach writing in teacher education and beyond. *Journal of Literacy Research, 32*(4), 631–662.

Grossman, P., Schoenfeld, A., & Lee, C. (2005). Teaching subject matter. In L. Darling-Hammond & J. Bransford (Eds.), *Preparing teachers for a changing world: What teachers should learn and be able to do*. San Francisco: Jossey-Bass.

Hoffman, J., Roller, C., Maloch, B., Sailors, M., Duffy, G., & Beretvas, S. N. (2005). Teachers' preparation to teach reading and their experiences and practices in the first three years of teaching. *Elementary School Journal, 105*(3), 1–24.

International Reading Association. (2003). *Prepared to make a difference: An executive summary of the national commission on excellence in elementary teacher preparation for reading instruction*. Newark, DE: Author.

Kosnik, C., Beck, C., Diamond, P., Kooy, M., & Rowsell, J. (2002). *Preservice teacher education in Ontario: Trends and best practices in an era of curriculum reform*. Report for the Ontario Ministry of Education, 92 pp.

Kosnik, C., & Beck, C. (2008a). We taught them about literacy but what did they learn? The impact of our preservice teacher education program on the practices of beginning teachers. *Studying Teacher Education: A Journal of Self-Study of Teacher Education Practices, 4*(2), 115–128.

Kosnik, C., & Beck, C. (2008b). In the shadows: Non-tenure-line instructors in preservice teacher education. *European Journal of Teacher Education, 21*(2), 185–202.

Kosnik, C., & Beck, C. (2009). *Priorities in teacher education: The 7 key elements of preservice preparation*. London: Routledge.

Kosnik, C., Beck, C., & Cleovoulou, Y. (2008). Using research on our graduates to restructure our courses: Challenges and promising practices. In M. L. Heston, D. L. Tidwell, K. K. East, & L. M. Fitzgerald (Eds.), *Pathways to change in teacher education: Dialogue, diversity and self-study. Proceedings of the Seventh International Conference on the Self-Study of Teacher Education Practices, Herstmonceux Castle, East Sussex, England* (pp. 202–206). Cedar Falls, IA: University of Northern Iowa.

LaBoskey, V. (2004). The methodology of self-study and its theoretical underpinnings. In J. J. Loughran, M. L. Hamilton, V. K. LaBoskey, & T. Russell (Eds.), *International handbook of self-study of teaching and teacher education practices* (pp. 817–869). Dordrecht: Kluwer.

Lasely, T., Siedentop, D., & Yinger, R. (2006). A systemic approach to enhancing teacher quality: The Ohio model. *Journal of Teacher Education, 57*(1), 13–21.

Maloch, B., Flint, A. S., Eldridge, D., Harmon, J., Loven, R., Fine, J., et al. (2003). Understandings, beliefs, and reported decision making of first-year teachers from different reading teacher preparation programs. *The Elementary School Journal, 103*(5), 431–457.

Noell, G., & Burns, J. (2006). Value-added assessment of teacher preparation: An illustration of emerging technology. *Journal of Teacher Education, 57*(1), 37–50.

Phelps, G., & Schilling, G. (2004). Developing measures of content knowledge for teaching reading. *The Elementary School Journal, 105*(1), 33–48.

Punch, K. (2005). *Introduction to social research: Quantitative and qualitative approaches* (2nd ed.). London: Sage.

Rowsell, J., Kosnik, C., & Beck, C. (2008). Fostering multiliteracies pedagogy through preservice teacher education. *Teaching Education, 19*(2), 151–164.

Samaras, A., & Freese, A. (2006). *Self-study of teaching practices*. New York: Peter Lang.

Snow, C., Griffin, P., & Burns, M. S. (Eds.). (2005). *Knowledge to support the teaching of reading: Preparing teachers for a changing world*. San Francisco: Jossey-Bass.

Teachers for a New Era. Retrieved from: http://www.teachersforanewera.org/

U.S. Department of Education. (2002). *Strategic plan for 2002–2007*. Retrieved from http://www/ed/gov/pubs/stratplan2002-2007/index.html

Author Index

Subject Index

Lightning Source UK Ltd.
Milton Keynes UK
18 March 2010

151537UK00006B/128/P

584723